Coursebook

Margaret O'Keeffe
Lewis Lansford
Ed Pegg

A2

Business Partner

FT Publishing
FINANCIAL TIMES

GSE
Global Scale of English

Contents

UNIT 1 › WORKING DAY p.7
Videos: 1.1 Working day   1.4 What do you do?

1.1 › Daily tasks
Vocabulary: Jobs and tasks
Pronunciation: → The -s ending (p.96)
Communicative grammar: Facts and routines
Video: ▶ Working day
Task: Introducing yourself and talking about your job and routine

1.2 › A work plan
Vocabulary: Work tasks and activities
Reading and listening: ◆ Scheduling meetings
Writing: An email to schedule a meeting

1.3 › A survey
Reading: An employee survey
Communicative grammar: Questions
Pronunciation: → Questions (p.96)
Writing: A survey about facilities in the workplace

1.4 › Work skills: Talking about people and roles
Video: ▶ What do you do?
Speaking: Talking about people and roles

1.5 › Business workshop: We want to meet you ...
Reading: A webpage; an email
Speaking: Arranging to meet; an interview about your job; talking about your company and travel

Review p.87

UNIT 2 › DOING BUSINESS p.17
Videos: 2.1 The Good Eating Company   2.4 Agreeing contract details

2.1 › Orders and deliveries
Vocabulary: Orders and deliveries
Communicative grammar: Things you can and can't count
Video: ▶ The Good Eating Company
Task: Asking and answering questions about quantities

2.2 › Placing orders on the phone
Listening: ◆ An order by phone
Vocabulary: An order by phone
Pronunciation: → /iː/, /ɪ/ and /aɪ/ (p.96)
Grammar: can/can't
Speaking: Placing an order

2.3 › Email enquiries
Reading: Frequently Asked Questions (FAQs)
Pronunciation: → /tʃ/ and /dʒ/ (p.97)
Communicative grammar: Saying something exists
Writing: A response to an email enquiry

2.4 › Work skills: Making agreements
Video: ▶ Agreeing contract details
Speaking: Making agreements

2.5 › Business workshop: Planning a work party
Reading: Information from a catering company
Speaking: Comparing information about an order
Writing: reply to an order enquiry

Review p.88

UNIT 3 › CHANGES p.27
Videos: 3.1 How we started   3.4 How did the project go?

3.1 › A company's story
Vocabulary: A company's story
Communicative grammar: Talking about the past (1)
Pronunciation: → The -ed ending (p.97)
Video: ▶ How we started
Task: Completing a timeline

3.2 › New office
Vocabulary: Email phrases
Grammar: Giving instructions
Reading: An email about meeting room rules
Listening: ◆ A conversation about an office move
Writing: An email giving instructions

3.3 › Company performance
Reading: Past successes and challenges
Pronunciation: → /ɜː/ and /ɔː/ (p.98)
Communicative grammar: Talking about the past (2)
Writing: An email describing successes and challenges

3.4 › Work skills: How did it go?
Video: ▶ How did the project go?
Speaking: Talking about projects

3.5 › Business workshop: Our first year
Reading: A timeline about a new company
Writing: Preparing for a move
Speaking: Asking questions about a new company; discussing a project

Review p.89

UNIT 4 › TRAVELLING FOR WORK p.37
Videos: 4.1 Away on business   4.4 Technical problems

4.1 › I'm flying to Tokyo tomorrow
Vocabulary: Travel arrangements
Communicative grammar: Talking about arrangements
Pronunciation: → /ŋ/, /ŋk/ and /n/. The -ing ending (p.98)
Video: ▶ Away on business
Task: Arranging a time to meet

4.2 › The 12.05 is delayed
Vocabulary: Airports and train stations
Reading and listening: ◆ Dealing with delays
Grammar: will/won't
Writing: Writing a text message about an announcement

4.3 › An update email
Reading: Emails to a project manager
Communicative grammar: Things happening now
Writing: An update email

4.4 › Work skills: Setting up a video call
Video: ▶ Technical problems
Grammar: Making suggestions
Speaking: Problems with teleconferencing
Pronunciation: → /ɪə/ and /eə/ (p.98)

4.5 › Business workshop: A business trip
Reading: Travel arrangements
Listening: ◆ A change in plans
Speaking: Arranging a meeting
Writing: Text messages giving updates

Review p.90

UNIT 5 > ORGANISING p.47

Videos: 5.1 Graduate Fashion Week   5.4 What do you think of the trade fair?

5.1 > Trade shows and exhibitions	5.2 > Phoning about a conference	5.3 > Invitations	5.4 > Work skills: Socialising with clients	5.5 > Business workshop: The conference
Vocabulary: Organising an exhibition **Communicative grammar:** Talking about intentions **Pronunciation:** /æ/, /e/ and /eɪ/ (p.99) **Video:** Graduate Fashion Week **Task:** Talking abut plans for a trade fair	**Vocabulary:** Leaving a message **Listening:** Organising a conference **Speaking:** Taking and leaving phone messages	**Reading:** Messages about an invitation **Communicative grammar:** Invitations with *would* and *want* **Pronunciation:** /θ/ and /ð/ vs. /s/, /z/, /f/, /v/, /t/, /d/ (p.99) **Writing:** Informal messages of invitation	**Video:** What do you think of the trade fair? **Speaking:** Socialising with clients	**Speaking:** Phoning to compare conference details **Writing:** An email about a conference **Speaking:** Making conversation at a conference dinner

Review p.91

UNIT 6 > PRODUCTS p.57

Videos: 6.1 Industry futures   6.4 How many do you want to order?

6.1 > Future products	6.2 > A problem with an order	6.3 > The production process	6.4 > Work skills: Placing an order	6.5 > Business workshop: Buy natural
Vocabulary: Technology and the environment **Communicative grammar:** Speculating about the future **Video:** Industry futures **Task:** Talking about the future	**Listening:** A problem with an order **Vocabulary:** Helping with a problem **Pronunciation:** /ɑː/ and /ʌ/ (p.99) **Speaking:** Phoning and answering as customer services	**Reading:** Environment and ethics **Communicative grammar:** Describing production **Pronunciation:** /uː/ and /ʊ/ (p.100) **Writing:** A description for a company website	**Video:** How many do you want to order? **Speaking:** Placing an order	**Reading:** A company website about ethical products **Speaking:** Placing an order; making a complaint about an order

Review p.92

UNIT 7 > COMPETITION p.67

Videos: 7.1 Comparing sports cars   7.4 Our products and services

7.1 > Should I upgrade?	7.2 > Services	7.3 > The best providers	7.4 > Work skills: Presentations	7.5 > Business workshop: The big contract
Vocabulary: Product qualities **Listening:** Talking about using a product **Communicative grammar:** Comparing (1): comparatives **Video:** Comparing sports cars **Task:** Comparing two models	**Vocabulary:** Fees **Pronunciation:** /əʊ/ and /aʊ/ (p.100) **Listening:** Comparing recruitment agencies **Writing:** An advertisement for services	**Reading:** An email comparing services **Communicative grammar:** Comparing (2): superlatives **Writing:** An email summarising survey results **Pronunciation:** /p/, /b/, /f/ and /v/ (p.100)	**Video:** Our products and services **Speaking:** Presenting	**Reading:** An email about a trade show **Speaking:** Giving presentations **Writing:** A summary email giving a recommendation

Review p.93

UNIT 8 > JOBS p.77

Videos: 8.1 Skills and experience   8.4 The job interview

8.1 > Work experience	8.2 > The best person for the job	8.3 > Professional profiles	8.4 > Work skills: A job interview	8.5 > Business workshop: The interviewer and the candidate
Vocabulary: Skills and personal qualities **Communicative grammar:** Talking about experience **Video:** Skills and experience **Task:** Asking and answering interview questions	**Vocabulary:** Job requirements **Listening:** Choosing job candidates **Pronunciation:** The vowel /ɒ/. The letter 'o' as /ɒ/, /əʊ/ and /ʌ/ (p.101) **Speaking:** Describing and comparing candidates	**Reading:** A professional profile **Communicative grammar:** Talking about experiences and completed past events **Pronunciation:** Silent letters (p.101) **Writing:** An employee profile	**Video:** The job interview **Speaking:** Job interviews	**Speaking:** Interview questions; choosing the best candidate for the job

Review p.94

Pronunciation p.95 | Grammar reference p.102 | Irregular verbs list p.114 | Additional material p.115 | Videoscripts p.129 | Audioscripts p.133

Introduction

**Who ...
is Business Partner for?**

- *Business Partner* A2 is for learners who have studied English before, at school or privately, but what they learnt has not been very useful for them in their job, or they simply don't remember much of it.
- Now they need to study business English in order to better communicate in a workplace that is increasingly international.
- To achieve this, they need to improve their knowledge of the English language, but also develop key work skills.
- They need a course which is relevant to their professional needs.

**Why ...
a communicative methodology?**

Students of *Business Partner* may be working in different industries, different job positions or different countries, but they all have in common the need to communicate in English in an international workplace, in an effective manner.

The objective of the course is to equip students with the skills they need to use English effectively, without anxiety about their language ability.

**Why ...
work skills training?**

Business Partner focuses on delivering practical language and skills training that learners need for successful communication when working with people from different countries, even if those learners begin the course with limited language ability.

In *Business Partner*, every unit has a video-based lesson on 'Work skills', to expose students to best-practice scenarios of various business situations that they can use as models.

The objective of this training is to give learners a better chance of getting a job, or of moving jobs in an organisation.

What's in each unit?

Each unit is divided into five lessons and each lesson starts with a Lesson outcome and ends with a short Self-assessment section: this is to help learners think about the progress that they have made.

Vocabulary and functional language

In order to meet the course objectives, the vocabulary and functional phrases in each unit focus on industries, jobs and work environments that are relevant to students to help them function in a variety of professional situations.

This vocabulary has been selected to answer learners' needs at work and may seem high-level or technical compared to a general English course. It is, however, basic professional vocabulary that learners need to function in their jobs.

Grammar

Similarly, the approach to grammar is to help students acquire language to survive in these situations. The grammar content comes from the communicative needs of learners and is given in chunks, with a light approach to rules. The grammar reference section at the back of the book provides additional practice of grammar points and a recorded list of irregular verbs.

Listening and video

There are many listening activities to help students develop comprehension skills and hear language in context. All of the video and audio material is available in MyEnglishLab and includes a range of British, U.S. and non-native English speakers, so that learners are exposed to a variety of accents, to reflect the reality of their working lives.

Learners will be able to watch short, authentic videos, which they can also use as a model for the group speaking tasks.

Speaking

There are plenty of opportunities for speaking practice in relevant and engaging activities in each lesson. The objective is to make all students feel comfortable developing this essential skill for the workplace.

Writing

Learners at this level need to respond to emails and other functional pieces of writing. Writing lesssons provide a model for students to follow, grammar practice of the structures they need to use when writing and functional language phrases to help them. Writing tasks allow freer practice of target vocabulary and grammar, and offer elements of personalisation where possible.

Work skills

Through authentic videos, students are shown best-practice scenarios in different work situations and have the chance to study and practise the relevant functional language from each situation. Finally, students are encouraged to activate the skills and language they have learnt and practised by collaborating on group tasks.

Business workshops

Business workshops allow learners to focus mostly on speaking and writing, and offer a practical application and review of the content of the unit.

Pronunciation

Two pronunciation points, linked to the unit content, are presented and practised in every unit. The Pronunciation bank is at the back of the book, with signposts from the relevant lessons. This section also includes a phonetic chart for British English and American English.

Reviews

There is a one-page review for each unit at the back of the coursebook. The review recycles and revises the key vocabulary, grammar and functional language presented in the unit.

Signposts, cross-references and the Pearson English Portal

T **Signposts for teachers** in each lesson indicate that there are extra activities in the Portal which can be printed or displayed on-screen. These activities can be used to extend a lesson or to focus in more depth on a particular section.

➔ **page 000**
Cross-references refer to the Pronunciation bank and Grammar reference pages.

Pearson English Portal

Access to the Pearson English Portal is given through a code printed on the inside front cover of this book.

The code will give you access to:

Interactive eBook: a digital version of the coursebook including interactive activities, all class video clips and all class audio recordings.

Online Practice on MyEnglishLab: a self-study interactive workbook with instant feedback and automatic gradebook. Teachers can assign workbook activities as homework.

Digital Resources: including downloadable coursebook resources, all video clips, all audio recordings.

The **Global Scale of English (GSE)** is a standardised, granular scale from 10 to 90 which measures English language proficiency. The GSE Learning Objectives for Professional English are aligned with the Common European Framework of Reference (CEFR). Unlike the CEFR, which describes proficiency in terms of broad levels, the Global Scale of English identifies what a learner can do at each point on a more granular scale – and within a CEFR level. The scale is designed to motivate learners by demonstrating incremental progress in their language ability. The Global Scale of English forms the backbone of Pearson English course material and assessment.

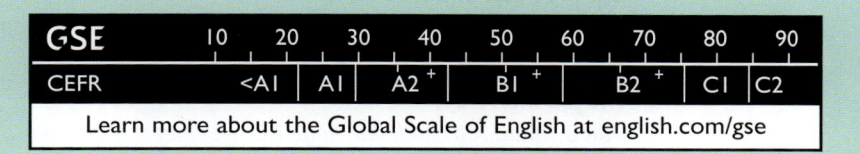

GSE	10	20	30	40	50	60	70	80	90
CEFR		<A1	A1	A2+	B1+	B2+	C1	C2	

Learn more about the Global Scale of English at english.com/gse

WORK SKILLS
Video introduction

Introduction

The Work skills videos in Lesson 4 of each unit show people in situations at work.

Sleek is a new, small fashion design company. They sell directly to customers in their own boutique shops in the UK and Western Europe and also sell their products to larger department stores. Max Hartmann is the Director of Operations in the UK, and Maria Stavrou is a Sales Manager in Spain. In the videos we see Max, Maria and other Sleek employees at work: in meetings, presentations and other day-to-day interactions.

Characters

- **Max Hartmann, German** — Director of Operations UK, (Units 1, 4, 5, 7)
- **Izabel Nowak, Polish** — Office Manager (Units 1, 2)  
- **William James, Australian** — Product Manager (Units 3, 4)
- **Haru Sakai, Japanese-British** — Lead Designer (Units 3, 4) 
- **Maria Stavrou, Greek** — Sales Manager (Units 1, 4, 5, 6)
- **Ellen Morgan, British** — Junior Clothing Designer (Unit 3)  
- **Josie Marr, British** — Administration Assistant (Unit 1)
- **Robert Harris, British** — Cleaning company owner (Unit 2) 
- **Julia Anderson, Brazilian-British** — External client (Unit 5) 
- **Matt Reece, British** — Human Resources Manager (Unit 8)
- **Eduardo Dias, Brazilian-Portuguese** — External client (Unit 6) 
- **Jonathan Potts, British** — External client (Unit 7) 
- **Angela Davies, British** — Job candidate (Unit 8)

Video summary

1 What do you do?
Unit 1 video: *Maria visits the London office for some meetings and meets the team.*

2 Agreeing contract details
Unit 2 video: *Izabela has a meeting with Robert to agree the details of an office cleaning contract.*

3 How did the project go?
Unit 3 video: *William holds a feedback meeting with designers Haru and Ellen.*

4 Technical problems
Unit 4 video: *Members of the team have technical problems on their video calls.*

5 What do you think of the trade fair?
Unit 5 video: *Max and Maria meet external client Julia Anderson and make small talk.*

6 How many do you want to order?
Unit 6 video: *External client Eduardo meets Maria to place an order for some T-shirts.*

7 Our products and services
Unit 7 video: *External client Jonathan Potts presents his company's products and services to a group, including Max.*

8 The job interview
Unit 8 video: *Job candidate Angela Davies meets Human Resources Manager Matt Reece for a job interview.*

Working day

> *What do you do?*

Unit overview

1.1	**Daily tasks** **Lesson outcome:** Learners can describe work activities and tasks.	**Vocabulary:** Jobs and tasks **Communicative grammar:** Facts and routines **Video:** Working day **Task:** Introducing yourself and talking about your job and routine
1.2	**A work plan** **Lesson outcome:** Learners can schedule tasks.	**Vocabulary:** Work tasks and activities **Reading and listening:** Scheduling meetings **Writing:** An email to schedule a meeting
1.3	**A survey** **Lesson outcome:** Learners can ask and answer questions for a survey about their workplace.	**Reading:** An employee survey **Communicative grammar:** Questions **Writing:** A survey about facilities in the workplace
1.4	**Work skills:** Talking about people and roles **Lesson outcome:** Learners can greet a visitor, make introductions and talk about people and roles.	**Video:** What do you do? **Speaking:** Talking about people and roles
1.5	**Business workshop:** We want to meet you … **Lesson outcome:** Learners can answer questions about jobs.	**Reading:** A webpage; an email **Speaking:** Arranging to meet; an interview about your job; talking about your company and travel

Review 1: p.87 | **Pronunciation:** 1.1 The -s ending 1.3 Questions p.96 | **Grammar reference:** 1.1 Facts and routines 1.3 Questions 1.4 Subject and object questions p.102

1.1 Daily tasks

Lesson outcome — Learners can describe work activities and tasks.

Lead-in

1A Match the photos (A–D) with the correct jobs (1–8).

1. Production Engineer
2. Sales Manager
3. Sales Assistant
4. Digital Designer
5. Admin Assistant
6. Finance Officer
7. Project Manager
8. IT Specialist

B Which of the jobs in Exercise 1A do people do where you work?

Vocabulary Jobs and tasks

2A Read about two jobs. Choose a job from Exercise 1A to complete the descriptions.

A I'm a(n) _____ . I'm responsible for a team of five people. They often have meetings with customers. They sometimes work in the office and **call customers** on the phone. At the end of the week, they **do research** to find new clients. I sometimes **go to meetings** with important customers, so I often **travel for work**. I **analyse** sales **data**, and I often **write reports**. I also **do research** to find new clients. At the end of the day, I usually **make calls** to the other managers and to my boss, who works in a different location. My office hours are 9 a.m. to 5.30 p.m. but I'm so busy I never **finish work** before 5.30 p.m.

B Elena is a(n) _____ . She usually **starts work** at 7 o'clock and she always has a lot of work to do. She **answers the phone** and **makes calls** or **writes emails**. She works with the sales team and often **processes orders** for them. She sometimes **goes to meetings** and takes notes. She rarely **travels for work**.

B Complete the expressions with words from Exercise 2A.

1. _go to_ meetings
2. _____ customers
3. process _____
4. do _____
5. _____ calls
6. _____ for work
7. _____ (sales) data
8. write _____ /emails
9. answer _____
10. _____ / _____ work

3 Work in pairs. Ask and answer the questions. Use the words in the box.

0%					100%
never	rarely	sometimes	often	usually	always

How often do you …

1. do research?
2. go to meetings?
3. start work at 8 o'clock?
4. finish work at 5 o'clock?
5. write reports?
6. write emails?
7. analyse data?
8. answer the phone?
9. make calls?
10. process orders?

T Extra activities

→ **page 96** See Pronunciation bank: The *-s* ending

1.1 ▶ Daily tasks

Communicative grammar

FACTS AND ROUTINES
➔ Grammar reference: page 102

+ I **am**/**'m** a Sales Manager.
  You/We/They **are**/**'re** Production Engineers

  He/She **is**/**'s** an IT Specialist.

+ I/You/We/They **always start** work at 8 o'clock.
  I/You/We/They **usually come** to the office on Mondays.

  He/She **often has** meetings.
  It **usually finishes** at midnight.

− I **am**/**'m not** a Finance Officer.
  I/you/we/they **do not**/**don't call** customers.

  He/She **is not**/**isn't** a Finance Manager.
  He/She **does not**/**doesn't call** customers.

4 Complete the text with the correct form of the verb in brackets.

Marek, Alberto, Ramona and I [1]_____ (work) in a computer shop. Marek sells computers, but he [2]_____ (not be) a Sales Assistant, he [3]_____ (be) a Sales Manager. Alberto and Ramona [4]_____ (be) IT Specialists. They [5]_____ (start) work at 9 o'clock. They [6]_____ (not finish) work before 7 o'clock.

I [7]_____ (analyse) sales reports, but I [8]_____ (not be) a Sales Manager, I [9]_____ (be) a Finance Officer.

5 Put the words in order to make sentences.
1 at / work / I / 8 o'clock / start / often _____
2 always / we / call customers / on Fridays _____
3 sometimes / they / a team meeting / have _____
4 after lunch / you / never / emails / write _____
5 data / don't / they / analyse _____
6 call / doesn't / she / customers / usually _____

T Extra activities

VIDEO

6A ▶ 1.1.1 Watch the video. Match the job titles with the speakers 1–3.

Chief Executive Officer (CEO)   Senior Research Manager   Student Services Manager

1 Liz   2 Ellen   3 Muj

B Watch the video again. Tick (✓) the things that each person does.

Who …	Liz	Ellen	Muj
starts work at 7.30?			
finishes work at 5.30?			
travels to other countries for work?			
has lunch at 1 o'clock?			
analyses data?			
writes reports?			

C Work in pairs. Talk about what each person does and doesn't do. Use the words in Exercise 3.

Liz never writes reports. Ellen …

7A Work in pairs. Take turns to introduce yourself. Talk about these things.
• Your name • Some tasks/things you do • Your job • Your routine

My name's Nick. I'm a factory worker. I help make cars. I always start work at seven-thirty.

B Now work with another pair. Take turns to talk about your previous partner.

This is Nick. He's a factory worker. He helps make cars. He always starts work at seven-thirty.

▶ TASK

Self-assessment   I can describe work activities and tasks.

1.2 A work plan

Lesson outcome Learners can schedule tasks.

Lead-in

1 Which of these tasks do you do in your job?

> answer the phone   do research   go to meetings   make calls
> process orders   travel for work   write reports

2 What type of meetings do you go to?

> budget   client   management   planning   project

Vocabulary Work tasks and activities

3 Read the calendar and to-do list. Match the words in bold with the correct definitions (a–g).

Susan's calendar

	Mon 25	Tue 26	Wed 27	Thu 28	Fri 29
11.00		Client meeting	¹**Budget** meeting		Factory
12.00			Management meeting		
1.00					
2.00	Project planning meeting				Client meeting
3.00					

SUSAN'S TO-DO LIST

Before planning meeting:
- ²**Book** a meeting room
- Create a ³**brief**
- Send out the ⁴**agenda**

Before budget meeting:
- Get data from production
- ⁵**Calculate** production costs

Before management meeting:
- Prepare a ⁶**presentation**
- Get an ⁷**update** from each team member

a instructions for a work task
b new information
c to make a reservation
d a plan about money
e to work with numbers to find an answer
f a list of things to talk about in a meeting
g a talk about a project, work task, etc.

4 Complete the sentences with the words in bold from Exercise 3.

1 She needs to _____ a room for ten people for the meeting.
2 Money isn't a problem. The _____ says we have $10,000 for the project.
3 The _____ says the meeting starts at 10 a.m. and we have five points to discuss.
4 The work isn't difficult. The _____ gives instructions about the job.
5 Jo and Sam have a new project. Their _____ about it was interesting.
6 How is your new job? Can you give me an _____ on it?
7 We need to prepare a budget. Please _____ the costs before the meeting.

T Extra activities

1.2 A work plan

Reading and listening

Scheduling meetings

5A Read the emails and number them in the correct order.

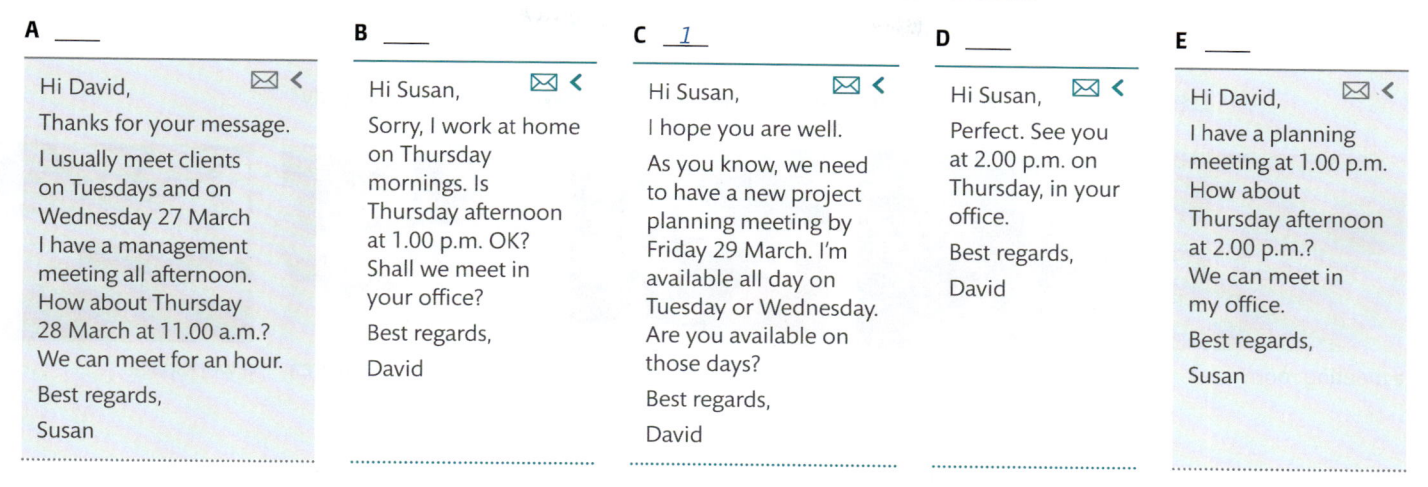

A ___

Hi David,
Thanks for your message. I usually meet clients on Tuesdays and on Wednesday 27 March I have a management meeting all afternoon. How about Thursday 28 March at 11.00 a.m.? We can meet for an hour.
Best regards,
Susan

B ___

Hi Susan,
Sorry, I work at home on Thursday mornings. Is Thursday afternoon at 1.00 p.m. OK? Shall we meet in your office?
Best regards,
David

C _1_

Hi Susan,
I hope you are well. As you know, we need to have a new project planning meeting by Friday 29 March. I'm available all day on Tuesday or Wednesday. Are you available on those days?
Best regards,
David

D ___

Hi Susan,
Perfect. See you at 2.00 p.m. on Thursday, in your office.
Best regards,
David

E ___

Hi David,
I have a planning meeting at 1.00 p.m. How about Thursday afternoon at 2.00 p.m.? We can meet in my office.
Best regards,
Susan

B Mark the new project planning meeting on David's calendar.

	1.00	1 o'clock
	2.15	two-fifteen
	3.30	three-thirty
	4.45	four-forty-five
	12.00	noon/midday (day)/ midnight (night)
	a.m.	morning
	p.m.	afternoon

David's calendar

	Mon 25	Tue 26	Wed 27	Thu 28	Fri 29
10.00					
11.00				Work at home	
12.00				Work at home	
1.00					
2.00					
3.00					

6A 🔊 1.01 Listen to a conversation between David and Susan. Write the work tasks in the correct place on David's calendar.
- Presentation • Phone call • New project planning meeting (new time)

B 🔊 1.02 Complete the sentences with the words in the box. Then listen and check your answers.

about available busy date fine see shall then

1 We need to change the _____ of the new project planning meeting.
2 Are you _____ on Friday 29th, in the morning?
3 How _____ Friday afternoon?
4 Sorry, I'm afraid I'm _____ then.
5 Friday lunchtime is good. _____ we meet in your office?
6 I usually have lunch at 1 o'clock. How about _____ ?
7 Yes, that's _____ . Then we can go to lunch for about an hour.
8 _____ you then.

T Extra activities

Writing

7 Work in pairs. You are going to schedule a meeting.
Student A: Look at page 115.
Student B: Look at page 117.

Self-assessment I can schedule tasks.

1.3 > A survey

Lesson outcome — Learners can ask and answer questions for a survey about their workplace.

Lead-in 1A Which of these facilities do you have at work / where you study?

a meeting room    a car park    an area for relaxing    a canteen or kitchen area    a workspace

B Which ones do you use?

Reading 2A Read the survey. Write the headings in the box in the correct place (A–D).

> Meetings and meeting rooms   Other facilities   The work day   The workplace

EMPLOYEE SURVEY > In order to make our workspace and facilities better, we would like your opinion on how to improve it. Please complete the survey and give extra information where possible.

A _____

1. How do you get to work?
   ○ Bicycle ○ Car ○ Motorcycle ○ Public transport ○ Walk ○ Other
2. What are your working hours?
3. How much time do you spend at your desk?

B _____

4. Which department do you work in?
5. Do you have a problem with noise in your work area? ○ Yes ○ Sometimes ○ No
6. Does your workspace have a desk lamp? ○ Yes ○ No

C _____

7. How many hours a week do you spend in meetings? ○ 0–2 ○ 2–5 ○ More than 5
8. Does your office have enough meeting rooms? ○ Yes ○ No
9. How often do you have problems booking meeting rooms?
   ○ Never ○ Sometimes ○ Often ○ Always ○ I don't book them

D _____

10. How often do you use the company gym?
11. How many times a week do you eat in the canteen?
12. Where do you take a break?

B Match the answers (a–f) with six questions in the survey.

a Production.
b From 9.00 a.m. to 5.30 p.m.
c About three times a week – I like to exercise in the evening.
d Five – I have lunch there every day.
e About six hours per day.
f In the kitchen area.

C Work in pairs. Ask and answer the questions in the survey.

1.3 A survey

Communicative grammar

> **QUESTIONS** → Grammar reference: page 102
>
> **What are** your working hours? **Do** you **have** problems booking meeting rooms?
> **Where is** your desk? **How often do** you use the company gym?
> **How do** you get to work? **Do** you **eat** in the canteen?
> **When does** your working day start? **Does** your workspace **have** a desk lamp?

3 Put the words in order to make questions.
1 are / working / your / what / hours / ? _____
2 office / your / workspaces / does / enough / have / ? _____
3 have / an area / does / for relaxing / your office / ? _____
4 gym / the / you / use / do / ? _____
5 is / where / area / the kitchen / ? _____
6 work / you / what / do / time / start / ? _____
7 does / your / when / finish / day / ? _____
8 your / does / have / company / a car park / ? _____

→ **page 96** See Pronunciation bank: Questions

4A Complete the questions with the correct word.
1 Where _____ the gym?
2 _____ the office have a kitchen area?
3 What time _____ you usually take a break?
4 What _____ the canteen's opening times?
5 How long _____ your lunch break?
6 _____ you usually work from home on Friday?
7 _____ the office have a space for relaxing?
8 _____ often do you book a meeting room?

B Match the answers (a–h) with the questions (1–8) in Exercise 4A.
a About 11.00 a.m.   e Yes, it does.
b Yes, I do.   f About forty-five minutes.
c On the second floor.   g About two or three times a week.
d 10.00 a.m. to 6.00 p.m. every day.   h Yes, it has a quiet room with sofas.

T Extra activities

Writing

5A You want to improve facilities in your workplace or where you study. Write a survey to find out what people do and what facilities they use now. Ask eight questions. Use these ideas to help you.
- The workspace
- Meetings and meeting rooms
- The canteen
- Available computers/IT (projectors, etc.)
- Access (stairs/lifts)
- Quiet areas
- Gym facilities
- Other facilities
- Your own ideas

B Give your survey questions to a partner. Write answers to your partner's questions.

Self-assessment I can ask and answer questions for a survey about my workplace.

1.4 WORK SKILLS
Talking about people and roles

Lesson outcome — Learners can greet a visitor, make introductions and talk about people and roles.

Lead-in

1 Put conversations 1–3 in the correct order. Then match the conversation with photos A–C.

1 a Nice to meet you, too.
   b Sylvia, this is Evan from the Tokyo office.
   c Nice to meet you.

2 a Sarah Jones? Yes. She works in my department.
   b She's fine.
   c How is she?
   d Do you know Sarah in the Beijing office?

3 a About ten.
   b That's the production team.
   c How many people work in production?

VIDEO

2A ▶ 1.4.1 Watch the video. Answer the questions.
1 Where are Max and Maria?
2 Do Izabela and Maria know each other?
3 Does Izabela know Josie?
4 Does Maria know Josie?

B Complete the sentences with one word. Watch the video again and check your answers.
1 **Max:** Izabela, _____ is Maria, _____ the Madrid office.
2 **Izabela:** _____ department do you _____ in?
3 **Izabela:** Oh, yes, I _____ Monica. She often _____ this office.
4 **Maria:** I _____ clients and I work with the local _____ teams.
5 **Maria:** I give a _____ about my work, and they give an _____ on their activities.

C Match the sentences with the answers. Watch the video again and check your answers.
1 Maria, do you know Josie?
2 Josie, this is Maria.
3 What do you do, Josie?
4 And which department do you work in?
5 And who manages that team?
6 What about you, Maria?

a Nice to meet you, Josie.
b I'm a Sales Manager with the Madrid team.
c Pietro Russo. Do you know Pietro?
d No. I don't.
e I'm an Admin Assistant.
f I work in office facilities.

T Extra activities

1.4 ▶ Work skills: Talking about people and roles

Speaking

> **TALKING ABOUT PEOPLE AND ROLES**
>
> **Introductions**
> Maria, do you know Josie? — No, I don't. / Yes, I do.
> Maria, this is Izabela. — Nice to meet you.
> He/She works in the Madrid office. — Nice to meet you, too.
> He/She's an Admin Assistant.
>
> **Asking about roles and activities**
> What do you do? — I'm an Admin Assistant.
> Which department do you work in? — (I work in) the Sales department.
> Who's your manager? — Monica Lopez.
> Do you travel for work a lot? — Yes, I do. / No, I don't.
>
> **Talking about roles and activities**
> Monica Lopez is/She's the Regional Sales Director for Southern Europe.
> I'm a Sales Manager with the Madrid team. I visit clients and …
> We usually have a planning meeting with the sales team when we visit.
> She's our Office Manager here in London. She manages office facilities.

> **SUBJECT AND OBJECT QUESTIONS** → Grammar reference: page 103
>
> **Subject question**
> Who **manages** the team? — Pietro **manages** the team.
>
> **Object question**
> Which team **does** Pietro **manage**? — He **manages the sales team**.

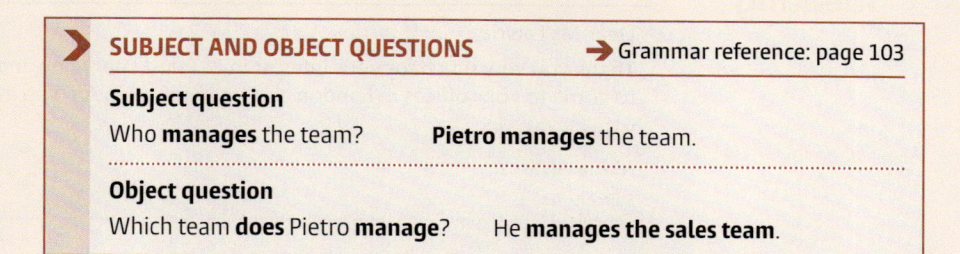

T Extra activities

3A Complete the information about yourself. Use the example to help you.

NAME:	Miguel Diaz
OFFICE:	Singapore
JOB:	Engineer
DEPARTMENT:	Design
ACTIVITIES:	I work with the Design Manager. We develop new products. I sometimes meet customers.

NAME:	
OFFICE:	
JOB:	
DEPARTMENT:	
ACTIVITIES:	

B Work in groups of three. Use the information from Exercise 3A and write a dialogue where one person introduces two others. Use the videoscripts on page 129 to help you.
Student A: You know Student B and Student C. Introduce them.
Student B: You are visiting from another country.
Student C: You are the Office Manager. Welcome Student B and ask questions about Student B's job, department, manager, activities, etc.

C Practise the dialogue. Changes roles and practise again.

Self-assessment I can greet a visitor, make introductions and talk about people and roles. 🙂 ☹

BUSINESS WORKSHOP

We want to meet you ...

Lesson outcome: Learners can answer questions about jobs.

Introduction

1 Read the webpage. Answer the questions.
1. What is *U-Trav-L*?
2. Why do they interview business professionals?
3. Why do they ask you to contact them?

> *U-Trav-L* is a travel sales website for business travellers. Every month, we interview business professionals around the world for the blog on our website. With their help, our blog shows work life and business travel and how it really is. Readers also see their business profile and what their company does.
>
> We always need business professionals for our blog so we'd like to interview you about your job and business travel. Please contact us by email if you would like to be on our website.

Arranging a meeting

2A Work in pairs. Read the email. What does Maria want to do? When?

> Dear Ms Lawrie,
>
> Thank you very much for your interest in *U-Trav-L* magazine and website. We would like to come to your offices in London and interview you. Are you available in March?
>
> Yours sincerely,
>
> Maria Alvarez
> Editor, *U-Trav-L*

B Arrange a meeting by email. Student A: Look at page 115. Student B: Look at page 117.

A phone call

3 Maria Alvarez cannot meet on Friday. She needs to call Angela Lawrie and change the time of the interview. Student A: Look at page 118. Student B: Look at page 116.

The interview

4A Complete Maria's questions for the interview.

1. Which / department / work in / ? *Which department do you work in?*
2. What / do / ?
3. Where / work / ?
4. How / get to work / ?
5. How long / be / your journey / to work / ?
6. How often / travel / abroad / ?
7. Where / travel / to / ?
8. Why / travel for work / ?
9. Do / work on the train/plane / ?
10. What / favourite travel destination / ?

B Maria Alvarez wants to interview Angela Lawrie. Work in pairs. Look at page 116. Take turns to be Maria and Angela.

Talking about your company and travel

5A Work in pairs. You are going to have an interview.

Student A: You are Maria Alvarez. Look at page 115.
Student B: You own a business. Look at page 117.

B Work with a different partner. Take turns to tell each other about the person you interviewed in Exercise 5A. Then decide the best person for Maria to write about in *U-Trav-L* magazine next month.

Self-assessment: I can answer questions about jobs.

Doing business

2

> Can you deliver tomorrow?

Unit overview

2.1 Orders and deliveries
Lesson outcome: Learners can talk about deliveries, orders and quantities.

Vocabulary: Orders and deliveries
Communicative grammar: Things you can and can't count
Video: The Good Eating Company
Task: Asking and answering questions about quantities

2.2 Placing orders on the phone
Lesson outcome: Learners can place a simple order on the phone.

Listening: An order by phone
Vocabulary: An order by phone
Speaking: Placing an order

2.3 Email enquiries
Lesson outcome: Learners can write a short email responding to an enquiry.

Reading: Frequently Asked Questions
Communicative grammar: Saying something exists
Writing: A response to an email enquiry

2.4 Work skills: Making agreements
Lesson outcome: Learners can make a simple business agreement.

Video: Agreeing contract details
Speaking: Making agreements

2.5 Business workshop: Planning a work party
Lesson outcome: Learners can make simple email enquiries and business arrangements on the phone and in person.

Reading: Information from a catering company
Speaking: Comparing information about an order
Writing: Reply to an order enquiry

Review 2: p.88   **Pronunciation:** 2.2 /iː/, /ɪ/ and /aɪ/ 2.3 /tʃ/ and /dʒ/ p.97   **Grammar reference:** 2.1 Things you can and can't count 2.2 can/can't 2.3 Saying something exists p.103

2.1 Orders and deliveries

Lesson outcome — Learners can talk about deliveries, orders and quantities.

Lead-in 1 Do you use food delivery apps? Which ones?

Vocabulary Orders and deliveries

2A Read the text. Are the words in bold verbs or nouns?

What is Jangle?

Jangle ¹**delivers** meals to customers from their favourite restaurants. You can ²**order** your food on our website or with our app. Use your postcode to find restaurants in your area, choose your food and place your ³**order**. The ⁴**supplier** prepares your food and our rider ⁵**delivers** it to you. We make ⁶**deliveries** every day of the year.

B Complete the sentences about the Jangle app with the correct form of the words in Exercise 2A.

1 We often _____ food with the Jangle app. It's quick and easy.
2 Jangle _____ food to homes and offices.
3 Jangle makes thousands of _____ every day.
4 Jangle isn't a food _____ , it's a delivery service.
5 They place a big _____ with Jangle every Friday and the service is great.

3 Look at the webpage about a distribution centre for a supermarket chain. Match the questions (a–d) with the paragraphs (1–4).

a **How many** products do you have here?
b What does a distribution centre do?
c **How much** food do the supermarkets order?
d **How many** people work at the distribution centre?

Jess Patel
Distribution Centre Manager

1 ___ We prepare the orders and deliver them to our supermarkets in each region. We have fifteen regional centres in the country. The supermarkets send their orders via the online platform. We don't have **much** time to prepare **an** order. Our delivery trucks leave here the next day with the order.

2 ___ We have over 400 warehouse workers and about fifty drivers here. It's **a** big centre. We deliver food to supermarkets in the London area and operate twenty-four hours a day.

3 ___ We have over 2,000 products including **some** fresh fruit and vegetables, drinks, tinned food, rice, pasta, cereals and cleaning products. We sell **a lot of** bananas. It's the top-selling product.

4 ___ It depends on the size and location of the store. For example, **a lot of** office workers and tourists use the small city-centre shops. **A** customer usually wants **a** sandwich or **some** sushi for lunch, or **some** snacks and water. **Not many** customers buy fresh fish and meat.

Communicative grammar

> **THINGS YOU CAN AND CAN'T COUNT** ▶ Grammar reference: page 103
>
> **Things you can count**
> **A** sandwich, **an** order, **a** delivery
> **How many** deliveries do you have a week?
> We have **a lot of** / (not) many / some deliveries on Tuesdays.
> We don't have **any** deliveries on Saturdays.
>
> **Things you can't count**
> some / a lot of / not much + coffee, food, fruit, information, money, time
> **How much** coffee do you sell?
> We sell **a lot of** coffee. / We don't sell **much** coffee. / We don't sell **any** coffee.

2.1 Orders and deliveries

4A Look at the words in bold in Exercise 4B. Write (C) for things you can count or (U) for things you can't count.

B Complete the sentences with *a lot of*, *any*, *much* or *many*.

1 Our company sells _____ **T-shirts** in the summer.
2 The shop doesn't sell _____ **winter jackets**, only summer jackets.
3 The factory makes _____ **coffee**. It's a big export for us.
4 We don't make _____ **money** doing this. We do it for free.
5 We don't eat _____ **pasta**. Only a small amount.
6 This shop doesn't sell _____ **jumpers**. Maybe one or two a week.

5 Complete the sentences with *a*, *an* or *some*.

1 This is _____ old warehouse but _____ people still work here.
2 He usually has _____ sandwich and _____ fruit for lunch.
3 The truck arrives in _____ hour to deliver to _____ UK cities.
4 I write _____ email to _____ customer in England every week.

6 Complete the questions with *many* or *much*. Then match the questions and answers.

1 How _____ people work in your company?
2 How _____ money do you spend on travel each week?
3 How _____ emails do you receive every day?
4 How _____ time do you have for lunch at work/college?
5 How _____ coffee do you drink every day?
6 How _____ hours do you work each week?

a On some days, I don't get any. When we're busy, I receive a lot.
b A lot. The train to work costs £50 a week!
c Not many. Twenty in the office and twelve in the warehouse.
d About forty a week, from Monday to Friday.
e Not much. About thirty minutes to an hour.
f A lot! It helps me concentrate in meetings.

T Extra activities

VIDEO

7A ▶ 2.1.1 Watch the video introduction. What do The Good Eating Company do?

B Watch the complete video. Complete the information about the company.

They run around [1]_____ cafés and restaurants. [2]_____ people work at Maxwell's café. The café serves breakfast, lunch and snacks. They sell [3]_____ different types of coffee and also serve over [4]_____ cups of coffee a week. They have lots of different suppliers. They get about [5]_____ deliveries a week. To make their food, they use over [6]_____ kilos of potatoes, thirty kilos of carrots, ten kilos of lettuce and [7]_____ eggs per week.

C Watch the video again. Choose the correct option.

1 Jodie is *Operations Manager / CEO* at The Good Eating Company.
2 The Good Eating Company have cafes in London and *Scotland / Ireland*.
3 Maxwell is a *Chef / Café Manager* at The Good Eating Company.
4 The café *sells a lot of / doesn't sell many* flat whites.
5 The Good Eating Company like to use *international / local* suppliers.
6 Jodie speaks to *delivery companies / suppliers* on the phone.
7 Fresh produce arrives in the *morning / afternoon*.
8 For lunch customers buy sandwiches, salads, fruit and *hot dishes / dessert*.

*produce = a large amount of food (often fresh) from farms, e.g. fruit and vegetables

*run a business = manage a business

TASK

8A Work with a partner. Ask and answer the questions in Exercise 6.

B Look at page 126. Follow the instructions.

Self-assessment: I can talk about deliveries, orders and quantities.

2.2 Placing orders on the phone

Lesson outcome — Learners can place a simple order on the phone.

Lead-in

1 Work in pairs. Student A: Look at the order form below. Ask student B questions to complete the information. Student B: Look at page 118.

- What's the order number?
- What's the company address?
- What's the product code number?

ORDER NUMBER	1
CUSTOMER NAME	Donaldson Group
COMPANY ADDRESS	3
CUSTOMER REFERENCE NUMBER	CR88510765V
PRODUCT	Green one-litre bottles
PRODUCT CODE NUMBER	5
QUANTITY	250

Listening — An order by phone

2 A 🔊 2.01 Look at the catalogue for Eco Boxes and listen to a phone call. What information does the customer need from Eco Boxes?

ECOBOXES: Takeaway boxes

PRODUCT	REFERENCE NUMBER	SIZE	COLOUR	QUANTITY
Small box	TGB01	57 x 115 x 75 mm	Two colours	25 units
Medium box	TGB02	62 x 145 x 95 mm	Two colours	20 units
Big box	TGB03	70 x 225 x 95 mm	Two colours	10 units

B Listen again. Choose the correct option (1–8) below.

PRODUCT PRICES
- Small Box   TGB01 [1]£2.50 / 2.60
- Medium Box   TGB02 [2]£2.00 / 3.00
- Big Box   TGB03 [3]£2.00 / 3.00
- Colours   [4]natural / black / white / beige
- Quantity   [5]400 / 500 TGB01 and [6]400 / 500 TGB02
- Delivery date   [7]Monday 25th / 26th
- Total cost   [8]£115 / 150
- Delivery   free of charge

Vocabulary — An order by phone

3 🔊 2.02 Complete the phrases from the dialogue. Then listen and check.

1. Eco Boxes. Laura _____ . How can I help you?
2. I'd like to _____ some of your new takeaway boxes.
3. Do you _____ the product reference numbers?
4. How _____ are the three boxes?
5. How much does _____ cost?
6. How _____ boxes do you need?
7. Can you _____ by Monday 26th?
8. I'm very _____ , we can't. We don't have any in stock*.
9. Certainly, I'll _____ your order on the system.
10. How _____ is that in total?

*in stock = the product is in the shop / the supplier has the product you want to buy

T Extra activities

4 Categorise the phrases in Exercise 3. Write *customer* (C) or *salesperson* (S).

➔ page 96 See Pronunciation bank: /iː/, /ɪ/ and /aɪ/

2.2 Placing orders on the phone

> **CAN/CAN'T** → Grammar reference: page 104
>
> We use *can* to say something is possible. We use *can't* when something is not possible.
>
> +/− We **can** deliver the order on Monday. They **can't** deliver today.
> ? **Can** you deliver the order on Monday? Yes, we **can**. / Sorry, we **can't**.

Extra activities

Speaking

5 Work in pairs. Student A: Read the instructions below. Student B: Look at page 116.

Roleplay 1: You are the customer. You own Super Sun sushi restaurant and need to order some boxes.

- Look at the catalogue.
- Phone your partner and order some boxes.
- You want to know:
  – the colours, prices and delivery costs.
- You would like:
  – 100 small white boxes and 200 big white boxes.
  – to know the total cost of the order.
  – delivery tomorrow.
- Use the phrases in Exercise 3 to help you.

ECOBOXES: Salad and sushi boxes

PRODUCT	REFERENCE NUMBER	SIZE	COLOUR	QUANTITY	PRICE	PRICE PER 100
Small salad and sushi box	SUB01	57 x 115 x 75 mm	Two colours – _____ , _____	25 units	_____	£20
Big salad and sushi box	SUB02	70 x 225 x 95 mm	Two colours – _____ , _____	20 units	_____	£30

Roleplay 2: You work for Eco Boxes.

- Look at the catalogue.
- Answer the phone and take the customer's order.
- You need to know:
  – the customer's name and company name.
  – details of the order (quantities and colours).
- Use the phrases in Exercise 3 to help you.
- You need to tell the customer:
  – You only have blue boxes in stock.
  – Delivery cost: £6 all orders under £40, free of charge over £40.
  – Delivery time: two working days.

ECOBOXES: Sandwich and burger boxes

PRODUCT	REFERENCE NUMBER	SIZE	COLOUR	QUANTITY	PRICE	PRICE PER 100
Sandwich box	SAB01	57 x 115 x 75 mm	Two colours – blue and white	20 units	£4	£17.50
Burger box	BBB03	70 x 225 x 95mm	Two colours – blue and white	20 units	£6	£22.50

Self-assessment I can place a simple order on the phone.

2.3 Email enquiries

Lesson outcome Learners can write a short email responding to an enquiry.

Lead-in

1A Match the words (1-4) with the definitions (a-d).
1 exchange   a things you buy
2 purchases   b take or send back something you buy in a shop or online
3 refund   c get something different for something you buy and don´t want
4 return   d get money back for something you buy but don't want

B Discuss the questions.
1 Do you sometimes return things you buy in shops or online?
2 Do you prefer to exchange your purchases or get a refund?

Reading

2 Read a company's Frequently Asked Questions (FAQs) about orders. Match the questions (a-d) with the correct section (1-4) on the webpage.
a Can I return my order?   c Can I exchange or cancel my order?
b **Is there a** delivery charge?   d **Are there any** discounts for large orders?

Orders and returns FAQs

1 _____
Delivery is free of charge in the EU for orders of €50 and over. **There is a charge** for orders under €50. **Click here** for delivery charges.

2 _____
Yes, **there are some discounts**. Please contact **Customer Services** for information.

3 _____
Yes, **there is some time** to change or cancel your order before delivery. Please contact **Customer Services** as soon as possible.

4 _____
Yes, you have thirty days to return your online purchases free of charge. **There are two easy ways** you can return your order. **Click here** for details.

3A Read the replies to two customers' enquiries. Which FAQ does each enquiry refer to?

Dear Ms Mayer,
¹_____ **there are two ways** you can return your order. You can go to one of our stores and they can exchange the goods or refund your money. ²_____ a list of our stores. We can also collect the goods from your home address free of charge. Please click on this link to complete the return form.
³_____ if you have any questions.
Regards,

Dear Mr Weber,
⁴_____ **There aren't any delivery charges** in the EU for orders over €50. **There is a charge** for orders €50 and under. Standard delivery costs €4.50 and express delivery costs €6.50.
Please contact us if you have any questions.
Regards,

B Complete the replies with the phrases in the box.

Please find attached
Please contact us
Thank you for your enquiry.
In response to your enquiry,

T Extra activities

➡ **page 97** See Pronunciation bank: /tʃ/ and /dʒ/

2.3 | Email enquiries

Communicative grammar

> **SAYING SOMETHING EXISTS** → Grammar reference: page 104
>
> + **There is (There's) a** delivery **charge**.
>   **There is (There's) some time** to change your order.
>   **There are some discounts** on large orders.
>
> − **There is not (isn't) a store** near me.
>   **There are not (aren't) any** delivery **charges** within the EU.
>   **There is not (isn't) any information** on the website.
>
> ? **Is there a discount** for a large order?   Yes, **there is**. / No, **there isn't**.
>   **Are there any deliveries** at the weekend?   Yes, **there are**. / No, **there aren't**.
>   **Is there any time** to cancel my order?   Yes, **there is**. / No, **there isn't**.

4 Choose the correct option to complete the sentences.
1 There *is / are* some problems in the warehouse.
2 There *is / are* a problem with your order.
3 There *is / are* some products that you can't return.
4 There *is / are* some food in this order.
5 There isn't *any / some* information on the website.
6 There aren't *any / some* discounts on orders.
7 There *isn't / aren't* any white boxes in stock.
8 There *isn't / aren't* any space in the truck.

5A Complete the two dialogues with the correct form of *there is/isn't* or *there are/aren't*.

A: ¹_____ _____ any photocopy paper in the office?
B: Yes, ²_____ some pink A4 paper. Here you are.
A: No, I need white paper. ³_____ _____ any white paper?
B: Sorry! No, ⁴_____ _____. I'll order some now.

C: Three new employees start work today. ⁵_____ _____ any desks and computer chairs for them?
D: Yes, ⁶_____ some new furniture in the warehouse.
C: ⁷_____ _____ any office equipment for them?
D: No, ⁸_____ _____. What exactly do they need?
C: Three phones, three computers and a printer.

B 🔊 2.03 Listen and check your answers. In pairs, practise the dialogues.

Writing

6 Look at an email from another customer. Write a response to her enquiry. Use phrases from Exercise 3B to help you.

From:	Liudvika Kuliešienė
To:	Customers Services
Subject:	Prices and discounts for large orders

I'd like to place a large order for photocopy paper. I can't find any prices on the website. Is there a discount for a large order? Are there any delivery charges?
Regards,
Liudvika Kuliešienė

T Extra activities

Self-assessment   I can write a short email responding to an enquiry.

2.4 WORK SKILLS
Making agreements

Lesson outcome — Learners can make a simple business agreement.

Lead-in 1 Look at the photos and the phrases. Do you have a cleaning service where you work, live or study? What do cleaners do?

clean the floor  — empty the bins  — clean the desks  — vacuum the carpet  — wash dishes/cups

VIDEO 2 ▶ 2.4.1 Izabela, an office manager, has a meeting with Robert, a cleaning company owner. They discuss a cleaning contract. Watch the video. In what order do they talk about these things? Number the items 1–5.

a the cost of the service ____
b the working days ____
c the cleaning tasks ____
d the description of the office ____
e the working hours ____

3 Watch the video again and complete Robert's notes with a word, number or phrase.

> **ROBERT'S CLEANING SERVICES**
> - Places to clean: reception area, one big office, two ^{1}_____ , a staff kitchen on the first floor; one big office, four individual ^{2}_____ on the second floor; two staff toilets (one on each floor) and the stairs.
> - Jobs to do: clean the desks; empty the bins and ^{3}_____ , clean the toilets, the kitchen area and wash the coffee cups.
> - Days of work: ^{4}_____
> - Hours of work: Before ^{5}_____ a.m.
> - Total hours of contract ^{6}_____ (per day), ^{7}_____ (per week).
> - Agreed price: ^{8}£_____ including charge for the cleaning products.
> - Cleaning equipment in the cupboard in the ^{9}_____ .

4 Match the questions with the answers. Watch the video again and check your answers.

1 What do you want the cleaner to do, exactly?
2 Can the cleaner wash the coffee cups?
3 Do you want us to clean the windows?
4 How many cleaners are there?
5 How much time does the cleaner need?
6 Does the price include cleaning products?
7 How much is that?
8 When can the cleaner start?

a It's usually one cleaner for an office this size.
b About three hours a day.
c How about next Monday?
d Yes, of course.
e No, we have a specialist company to clean the windows.
f Clean the desks, empty the bins and clean the floors.
g No, it doesn't. There's a small charge for those.
h It's ten pounds a week.

T Extra activities

24

2.4 Work skills: Making agreements

Speaking

> **MAKING AGREEMENTS**
>
> **Asking about the company's service**
> How many [workers / chefs] are there?
> How about (coming) [before / after] [8 o'clock / we start work]?
> Can [you / your team] do that?
> How much time do you need?
> Can [you/your team] provide the [materials / plates / cleaning products]?
> How much is that [for fifteen / twenty hours a week]?
> Does the price include [materials / cleaning products / delivery]?
> When can [you / your team] start?
>
> **Asking the client questions**
> What do you want [the cleaner / us] to do (exactly)?
> How many [days / hours] do you need the [cleaning / catering] service?
> What time do you want the [cleaner / chef] to come?
> Is there a place for the [cleaning products / materials]?
> How about [on Monday / on the 14th]?
>
> | **Saying yes** | **Saying no** |
> |---|---|
> | Yes, we can. / Yes, it does. | No, we can't. (I'm sorry). |
> | Yes, that's fine/right. / Yes, of course. | No, it doesn't. (I'm sorry). |

5 Work in pairs. Read your information. Roleplay the situation.
   Student A: You represent Robert's Cleaning Services. Look at page 117.
   Student B: Your need a cleaner for your office. Look at page 122.

6 Work in pairs. Read your information. Roleplay the situation.
   Student A: You need a catering service for your office party. Look at page 117.
   Student B: You represent a catering service. Look at page 120.

Student A / **Student B**

- Student B: Ask if Student A wants a hot or cold buffet.
- Student A: Answer with details about the buffet you want.
- Student B: Ask how many people the buffet is for.
- Student A: Answer.
- Student B: Ask what day/time the party is.
- Student A: Answer.
- Student B: Ask if there is a kitchen at Student A's office.
- Student A: Answer. Ask how many catering staff they provide.
- Student B: Tell Student A how many staff you provide for hot/cold buffets.
- Student A: Ask Student B if their staff can clean the room after the party.
- Student B: Answer.
- Student A: Ask Student B if their company provides plates/glasses.
- Student B: Answer.
- Student A: Ask Student B how much they charge for the service.
- Student B: Answer.

Self-assessment: I can make a simple business agreement.

BUSINESS WORKSHOP

Planning a work party

Lesson outcome: Learners can make simple email enquiries and simple business arrangements on the phone and in person.

Introduction

1 You work in the human resources department at Benham Engineering. You receive this email. What do you need to do?

Subject: Emilia's 20th Anniversary Party

We'd like to celebrate Emilia's twenty years with Benham Engineering. Can you organise a party for everyone? Here are the details:

Date: Wednesday 14 March
Time: 12.00 to 14.00
Place: Conference room
Number of people: Sixty
Catering: a light buffet lunch with sandwiches, canapés, fruit and desserts

Please arrange for a catering company to do the food service. We can buy the drinks. Can you also arrange the extra cleaning service with the cleaners after the party?

Best regards,

Reading

2 Look at the information from a catering company and complete the questions in the email.

Carter-Villiers CATERERS

Sandwich platters
£16.50 per platter
Each platter serves six people. We provide a selection of sandwiches and baguettes on white and brown bread. Please select from the menu.

Canapés
£9.95 per person
Please select from the menu.

Cake platters
£14.50

Cut fruit platter
£12.50

Please place your orders online before 1.30 p.m. for next-day deliveries. Minimum order is £30.
If you have any questions, call 0938 665 0123 or email customerservice@carter-villiers.

- Any vegetarian options?
- Number of canapés per person?
- Number of people one platter serves?
- Cost of delivery?
- Discount for large order?

To: customerservice@carter-villiers
From: Anita Patterson
Subject: Enquiry about a catering order

Dear Sir/Madam,

We would like to order food for lunch at Benham Engineering on Wednesday 14 March and I have some questions. Firstly, ¹a_____ t_____ any sandwiches for vegetarians? I couldn't find any on the website.

The selection of canapés is very good. ²H_____ m_____ canapés are there per person? We also want to order cake and cut fruit platters. ³H_____ m_____ people does each platter serve? Finally, ⁴h_____ m_____ does delivery cost and ⁵i_____ t _____ a discount for large orders? We want to order food for sixty people.

Regards,

Anita Patterson
Human Resources Assistant
Benham Engineering

---

3 Write a reply to the email in Exercise 2.

Speaking

4A Work in pairs. Student A: Read the information below. Student B: Look at page 119.

You are Anita Patterson from Benham Engineering. Read the information and phone Carter-Villiers caterers to order food for the party.

Write the cost of the order in your notes.

BENHAM ENGINEERING

Lunch order for 14 March
Order details
- Selection of canapés for sixty people
- Ten sandwich platters: five meat, three fish, two vegetarian
- Ten cake platters
- Eight cut fruit platters

Delivery time: 11.30 a.m.
Total cost with five percent discount? _____

B Compare your information. Are all the details of the order correct?

5 Work in pairs. Student A: Look at page 127. Student B: Look at page 119.

Self-assessment: I can make simple email enquiries and simple business arrangements on the phone and in person.

Changes

> How old is your company?

Unit overview

3.1	**A company's story** **Lesson outcome:** Learners can describe changes at work.	**Vocabulary:** A company's story **Communicative grammar:** Talking about the past (1) **Video:** How we started **Task:** Completing a timeline
3.2	**New office** **Lesson outcome:** Learners can write about a change at the workplace.	**Vocabulary:** Email phrases **Reading:** An email about meeting room rules **Listening:** A conversation about an office move **Writing:** An email giving instructions
3.3	**Company performance** **Lesson outcome:** Learners can write about a company's performance.	**Reading:** Past successes and challenges **Communicative grammar:** Talking about the past (2) **Writing:** An email describing successes and challenges
3.4	**Work skills:** How did it go? **Lesson outcome:** Learners can talk about how a project went.	**Video:** How did the project go? **Speaking:** Talking about projects
3.5	**Business workshop:** Our first year **Lesson outcome:** Learners can write an email about their company.	**Reading:** A timeline about a new company **Writing:** Preparing for a move **Speaking:** Asking questions about a new company

Review 3: p.89 | **Pronunciation:** 3.1 The -ed ending p.97 3.3 /ɜː/ and /ɔː/ p.98 | **Grammar reference:** 3.1 Talking about the past (1) 3.2 Giving instructions 3.3 Talking about the past (2) p.104

3.1 A company's story

Lesson outcome — Learners can describe changes at work.

Lead-in

1 Work in pairs. Think of a businessperson and answer the questions.
1 What's his/her name?
2 What's the name of his/her company?
3 What does his/her company do, make or sell?

Vocabulary — A company's story

TIMELINE: COSTA COFFEE

2A Read the timeline. In how many countries does Costa Coffee operate?

1960s The Costa family, with sons Sergio and Bruno, ¹**move** from Italy to London.

1978 The Costa brothers ⁴**open** a coffee shop – Costa Coffee.

1985–1995 Costa opens more shops and ⁶**hires** more employees. By 1995, there are forty-one shops in the UK.

2006 Costa ⁸**launches** the Costa Book Awards, giving prizes to the best writers in England and Ireland.

1971 Brothers Bruno and Sergio Costa ²**start** a coffee supply company in London. They ³**produce** coffee for local food sellers.

1985 Bruno leaves the business and ⁵**creates** a different company.

1999 Costa ⁷**expands** its market – the company opens a shop in Dubai.

2019 Costa has more than 3,800 shops in thirty-one countries.

B Match the verbs in bold (1–8) in Exercise 2B with their past form in the sentences (a–h).

a No, they didn't. In their first year, Costa Coffee **produced** coffee for local food sellers.
b Yes, he did. In 1985, Bruno **created** a different company.
c The Costa brothers **moved** from Italy in 1960.
d In 1999, Costa **expanded** its market and opened a shop in Dubai.
e In 1971, the Costa Brothers **started** a coffee supply company in London.
f They **opened** a Costa Coffee shop in 1978.
g Costa Coffee opened more shops in the UK and **hired** more employees from 1985 to 1995.
h In 2006, they **launched** the Costa Book Awards.

C Match the questions (1–8) with the sentences (a–h) in Exercise 2B.

1 Where did the Costa family move from?
2 Who started Costa Coffee?
3 Did they open a coffee shop at the beginning?
4 When did they open a Costa Coffee shop?
5 Did Bruno start his own company in 1985?
6 When did Costa open more shops in the UK?
7 When did Costa expand its market to other countries?
8 What did the company launch in 2006?

T Extra activities

Communicative grammar

> **TALKING ABOUT THE PAST (1)** → Grammar reference: page 104
>
> **+** The Costa brothers **moved** from Italy to London in 1960.
> I **joined** the company eight years ago.
>
> **?** **Did** Sergio **start** his own company? — Yes, he **did**. / No, he **didn't**.
> **Did** they **start** Costa Coffee? — Yes, they **did**. / No, they **didn't**.
> **Did** the company **change** its name? — Yes, it **did**. / No, it **didn't**.
>
> **?** When **did** they **open** a shop? — In 2002. / They **opened** a shop in 2002.
> What year **did** the company **expand**? — Last year. / It **expanded** last year.
> Who **did** you **hire** last year? — An HR Manager. / I **hired** an HR Manager.
>
> **?** Who **started** the company? — The two brothers **started** the company.
> Who **designed** the product? — Angela **designed** the product.
> Which company **launched** Windows? — Microsoft **launched** Windows.

→ page 97 See Pronunciation bank: The *-ed* ending

3.1 A company's story

TIMELINE – BILL GATES

- **1973** Finishes school.
- **1975** Starts Microsoft.
- **1973–1975** Studies at Harvard University – doesn't finish.
- **1985** Launches Windows.
- **2000** His job changes at Microsoft from CEO to Chairman.
- **2014** His job changes from Chairman to Technology Advisor.
- **2017** Plays a tennis match with Roger Federer to make money for charity.

3A Complete the sentences with the correct verb in the past.

1 He _____ school in 1973.
2 He _____ at Harvard for about two years.
3 He _____ Microsoft in 1975.
4 He _____ Windows in 1985.
5 His job _____ at Microsoft in 2000.
6 He _____ tennis with Roger Federer in 2017.

B Put the words in the correct order to make questions.

1 1973 / did / what / Bill Gates / in / do / ? _____
2 he / finish / university / did / ? _____
3 did / when / he / Microsoft / start / ? _____
4 1985 / did / what / in / launch / he / ? _____
5 his job / at Microsoft / did / change / in 2000 / ? _____
6 who / he / did / tennis with / play / in 2017 / ? _____

C Work in pairs. Ask and answer the questions in Exercise 3B.

4 Work in pairs. Ask and answer the questions.

1 When did you start school?
2 What was your first job?
3 Who was your first boss?
4 When did you start your job?
5 When did you last change job or move city?

VIDEO

5A ▶ 3.1.1 Watch the video introduction. What do Postmark and The Cambridge Satchel Company sell?

B Watch Part 1 of the video. Answer the questions.
1 Who started Postmark?
2 When did Postmark start?
3 What was the annual turnover in a) 2006? b) last year?
4 How many stores and employees does Postmark have?
5 When did Morgan arrive in the UK and what did she do?
6 When did Morgan join Postmark?

C Watch Part 2 of the video. Are the sentences *true* (T) or *false* (F)? Correct the false sentences.
1 At the beginning, The Cambridge Satchel Company only had three colours of bags.
2 The company opened a factory in 2012.
3 The company now has 150 employees.
4 The company has two shops – one in Cambridge and one in London.
5 Max is the manager of The Cambridge Satchel Company shop in London.
6 Max designed the first shop for Cambridge Satchel Company.

annual turnover = the total sales of a business in one year

6 Work in pairs. Ask and answer questions and complete the timeline.
Student A: Look at page 115. Student B: Look at page 119.

> TASK

Self-assessment — I can describe changes at work.

3.2 New office

Lesson outcome Learners can write about a change at the workplace.

Lead-in

1 Answer the questions.
1 Do you work/study in the same place every day? Where?
2 How often do you have to change your work/study location?
3 Do you prefer to stay in one location, or do you like change?
I prefer to have the same desk every day because ...

Vocabulary Email phrases

2A Read the email. Answer the questions.
1 Who wrote the email?
2 What do employees need to do?

Subject: New workspaces

¹To all staff,

This week, the new Hong Kong project started and we are now in new teams. Next week, there are new arrangements for all teams, and new workspaces for everyone. In preparation for this on Friday, ²please do the following:

- remove everything from your desk.
- put all of your things in a box.
- write your name on the box.
- please don't move the box. That job is for the warehouse workers.
- look at the plan attached and find your new workspace.

³Thank you for your help. Have a great weekend!

⁴Best wishes,

Beth Lowry
Office Manager

B Match the phrases (a–d) with the phrases (1–4) in the email.
a Regards, ____
b Dear employees, ____
c We appreciate your cooperation. ____
d Please follow these instructions. ____

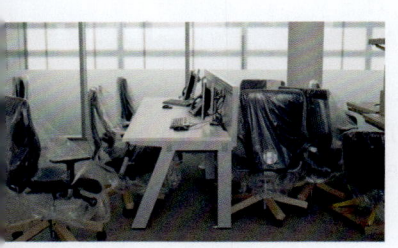

> **GIVING INSTRUCTIONS** → Grammar reference: page 106
>
> **What to do**
> **Remove** everything from your desk.
> **Put** all your things in a box.
> **Please use** two boxes.
>
> **What *not* to do**
> **Don't put** all your things in one box.
> Please **don't move** the box.

3 Match the sentence halves.

1 Please arrive   a your things on your new desk.
2 Don't be   b at the new office at 8.00 a.m. on Monday morning.
3 Find   c your new workspace on the office plan.
4 Don't change   d the lunch party at 12.30 p.m.
5 Put   e desks with other employees, please.
6 Please join   f late.

T Extra activities

3.2 New office

Reading and Listening

4 Complete the instructions with the correct form of the words and phrases in the box.

> dear all   don't have   don't use   for your cooperation   go   make   regards   talk

Subject: Meeting room rules

¹_____ ,

We love the new offices, but we had some problems last week with meeting rooms. Please ²_____ a meeting room without a reservation. When you need a room, please ³_____ to Agnes and ⁴_____ a reservation. Please ⁵_____ lunch in meeting rooms. ⁶_____ to the company canteen for food.
Thank you ⁷_____ .

⁸_____ ,

Denise Woo
Admin Assistant

5A 🔊 3.01 Listen to the conversation and answer the questions.
1. Why does the company need to move?
2. What event is on Friday evening?

B Listen again. Complete the notes.

Company hired ¹_____ new employees last month, need to move to ²_____ , _____ offices.

Thursday:
- Everyone in the office: ³_____ a.m.
- Desk items in boxes. Boxes stay in ⁴_____ .
- No staff in office after ⁵_____ .

Friday:
- Morning – no work. Arrival time – ⁶_____ .
- Employees find desks – don't ⁷_____ desks!
- Items on new desks.
- ⁸_____ – party for new office.

Writing

6A Write instructions about the notes in Exercise 5A. Use the words and phrases in the box.

> arrive   find (x2)   join   not change   not come   not stay   put

1. Thursday: Please _____ at the office by 9.00 a.m.
2. _____ all desk items in boxes.
3. Thursday: _____ in the office after 12.30 p.m.
4. _____ to work on Friday morning.
5. _____ your new desk and please _____ it!
6. You can _____ your office items on your new desk.
7. Please _____ us for a celebration at 6.00 p.m.

B Write an email giving instructions for the office move in Exercise 5B.

Self-assessment   I can write about a change at the workplace.

3.3 Company performance

Lesson outcome — Learners can write about a company's performance.

Lead-in **1A** How do you receive communication from your place of work/study?

- ☐ blog post
- ☐ website
- ☐ newsletter
- ☐ emails
- ☐ intranet
- ☐ other _____

B How often do you receive this type of communication? What is it usually about?

Reading Past successes and challenges

2A Read the email about KwikBike. Did they succeed? Tick (✓) *Yes* or *No* for points 1–6.

Target	Yes	No
1 Hit the target number of new shops		
2 Get to know corporate customers very well		
3 Advertise to win more customers		
4 Win customers in the Overton area		
5 Create a booking system		
6 Make booking fast		

✉
To: all staff
From: simon.owen@kwikbike
Subject: Another great year for KwikBike – Thank you

Monday 22 December

Dear Team,

First, a big thank you for all your hard work in the last year. We **made** good progress at KwikBike. We **grew** our retail business from ten stores to twelve and we **built** strong relationships with important corporate customers. Unfortunately, we **didn't hit** our target of fourteen stores, so we need to investigate new areas for business.

We also **went** to bike events, **bought** advertising there and offered discounts, and this **won** new business, especially in the Northside area. However, we **didn't win** any new business in the Overton area so we want to make progress there next year. We also **spent** $10,000 on our online booking system. Our sales started to increase, but some customers **had** problems with it. We need to improve this system as soon as possible so we don't lose sales.

Overall, it **was** a great year. Well done everyone! I look forward to next year.

Best regards,

Simon Owen

B Match the verbs in bold in the email with their present form.

- **a** hit – *hit*
- **b** make
- **c** win
- **d** have
- **e** build
- **f** grow
- **g** buy
- **h** spend
- **i** be
- **j** go
- **k** don't hit
- **l** don't win

C Answer the questions.

1. How many shops did KwikBike have at the beginning of last year? _____
2. How many shops do they have now? _____
3. Where did they advertise? _____
4. Where did the advertising win new business? _____
5. How much did they spend on their online booking system? _____

➔ **page 98** See Pronunciation bank: /ɜː/ and /ɔː/

3.3 Company performance

Communicative grammar

TALKING ABOUT THE PAST (2)
→ Grammar reference: page 106

+/- Irregular verbs
We **grew** our retail business.
It **was** a great year. We **made** good progress.

Negatives
We **didn't grow** our retail business.
It **wasn't (was not)** a good year.

3 Complete the sentences with the correct form of the words in the box.

| buy | hire | make (x2) | miss | not buy | not grow | not meet | win |

1 We _____ our sales targets, so we need to find new customers.
2 We _____ new desks, but we _____ any new chairs.
3 We _____ a new Sales Manager and we hired a new Office Manager.
4 We _____ new business, but we also _____ some mistakes.
5 We _____ our retail business, so we need to work on this next year.
6 We _____ some sales targets. However, we _____ a lot of money in other areas.

T Extra activities

4 Complete the summary with the correct past form of the verbs in brackets.

Summary of last year

We ¹ _didn't have_ (not have) any problems in our retail business and we ² _____ (make) good progress.
We:
- ³ _____ (hit) our sales targets.
- ⁴ _____ (buy) new equipment and made production faster.
- ⁵ _____ (win) new customers in some areas.
- ⁶ _____ (not spend) too much money. We were €150,000 under budget.

What we need to do next.
We:
- ⁷ _____ (not build) any new business relationships in new markets. We need to build more next year, especially in South America. We have plans for the sales team to visit new customers very soon.
- ⁸ _____ (not grow) our sales profit in China. This is a key market for us, and we want to continue to grow here.

Writing

5 Read the notes about a company's performance last year. Write an email about the performance to the new Sales Manager.

SUCCESSES
spent €16,000 on advertising = won a lot of new business in North America; made progress in areas with lots of competition – Japan, South Korea

CHALLENGES
no growth of export business because sales targets not hit in Europe – customers didn't buy new product immediately

REASONS TO BE POSITIVE
good relationships built with new customers in Europe last year – we can increase sales in first six months this year

AIMS
hire more Sales Reps to sell new products in Europe

Dear Anthony,
Welcome to the team! Here is a summary of last year's sales report.
At the start, …

Self-assessment I can write about a company's performance.

3.4 WORK SKILLS
How did it go?

Lesson outcome   Learners can talk about how a project went.

Lead-in **1A** Match each picture (A–I) with a process step (1–3).
1 Design   2 Manufacturing   3 Delivery to shops

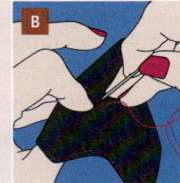

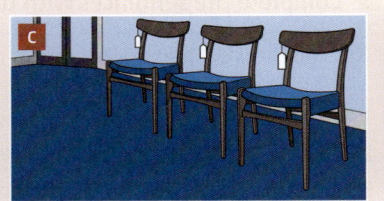

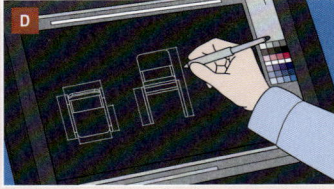

B Which three pictures show the design to delivery process for
1 a car? ___ , ___ , ___   2 a jacket? ___ , ___ , ___   3 a chair? ___ , ___ , ___

C Do you own or use products similar to these? Describe them (colour, design, manufacturer, etc.).

VIDEO **2A** ▶ 3.4.1 Watch the start of the video. Why did William arrange a meeting with the designers?

B Watch the complete video. Tick (✓) the topics they talk about.
- [ ] The customers' comments about the new jacket
- [ ] Ellen's other new clothing designs
- [ ] Problems with teamwork
- [ ] The design of the jacket
- [ ] Problems with manufacturing
- [ ] Problems with money
- [ ] Communication problems
- [ ] Something that needs to change
- [ ] Ellen's pay for the work

C Watch the video again. Put the stages of the project (a–f) in the correct order.
a They had a problem with the material from the supplier.   ___
b Ellen started designing the jacket.   ___
c They had a problem with the schedule – manufacturing were late.   ___
d The team helped her and answered her questions.   ___
e They were didn't meet the delivery deadline for the shops.   ___
f They changed to a different supplier.   ___

3A Match the questions with the answers. Look at the videoscript on page 130 if necessary.
1 How did it go, generally?
2 What went well in particular?
3 What didn't go well?
4 What did you do?
5 What was the problem?
6 Why did this happen?
7 What do we need to change?

a There were one or two problems with the jackets.
b They didn't meet the deadline.
c The teamwork.
d We didn't communicate the new dates for delivery.
e Communicate the dates to everyone. We need to have regular update meetings.
f We changed to a different supplier.
g I think it went well.

T Extra activities

B Look at page 130. Practise reading the script with a partner.

3.4 Work skills: How did it go?

Speaking

1 Mark designs the shoe.

2 The team tests the design. The teamwork was really good.

3 They start to produce the shoe, but they have a problem with the material.

4 They change to a different material.

5 They miss a deadline. They have communication problems with the shipping company – the shipping instructions aren't clear.

6 The shoes are in the shops – and customers really like them!

> **TALKING ABOUT PROJECTS**

Asking about projects	Saying how it went
How did it go, generally?	It went well. / Not very well. It was OK. / There were one or two problems.
What went well, in particular?	We met each (project) deadline.
What didn't go well?	We had a problem with [the suppliers / our client]. There was a problem with [our materials / some of the team].
What was your experience?	The [project / teamwork] was [good / great]. There were one or two problems with [the clients / the designs].
What did you do?	We changed to a different factory. I started to ask more questions.
What happened? / Why did this happen?	We didn't communicate the changes well. We made some mistakes in planning.
What was the problem?	The supplier didn't explain the changes. We didn't meet the deadline.
What do we need to change?	Next time … We need to improve our design. I want to make the process clearer.

4A Look at the pictures (1–6) and read about a product. Answer the questions.
1 What is the product?
2 What three problems did the team have?
3 Did the shops like the product?

B Work in pairs. Look at page 116 and write a dialogue about a shoe-design project. Use the photos to help you.

Student A   **Student B**

Congratulate Student B.
→ Thank Student A.
Ask how the project went.
← Answer.
Ask what went well.
← Answer.
Ask what didn't go well.
← Answer, and explain the problems.
Ask what you need to change.
← Say what you want to change.
Say that it's OK now and everyone's happy.

A: Congratulations! The shoes are in the shops today!
B: Thanks. Yeah, I'm very happy!
A: So how did the project go, generally?
B: It went well, thanks.
A: Tell me about it. What went well, in particular?
B: The teamwork. It was …

C Practise the dialogue.

Self-assessment

I can talk about how a project went.

BUSINESS WORKSHOP

Our first year

Lesson outcome: Learners can write an email about company changes.

A company's first year

1A Read the timeline. Complete the notes.

TIMELINE	SOFTWARE DE JOGO
January	Brother and sister João and Manuela Silva create a simple smartphone game called *Vai-Vai*. However, they don't launch the game. They want to make it better first. They hire two software engineers to make the game better. They don't open an office. They work from their home.
March	They create a software company and call it Software de Jogo.
April	They rent an office in their home city, Brasilia.
June	They launch *Vai-Vai* in Portuguese. It's an instant success in Brazil and Portugal.
August	They hire translators for an English version of *Vai-Vai*.
October	The Silvas move their office from Brasilia to Campinas – Brazil's Silicon Valley. They hire a product manager and two more engineers to produce more games.
December	Software de Jogo expands its range of games to five.

The name of João and Manuela's game:
1 _____

The name of their company:
2 _____

Original location of company:
3 _____

Location of company from October:
4 _____

How they expanded in October:
5 _____

Number of games in range from December:
6 _____

B Work in pairs. Student A: Look at page 118. Student B: Look at page 120. Ask and answer questions about Software de Jogo.

Preparing for a move

2 It is October and the company needs to move to Campinas next week. Use João's notes to write instructions to the team for the move.

Move to Campinas
- It's next week!
- Employees' jobs for Friday =
  – removing everything from desk
  – putting things in a box
  – writing name on box – boxes not be moved
    – should leave on desk!
- Remember to thank the team for cooperation.

3 João writes an email to his staff to thank them for the work they did last year. Put the sentences (a–i) in the correct order.

a We grew our range of games from one to five, and we built strong relationships with other businesses here in Campinas.

b Unfortunately, we didn't win any new business in other countries so we didn't hit our target of 100,000 sales.

c First, a big thank you to the team for your work, and for the progress we made at Software de Jogo last year – it was an amazing start for our new business.

d However, we know this is because we had some problems with the English translation of *Vai-Vai*, so we couldn't launch it in August.

e Last week, we fixed the problem, and we plan to launch the English version in January next year.

f We also bought advertising on social media in Portuguese and this won new business throughout Brazil and Portugal.

g Best regards, João and Manuela

h Overall, we had a great year and we look forward to working with you next year.

i Dear all,

How the first year went

4 Work in pairs. You are going to ask and answer some interview questions.

Student A: Look at page 118.
Student B: Look at page 125.

Self-assessment: I can write an email about company changes.

Travelling for work 4

> *Are you travelling for work next week?*

Unit overview

4.1 **I'm flying to Tokyo tomorrow**
Lesson outcome: Learners can talk about travel arrangements.

Vocabulary: Travel arrangements
Communicative grammar: Talking about arrangements
Video: Away on business
Task: Arranging a time to meet

4.2 **The 12.05 is delayed**
Lesson outcome: Learners can write a text message to apologise and explain why they are late.

Vocabulary: Airports and train stations
Reading and listening: Dealing with delays
Writing: Writing a text message about an announcement

4.3 **An update email**
Lesson outcome: Learners can write an update email about work they are doing now.

Reading: Emails to a Project Manager
Communicative grammar: Things happening now
Writing: An update email

4.4 **Work skills:** Setting up a video call
Lesson outcome: Learners can set up a video call and fix problems.

Video: Technical problems
Speaking: Problems with teleconferencing

4.5 **Business workshop:** A business trip
Lesson outcome: Learners can deal with arrangements for a business trip.

Reading: Travel arrangements
Listening and speaking: A change in plans
Writing: Text messages giving updates

Review 4: p.90 | Pronunciation: 4.1 /ŋ/, /ŋk/ and /n/. The *-ing* ending 4.4 /ɪə/ and /eə/ p.98 | Grammar reference: 4.1 Talking about arrangements 4.2 *will* / *won't* 4.3 Things happening now 4.4 Making suggestions p.106

37

4.1 I'm flying to Tokyo tomorrow

Lesson outcome — Learners can talk about travel arrangements.

Lead-in **1A** Match the words (1–6) with the photos (A–F).

1 a plane ____
2 an apartment ____
3 a bus ____
4 a hotel ____
5 a train ____
6 a coach ____

B Answer the questions.
1 Where do you usually stay when you travel a) for work b) for holidays?
2 When was the last time you travelled by plane/train/coach/bus?
3 When was the last time you stayed in a hotel / an apartment?

Vocabulary **Travel arrangements**

2A 🔊 4.01 Listen to a conversation between a PA and her manager about a business trip to Japan. Complete the dialogue.

Bea: Dom, I booked ¹_____ for your trip to Japan, on Japan Airlines.
Dom: Thanks, Bea. What about my hotel?
Bea: I need to book ²_____ room for you tomorrow.
Dom: **Am I going** by ³_____ from Osaka to Tokyo?
Bea: No, you **aren't flying**. You**'re going** by ⁴_____ . It's only two-and-a-half hours by train – the trains are very fast in Japan.
Dom: Where **am I staying**? For a two-week visit, I usually rent ⁵_____ .
Bea: Yes, that's what **we're doing**. It isn't big, but it's very comfortable. And it's near the office.
Dom: OK. Where **am I meeting** customers?
Bea: In the office. There's a meeting room there.

B Complete the table with the words in the box.

| a car   an apartment (x2)   a flight   coach   plane |

book	a hotel / a train ticket / an apartment / ¹_____
stay at	a hotel, ²_____
go by	bus / car / coach / ³_____ / ⁴_____
rent	⁵_____ / ⁶_____

C Match the sentence halves.
1 She usually books
2 On work trips, I stay
3 We go by
4 They rent

a in an apartment.
b a car and drive to the hotel.
c a hotel near the office.
d bus from home to the airport.

Extra activities

4.1 I'm flying to Tokyo tomorrow

Communicative grammar

TALKING ABOUT ARRANGEMENTS
➔ Grammar reference: page 106

+	I'm flying to Tokyo tomorrow. We/You/They're working in Tokyo next week.	She/He is meeting customers on Friday. You're staying in the city centre.
–	I'm not staying at a hotel. We/You/They aren't going to the factory on Tuesday.	He/She isn't going to the factory.
?	Where are you meeting the customers?	I'm meeting them at their office.
?	Is Claudia meeting you at the airport? Are they visiting the factory with you?	Yes, she is. / No, she isn't. Yes, they are. / No, they aren't.

➔ **page 98** See Pronunciation bank: /ŋ/, /ŋk/ and /n/. The -ing ending.

3 Complete the sentences with the correct form of *be* and the verb in brackets. Look at the examples in Exercise 2A to help you.
1 I _____ clients next Monday and you _____ a presentation to them at 9 a.m. (visit, give)
2 We _____ by bus, we _____ the train. (not go, take)
3 _____ they _____ in a company apartment? (stay)
4 Who _____ the flights to Moscow? (book)

Trip to Munich
MONDAY
Fly to Munich
Stay at Hotel Olympic (two nights)

TUESDAY
Morning: Claudia meets me at hotel
Afternoon: Visit factory with area managers

WEDNESDAY
Travel to Augsburg (go by train)

T Extra activities

4 🔊 4.02 Look at Barbara's arrangements for next week. Complete the dialogue with the correct verbs from the calendar. Then listen and check.

Pietro: When ¹__are__ you __flying__ to Munich?
Barbara: I ²_____ on Monday.
Pietro: ³_____ Claudia _____ you at the airport on Monday?
Barbara: No, she ⁴_____. She ⁵_____ me at the hotel on Tuesday morning. We ⁶_____ the factory in the afternoon.
Pietro: ⁷_____ the area managers _____ the factory with you?
Barbara: Yes, they ⁸_____ .
Pietro: And when ⁹_____ you _____ to Augsburg?
Barbara: On Wednesday morning. I ¹⁰_____ by train.

VIDEO

5A ▶ 4.1.1 Watch the video introduction. What are the reasons for travelling for work?

B Watch the video. Answer the questions with (C) for Claire or (M) for Michaela.
1 Who travels abroad ... a) sometimes? ____ b) often? ____
2 Who is traveling a) with a colleague? ____ b) alone? ____
3 Who is a) taking the train? ____ b) taking a plane? ____
4 Who is a) working with a client at their office? ____ b) going to a conference? ____

C Watch again. Choose the correct option.
1 Claire is going to Oxford for *one / two* day(s).
2 Claire is staying in a hotel in Manchester for *one / two* night(s).
3 Claire is going to a restaurant with *friends / her boss*.
4 Michaela is staying in Hong Kong for *one / two* week(s).
5 Michaela is building a website for her *clients / company*.
6 Michaela is planning to *do some sightseeing / rent a car for work*.
7 Michaela is going to a restaurant with clients in the *afternoon / evening*.

➔ TASK

6 Work in pairs. Student A: Look at page 121. Student B: Look at page 122. Read your travel arrangements and arrange a time to meet. Use the conversation in Exercise 4 to help you.

Self-assessment I can talk about travel arrangements.

4.2 The 12.05 is delayed

Lesson outcome: Learners can write a text message to apologise and explain why they are late.

Lead-in 1 Look at the signs. Which do you see …
1 at an airport? 2 in a train station? 3 in both places?

A TERMINAL 1
B PLATFORM 2
C GATE 32
D FLIGHT CONNECTIONS
E ARRIVALS DEPARTURES
F BAGGAGE CLAIM
G PASSPORT CONTROL
H CUSTOMS
I TAXI

Vocabulary Airports and train stations

2A Match each picture (1–4) with with the words in bold in Exercise 2B.

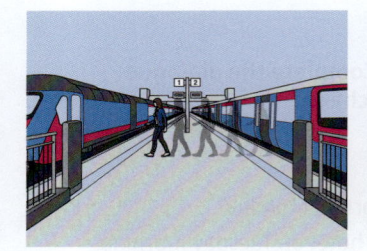

1  _____ 2  _____ 3  _____ 4 _____

B Put the sentences in the correct order to make a travel story.
a ____ The 7.00 train to Manchester airport was cancelled.
b ____ The train stopped at every station, so I arrived at the airport an hour late.
c _1_ I left my hotel at 6.30 in a **taxi**.
d ____ But there was good news. My plane was delayed!
e ____ I arrived at the train station at 6.45.
f ____ There was a queue to board the plane. It **departed** an hour late, but I was on it.
g ____ I went through **security**, but it was very slow. I ran quickly to the gate.
h ____ I took the 7.30 train from platform three. I had to **change trains** at Manchester Victoria Station.

C Complete the sentences with the words in the box.

> arrive cancelled change delayed depart gate late platform security stop

1 Flight 450 to Tokyo isn't departing today. It's _____ .
2 The train is _____ until 7.30 so I'll be fifteen minutes late.
3 We _____ at 10.00 and arrive at 12.30.
4 Does this train _____ at York?
5 Please _____ at Victoria Station for an airport train.
6 You need thirty minutes to go through _____ .
7 When you _____ at the airport, go through passport control.
8 Sorry I'm _____ ! There were no taxis.
9 The 6.30 train for Prague leaves from _____ ten.
10 Passengers on flight EZ 345 please go to _____ 28.

T Extra activities

40

4.2 The 12.05 is delayed

Reading and listening

Dealing with delays

3A 🔊 4.03 Listen to the announcements (1–8). Write (T) for train station or (A) for airport.

1 ___ 2 ___ 3 ___ 4 ___ 5 ___ 6 ___ 7 ___ 8 ___

B Listen again. Complete the sentences with one word.

1 AI663 to Rome is _____ .
2 The 10.15 to Paris is _____ .
3 The service to Leeds on _____ 7 is delayed by 30 minutes.
4 Flight EY825 to New York is _____ .
5 Passengers for Abu Dhabi need to go to a different _____ .
6 Passengers for Brussels need to go to a different _____ .
7 You need extra time to go through _____ today.
8 Follow the signs if you need to make a flight _____ .

C Complete the text messages about travel delays with the words in the box.

> hotel   meeting   security   train

a Hi Dan,
My train to Paris is cancelled because of the weather. But don't worry, I'll join the _____ online.
Sara

b Hello Bella,
My flight to JFK is cancelled. I'll stay in a _____ tonight and fly to New York tomorrow.
Roberto

c Martin
I'm sorry, but my _____ is delayed by thirty minutes. I'll be late for the meeting.
Liz

d Ella
Did you hear the announcement? _____ takes forty-five minutes! Meet me at the gate!
Naomi

D 🔊 4.04 Listen. Match the messages in Exercise 3C (a–d) with the correct announcement.

1 ___ 2 ___ 3 ___ 4 ___

> **WILL / WON'T** → Grammar reference: page 107
>
> **I'll be** late for the meeting.
> **I'll join** the meeting online.
> I **won't stay** in a hotel tonight.

T Extra activities

Writing

4A 🔊 4.05 Listen to two announcements. Make notes on the problems.

1 _____
2 _____

B Work in pairs. Compare your notes with a partner.

C Work in pairs.
Student A: write a message to student B about the problem in announcement 1.
Student B: write a message to student A about the problem in announcement 2.

_____
_____
_____

Self-assessment I can write a text message to apologise and explain why I am late.

4.3 An update email

Lesson outcome: Learners can write an update email about work they are doing now.

Lead-in 1 Match each sentence with the correct place on the world map.

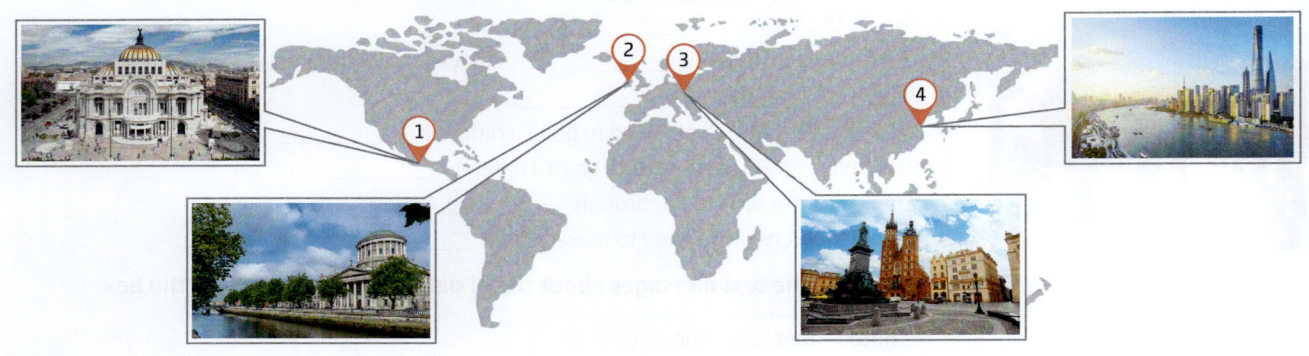

Right now, employees from World Computer Solutions Ireland are working in four countries.
a Alex is visiting the sales team in Shanghai, China. ____
b Alicia is managing the project in Dublin, Ireland. ____
c Liz is meeting customers in Mexico City, Mexico. ____
d Eduardo is setting up a computer system in Krakow, Poland. ____

Reading 2A Alicia is a Project Manager for World Computer Solutions based in Ireland. Read three emails from her colleagues. Answer the questions.

Alicia, Project Manager, Ireland

Which person …
1 has a problem with communication? _____
2 thinks they need to sell more? _____
3 needs some important information to prepare for a meeting? _____

A

Hello Alicia,
How are you? **I'm writing** to update you on the project. Yesterday's customer meetings in Mexico City were good, but we **aren't hitting** our targets this month. We need to make more sales. **I'm preparing** for more customer meetings tomorrow.
Best regards,
Liz

2

Dear Alicia,
How are things going in Dublin? **We're starting** work in the Krakow factory today. Right now, Roger **is managing** the computer delivery. **It's going** well – we **aren't having** any problems. This week, **I'm trying** to talk to a supplier about new computers for Mexico City, but he **isn't answering** my calls.
Speak soon,
Eduardo

3

Dear Alicia,
_____ Here's an update on what we're doing today. My team **are finalising** the sales figures for the meeting next week. **We're having** problems with some missing data from some markets, but **we're expecting** it today. **I'm writing** the sales report and preparing the presentation.
_____ ,
Alex

B Complete the beginning and ending of email 3. Use ideas from email 1 or 2.

C Read Alicia's replies to her team. Write the name of the person in each email.

A

Hi _____ ,
Good to hear from you. Thanks for the update. **I'm planning** my talk for the sales meeting now so I need the sales figures this week. Everything's going well here. I hope **you're having** a good week.
Best wishes,
Alicia

B

Hi _____ ,
That's great news! At the moment, **I'm preparing** the new price list. I'll send it to you before tomorrow's meetings. Good luck with the sales. I'm sure things will go well tomorrow.
Best wishes,
Alicia

C

Hi _____ ,
Thanks. That sounds good! Right now, **I'm dealing** with the paperwork for next week's job in Bremen. The order is for sixty computers, but the supplier says they have forty. **I'm trying** to find twenty more computers! I hope you hear from that supplier soon.
Best regards,
Alicia

4.3 An update email

Communicative grammar

> **THINGS HAPPENING NOW** → Grammar reference: page 107
>
> \+ I**'m planning** my talk for the sales meeting now.
> At the moment, we**'re preparing** the new price list.
> Right now, they**'re dealing with** the paperwork for next week's job in Bremen.
>
> − We **aren't having** any problems at the moment.
> It **isn't going** well today.
> Things **aren't going** well.
>
> ? **Are** you **working** in the Shanghai office today? Yes, I **am**. / No, I**'m not**.
> **Is** Henrik **writing** the report today? Yes, he **is**. / No, he **isn't**.
> What **are** you **working** on right now? I**'m finalising** the sales figures.
> What **is** Ellie **doing** at the moment? She**'s giving** a presentation.

3A Look at the pictures. Complete the sentences with the correct form of the verbs in brackets.

Mikhail, Rita, Pablo, Richard    Andres    Paola    Peter 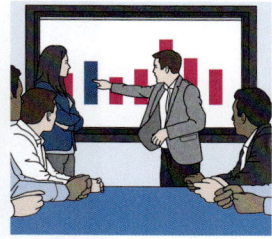   Katrina and Will

1 Mikhail, Rita, Pablo and Richard _____ (have) a meeting. It _____ (not go) well.
2 Andres _____ (not work) at his desk. He _____ (looking after) the machines in the factory. He _____ (not have) problems.
3 Paola _____ (not meet) customers. She _____ (write) a report.
4 Peter _____ (repair) the computer. He _____ (have) problems.
5 Katrina and Will _____ (not prepare) a report. They _____ (give) a presentation. It _____ (go) well.

B Complete the questions with the correct form of verbs in the box.

| do | give | have |
| talk | use | work |

1 _____ Mikhail, Rita, Pablo and Richard _____ a good meeting?
2 _____ Andres _____ at his desk?
3 _____ Paola _____ her computer?
4 What _____ Peter _____ ?
5 Who _____ Katrina and Will _____ to?
6 _____ Katrina and Will _____ a presentation?

C Match the answers with the questions in Exercise 3B.

a No, he isn't. ____   c No, they aren't. ____   e Yes, they are. ____
b Customers. ____   d Repairing a computer. ____   f Yes, she is. ____

Writing

4 Alicia is writing an update email to her boss Veronika in Zurich. Imagine you are Alicia. Use the information in the emails on Page 42 to write your email.
- Start the email and say you hope everything is going well in Zurich.
- Say why you are writing – give an update on work and the team.
- Give an update on the different activities happening now. Write one paragraph about Mexico sales and one paragraph about suppliers.
- Complete the email with an appropriate ending.

T Extra activities

Self-assessment I can write an update email about work I am doing now.

43

4.4 WORK SKILLS
Setting up a video call

Lesson outcome — Learners can set up a video call and fix simple problems.

Lead-in **1A** Which do you prefer, online or face-to-face meetings? Why?

Face-to-face meetings: You can see people, …
Online meetings: You can speak to people anywhere in the world, …

B Look at the pictures. Match each button (1–7) in the pictures with the correct description.

a start audio call ____
b stop video ____
c start video call ____
d end call / hang up ____

e open chat window ____
f mute/unmute microphone ____
g share screen button ____
h close window __

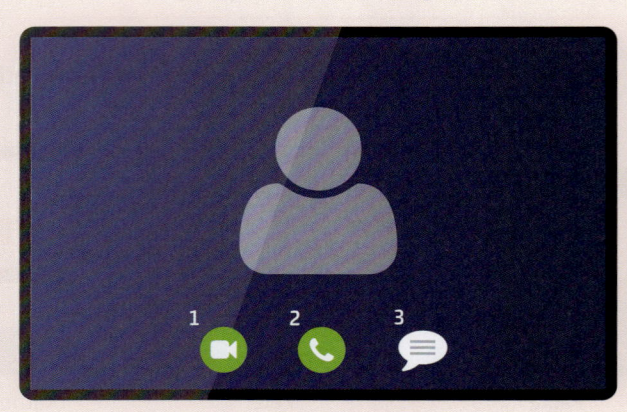

A Before the call

B During the call

VIDEO **2A** ▶ 4.4.1 Watch the video. Choose the problem in each call.

1 In Conversation 1 the *audio / video* isn't working.
2 In Conversation 2 the *camera isn't working / screen is frozen*.
3 In Conversation 3 the *camera / microphone* isn't working.

B Watch the video again. Are the statements *true* (T) or *false* (F)?

Conversation 1
1 At first, Haru can't hear William.
2 Haru is on mute.
3 William had a call from the material supplier.

Conversation 2
4 Haru's internet connection is slow.
5 Haru suggests an audio call.
6 William wants to discuss design changes.

Conversation 3
7 Maria and Max can't see William.
8 Maria shares her screen.
9 Max can't see the sales figures.

C Match each solution with the correct problem in Exercise 2A.

a Max stays on audio.
b William unmutes.
c William turns off his video.

> **MAKING SUGGESTIONS** → Grammar reference: page 108
>
> **Try turning** off your video. / **Try unmuting** your microphone.

T Extra activities

4.4 Work skills: Setting up a video call

D Watch the video again. Complete the sentences from conversations 1–3.

Conversation 1
1 I can't *see / hear* you, William. Are you *on mute / there*?
2 Try *unmuting / turning off* your microphone.
3 How about now? Can you *see / hear* me?

Conversation 2
4 The screen *is frozen / isn't working*.
5 The *internet / connection* isn't very good. You're *breaking up / slow*.
6 Try turning *off / on* your video.
7 Let's have a(n) *video / audio* call.

Conversation 3
8 I'm adding Max to the *screen / call*.
9 My camera isn't *working / on*.
10 I'm *sharing / turning on* my screen now.

Speaking

> ### PROBLEMS WITH TELECONFERENCING
>
> **Checking the connection**
> Can you see/hear me?   Yes, no problem.   Are you there?   Yes, I'm here.
>
> | **Talking about problems** | **Suggesting solutions** |
> |---|---|
> | (Sorry), the connection isn't very good. | |
> | You're breaking up. | Hang up. I'll call you back. |
> | My camera isn't working. | |
> | Sorry, I can't see you. | Let's have an audio call. |
> | The screen is frozen. | |
> | My internet connection is slow. | Try turning off your video. |
> | Sorry, can you repeat that, please? | |
> | I can't hear you. | Try unmuting your microphone. |
>
> | **Saying it's OK** | **Other** |
> |---|---|
> | It's OK now. | I'm sharing my screen. |
> | That's (much) better. | I'm adding Hitomi to the call. |

➜ **page 98** See Pronunciation bank: /ɪə/ and /eə/.

3A ▶ 4.4.2 Watch the video without sound. What are William and Max saying? Write the dialogue.

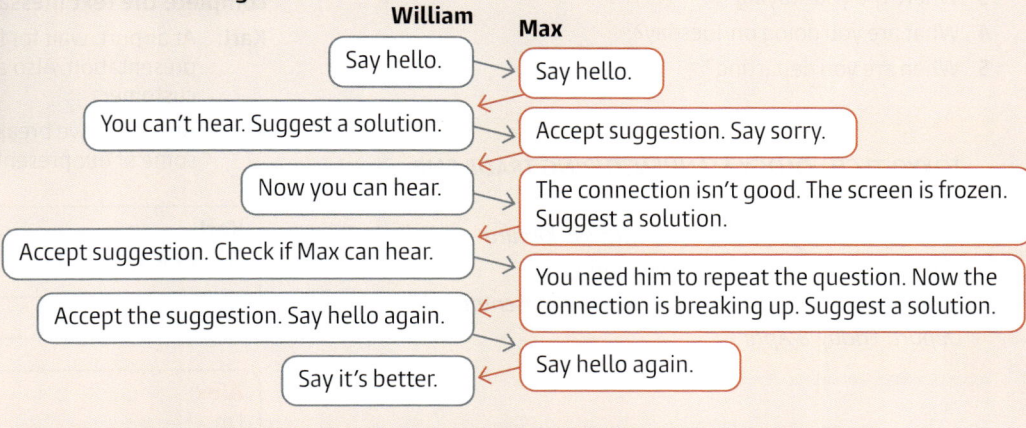

William → **Max**

- Say hello. → Say hello.
- You can't hear. Suggest a solution. → Accept suggestion. Say sorry.
- Now you can hear. → The connection isn't good. The screen is frozen. Suggest a solution.
- Accept suggestion. Check if Max can hear. → You need him to repeat the question. Now the connection is breaking up. Suggest a solution.
- Accept the suggestion. Say hello again. → Say hello again.
- Say it's better.

T Extra activities

B Watch the video again with sound. Was the conversation similar to yours?

C Practise the dialogue that you wrote in Exercise 3A.

Self-assessment I can set up a video call and fix simple problems.

BUSINESS WORKSHOP

A business trip

Lesson outcome — Learners can deal with arrangements for a business trip.

Introduction

1 Read the emails and answer the questions.

Hi Alex,

There's an important trade fair in Tokyo next week, but I can't go – I'm too busy. Karl from the Seoul office is attending and we need you to help him with our presentation. We also want you to meet customers and make new contacts.

I hope you can make the trip.

Best regards,

Rob

Hi Rob,

Thanks. I'd love to go!

Best regards,

Alex

---

1 Where is the trade fair?
2 When is it?
3 Why does someone need to go?
4 Who is going?

Arrangements

2 Work in pairs. Student A: Ask the questions (1–5). Student B: Look at the travel arrangements. Answer the questions.
1 When are you arriving?
2 What are you doing Monday evening?
3 Where are you staying?
4 What are you doing on Tuesday?
5 When are you departing?

TOKYO TECHNOLOGY MANUFACTURING TRADE FAIR
Arrive: Monday 4 April
Monday evening: Have dinner with Ms Kimura
Hotel: Hotel City Park (stay two nights)
Tuesday (a.m.): Meet Karl and practise presentation
Depart: Friday 8 April

A change in plans

3A 🔊 4.06 Karl is now at the airport waiting to depart for Tokyo. Listen. What problem does he have?

B 🔊 4.07 An airline employee is explaining the arrangement to Karl. Listen. When is he arriving in Tokyo?

C Write a message from Karl to Alex to explain the situation.

D Read Alex's reply to Karl's message. What does Alex want to do?

> Hi. Thanks for the message about your flight. That's bad luck. Can we have a quick online meeting this evening, when you get to your hotel? There's some new information that I want to discuss with you. And we need to arrange a new time to practise our presentation. Thanks!

4A 🔊 4.08 Listen to the beginning of Alex and Karl's online meeting. Answer the questions.
1 What problem does Alex have?
2 What problem does Karl have?

B What do you think Alex suggests for each problem? Complete the sentences with your ideas
1 Karl, try …   2 Try … , Karl

C Continue the call. Alex and Karl need to arrange a meeting to practise their presentation. Student A: Look at page 123. Student B: Look at page 121.

An update

5 It's Tuesday morning. Alex is at his hotel in Tokyo. Karl is at the airport, in Seoul. Use the information to complete the text messages.

Karl: At airport, wait for flight, have breakfast, plan our presentation. Also arrange lunch meetings with customers

Alex: At hotel, have breakfast, write emails. Also write some of our presentation.

Karl
I'm at the airport now. I'm waiting for _____
_____ .
What are you doing?

Alex
I'm _____
_____ .
Let me know when you arrive.

Self-assessment — I can deal with arrangements for a business trip.

Organising 5

> Do you organise events at work?

Unit overview

5.1 Trade shows and exhibitions
Lesson outcome: Learners can talk about intentions for future events in a simple way.

Vocabulary: Organising an exhibition
Communicative grammar: Talking about intentions
Video: Graduate Fashion Week
Task: Talking about plans for a trade fair

5.2 Phoning about a conference
Lesson outcome: Learners can leave a phone message and make simple arrangements on the phone.

Vocabulary: Leaving a message
Listening: Organising a conference
Speaking: Taking and leaving phone messages

5.3 Invitations
Lesson outcome: Learners can write a short message inviting and responding to invitations.

Reading: Messages about an invitation
Communicative grammar: Invitations with *would* and *want*
Writing: Informal messages of invitation

5.4 Work skills: Socialising with clients
Lesson outcome: Learners can talk about opinions on familiar topics using simple language.

Video: What do you think of the trade fair?
Speaking: Socialising with clients

5.5 Business workshop: The conference
Lesson outcome: Learners can talk and write about plans for future events in a simple way.

Speaking: Phoning to compare conference details
Writing: An email about a conference
Speaking: Making conversation at a conference dinner

Review 5: p.91 | **Pronunciation:** 5.1 /æ/, /e/ and /eɪ/ 5.3 /θ/ and /ð/ vs. /s/, /z/, /f/, /v/, /t/, /d/ p.99 | **Grammar reference:** 5.1 Talking about intentions 5.3 Invitations with *would* and *want* p.108

5.1 Trade shows and exhibitions

Lesson outcome — Learners can talk about intentions for future events in a simple way.

Lead-in

1A What type of events are these? Choose from the options in the box.

- business conference
- motor show
- technology exhibition
- tourism fair

B Do you go to trade shows and exhibitions? What shows and exhibitions do you want to go to?

Vocabulary — Organising an exhbition

2 Use the spidergram to write the names of the objects and places 1–5.

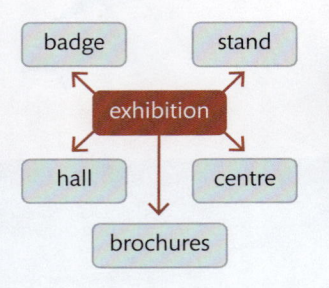

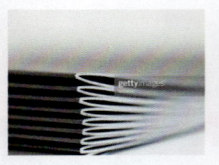

- badge
- stand
- exhibition
- hall
- centre
- brochures

1 *exhibition badge* 2 _____ 3 _____ 4 _____ 5 _____

3A Read the email about a trade fair. Are the sentences *true* (T) or *false* (F)?

1. The company went to the trade show last year.
2. They plan to have the same exhibition stand.
3. They want visitors to relax at the stand.
4. Exhibitors come from hundreds of countries.

Subject: Trade fair in Düsseldorf

We're attending the trade fair in Düsseldorf again this year and there are some exciting changes to the event. Last week we decided that we**'re going to set up** a bigger stand. We have a new space in the main exhibition hall so we **aren't going to be** in our usual location. We also decided that we**'re going to launch** our new app for online shopping at the show and we're designing a new, attractive brochure to help us! We**'re going to create** a really special experience at the stand with comfortable sofas and TV screens with videos of our new products. We**'re** also **going to provide** visitors with free coffee, a special cake and lots of freebies. There are 1,100 exhibitors from forty-five countries this year and thousands of visitors. This will be a great opportunity to meet clients and colleagues from our industry.

B Read the email again. Match the words from the box with the verbs (1–6).

- an app   a brochure   clients
- freebies   a stand   a trade fair

1 attend _____   3 launch _____   5 provide _____
2 design _____   4 meet _____   6 set up _____

Extra activities

4 Match the questions (1–6) with the replies (a–f).

1. **Are** we **going to be** in the same hotel this year?
2. How many people **are going to be** on the stand?
3. How big **is** the stand **going to be**?
4. **Are** we **going to have** some rest breaks this year?
5. **Are there going to be** any freebies for visitors?
6. When **are** we **going to receive** our badges?

a It**'s going to be** 20 square metres.
b There **are going to be** at least three people all the time.
c Of course. Everyone **is going to get** coffee breaks and lunch breaks.
d On the first day of the trade show. I**'m going to send** more details soon.
e No, we **aren't going to stay** in the same hotel.
f Yes, and we**'re going to organise** a competition this year.

5.1 Trade shows and exhibitions

Communicative grammar

> **TALKING ABOUT INTENTIONS** → Grammar reference: page 108
>
> \+ I'**m going to set up** a bigger stand. He**'s going to provide** free coffee.
> We**'re going to launch** our new app.
>
> \- We **aren't going to be** in our usual location. I**'m not going to stay** in the same hotel.
>
> ? **Are** there **going to be** any freebies? When **are** we **going to get** our badges?

→ page 98 See Pronunciation bank: /æ/, /e/ and /eɪ/

5 Complete the sentences with *be going to* and the verbs in the box.

have	not attend
not launch	not provide
phone	set

1 We _____ up a stand in the main hall this year.
2 She _____ the first day of the trade show. She's on holiday.
3 I _____ the exhibition organiser about the badges today.
4 We _____ new brochures at the next show.
5 They _____ the new product at the show. It isn't ready.
6 The conference centre _____ free parking this year.

6A Put the words in the correct order to make questions. The first word is given.

1 the exhibition hall / is / big / How / be / going / to / ?
How _____ ?
2 Are / freebies / we / to / provide / any / going / ?
Are _____ ?
3 we / are / the stand / going / to / When / set up / ?
When _____ ?
4 launch / going / we / to / any / products / Are / new / ?
Are _____ ?
5 are / to / Why / the brochures / they / going / change / ?
Why _____ ?

B Match questions (1–5) in Exercise 6A with the answers (a–e).

a The day before the show.
b Yes, we have some new office chairs.
c Yes, we're going to give away bags.
d Because they have new products.
e 1000 square metres.

T Extra activities

VIDEO

7A ▶ 5.1.1 Watch the video introduction. What is Graduate Fashion Week? Where is it?

B Watch the complete video. Which of the things in the box are mentioned? Tick (✓) the words you hear.

| app | awards | badges | brochures | cafes | entry cost |
| exhibition hall | freebies | stands | sponsors | shops | TV |

C Watch the video again. Are the sentences *true* (T) or *false* (F)?
1 The Graduate Fashion Week is going to open on 2 June.
2 13,000 people are going to visit Graduate Fashion Week.
3 There are going to be thirty-eight stands from international universities.
4 Givenchy, Ralph Lauren and LVMH are going to give presentations.
5 There is space for 400 people in the catwalk hall.
6 There are going to be twenty-four catwalk shows.

▶ TASK

8 Work in pairs. You are going to talk about an exhibition.
Student A: Complete the diary on page 128 and answer Student B's questions.
Student B: Complete the diary on page 128 and answer Student A's questions.

Self-assessment I can talk about intentions for future events in a simple way.

5.2 Phoning about a conference

Lesson outcome — Learners can leave a phone message and make simple arrangements on the phone.

Lead-in **1** Read the information about a hotel conference centre. What services and equipment does it provide?

| HOTEL | CONFERENCE CENTRE | MEETING ROOMS | GALLERY | ENQUIRE NOW |

WALLACE HOTEL & CONFERENCE CENTRE

Our centre team will work with you to organise a perfect event. Every meeting room has a data projector and screen. Large conference rooms also have a sound system. There is free Wi-Fi in the hotel and conference centre. We also provide free water, pens and paper.

Contact us on (+353) 064-6739000 or click here to enquire.

Vocabulary — Leaving a message

2 🔊 5.01 Listen to a client phoning the conference centre. Complete the message for the manager.

MESSAGE FOR MARY DUFFY

¹_____ Nakamura phoned from Dallas Corporation Europe.

It's about their ²_____ on ³_____ .

Please call her on ⁴_____ .

3A Complete the expressions from the phone call.
1. How can I h_____ you?
2. I'm s_____, she's not available right now.
3. Can I t_____ a message?
4. Yes, can you t_____ her Hinata Nakamura phoned?
5. Can you s_____ your name for me, please?
6. And it's a_____ the conference next month?
7. Sorry, c_____ you say that again, please?
8. OK, thank you. And can I h_____ your phone number?
9. So, t_____ 0044 3584 751 059.
10. I'll g_____ her your message.

B 🔊 5.02 Listen and check your answers.

50

5.2 Phoning about a conference

Listening: Organising a conference

4A 🔊 5.03 Listen to Mary Duffy's phone conversation with Hinata Nakamura. In what order (1–4) do they talk about these things?

a equipment ____ c catering ____
b hotel guests ____ d participants ____

B Listen again and answer the questions.
1 How many people are going to attend the conference?
2 How many people are going to stay at the hotel?
3 When is Ms Nakamura going to confirm this information?
4 What does Mrs Duffy need?
5 Who is going to help Ms Nakamura?
6 What time are they going to have the breaks and lunch?

T Extra activities

Speaking

5 Work in pairs. Take turns to take and leave phone messages. Use expressions from Exercise 3A.

Student A: Look at the information below.
Student B: Look at page 118.

Phone call 1

You are the client.

Your name is _____ . (invent a name)

You work for _____ . (choose a company)

You will attend a conference at Wallace Hotel on _____ . (choose a date)

Phone the Wallace Hotel Conference Centre. Leave a phone message for Angela Mulligan, the Assistant Manager.

Phone call 2

You represent the conference centre.

You work on reception for the Stanford Conference Centre in London. The Centre Manager Henri Dupont is in a meeting.

Answer the phone and take a message for him.

You want to know the caller's name, company and the date of the conference.

---

6 Work in pairs. Take turns to make phone calls. Use expressions from Exercise 3A to help you.

Student A: Look at page 125.
Student B: Look at page 122.

Phone call 1

Student A
- Answer the phone.
- Answer.
- Answer.
- Answer.
- Answer.
- Answer.

Student B
- Explain who you are and why you are phoning. Ask how many people are going to attend the conference.
- Ask how many participants are going to stay at the hotel.
- Ask when they can confirm the names and number of people.
- Ask what catering they are going to need.
- Ask what equipment they are going to need.
- Finish the call.

Self-assessment: I can leave a phone message and make simple arrangements on the phone.

5.3 Invitations

Lesson outcome — Learners can write a short message inviting and responding to invitations.

> Hi Carl. Free for ☕ this afternoon? Meet at 3 p.m.?

> Yes! But can we meet at 2 p.m?

1 Discuss the questions.
1. Do you write invitations to people? When? What type of invitations?
2. When do you use a) social media b) emails to write invitations? Which is a) informal b) more formal?

Reading

2 Read the messages from Carl Becker and his colleagues. What is the invitation? How many people can attend? Complete Carl Becker's last message.

Carl Becker
Hello everyone. Conference is going well. **Do you want to join** me for lunch?

A. Tanaka
Thanks! **I'd love to.** Where? What time?

Elisabeth Fischer
Yes, thanks. Where **do you want to have** lunch?

Pawel P.
Sorry, I'm with some clients at lunchtime.

Carl Becker
How about 1 p.m. in the hotel rooftop restaurant?

A. Tanaka
Yes! Sounds good!

Sakura
Yes, I'll be there. Thanks.

Anne Johnson
Thanks for the invitation, but I'm not free for lunch today.

Carl Becker
OK! I'll book a table for _____ people at _____ .

3 Read the email and the two responses. Answer the questions.
1. Does Carl know the clients?
2. Why are Carl and Danielle going to meet the clients next week?
3. What is Carl's invitation?
4. Do the clients accept the invitation?

From: Carl Becker
Re: Dinner

Danielle and I **would like to invite** you for dinner at the French restaurant in town.

Would you like to join us on 29 March after our sales presentation? I will send you details soon.

We look forward to meeting you next week.

Best regards,

Carl Becker

Thank you for the invitation. I **would love to join** you for dinner on 29 March.

I look forward to receiving the details.

Best wishes,

Oliver

Thank you very much for the dinner invitation. I am very sorry but I cannot come because I have an evening flight.

I look forward to meeting you on 29 March.

Kind regards,

Emma

5.3 Invitations

Communicative grammar

INVITATIONS WITH *WOULD* AND *WANT*
→ Grammar reference: page 109

Informal invitations	Formal invitations
Do you want to join us for dinner?	**Would you like to join** us for dinner?
Saying yes to informal invitations Thanks! **I'd** love to. Yes! Sounds good.	**Saying yes to formal invitations** Thank you for the invitation. I **would love to join** you for lunch. Yes, thank you very much for the invitation. **That would be** great.
Saying no to informal invitations Thanks for the invitation, but I'm not free today. Sorry, but I have other plans. Sorry, I'm with some clients at lunchtime.	**Saying no to formal invitations** Thank you very much for the invitation but I am not available today. I am very sorry, but I cannot come because I have an evening flight. I **would like to join you** but I am with some clients at lunchtime.

→ **page 99** See Pronunciation bank: /θ/ and /ð/ vs /s/, /z/, /f/, /v/, /t/, /d/

4A 🔊 5.04 Choose the correct option to complete the sentences. Then listen and check.
1. Would you *like / want* to join us for dinner? ____
2. *Do / Would* you want to see the factory? ____
3. *Thank / Thanks* you very much. That would be nice. ____
4. Thanks! *I'd / I'll* love to. ____
5. I would *like / want* to join you, but I have a meeting. ____
6. Thanks for the invitation, *and / but* I'm not free today. ____
7. I am *very / much* sorry but I am not available today. ____
8. Do you want to join *we / us* for coffee? ____

B Which phrases are informal (I) and which are more formal (F)? Write *I* or *F*.

5 Complete the formal emails and informal messages with the words in the box. What are they about?

> because invitation (x2) join like love much very want would

✉ The senior managers would ¹_____ to invite you to ²_____ them for lunch after your meeting next Monday. ³_____ you like to have a tour of the new factory after lunch?

✉ Thank you very ⁴_____ for the ⁵_____. We would ⁶_____ to join the senior managers for lunch. I am ⁷_____ sorry but we cannot do a tour of the factory after lunch ⁸_____ we have another visit in the afternoon.

T Extra activities

> Carl, do you ⁹_____ to join us for lunch with the new clients next Monday?

> Thanks for the ¹⁰_____, but I'm out of the office next Monday.

Writing

6 Work in groups of four. Write and respond to informal messages with invitations.
Student A: Look at page 119. Student B: Look at page 124. Student C: Look at page 122. Student D: Look at page 127.

7 Write a more formal email with an invitation to some clients or visitors to your company. Look at page 118.

Self-assessment I can write a short message inviting and responding to invitations.

5.4 WORK SKILLS
Socialising with clients

Lesson outcome — Learners can give their opinions on familiar topics using simple language.

Lead-in 1A Work in pairs. What do you talk about with colleagues when you don't talk about work? Choose from the topics in the box. Add any topics of your own.

> family   sport   TV shows   weather   work

B Do you ever spend time with clients or visitors at work? What do you talk about?

VIDEO

▶ Julia Anderson, Max Hartmann

▶ Maria Stavrou, Julia Anderson, Max Hartmann

2 ▶ 5.4.1 Watch Max and Julia's meeting. Choose the correct option.
1 *Julia / Max* was in Paris yesterday.
2 Julia arrived *last night / this morning*.
3 Max thinks that the conference will be *busy / great*.
4 Max invites Julia to join him for *lunch / dinner*.
5 Julia *knows / doesn't know* Maria Stavrou.
6 They are going to meet at 12.30 *in the conference hall / at the restaurant*.

3 Watch Maria, Julia and Max's conversation. Tick (✓) the four topics they mention.

> exhibitors   family   the city   the trade fair   the hotel   the weather

4 Watch Maria, Julia and Max's conversation again. Answer the questions.
1 What does Maria say about Julia's company?
2 What does Julia say about the presentations?
3 What presentation did Maria see?
4 How does Max describe the hotel?
5 What does Julia say about the hotel?
6 What do Maria and Max agree to do?

5A Match the questions from the video (1–4) with the answers (a–d).
1 When did you arrive?
2 What do you think of the trade fair?
3 Where are you staying?
4 Do you like the hotel?

a Well, it's comfortable and it's near a park.
b I think there are some good presentations.
c I flew here this morning.
d At the Mason Park Hotel.

B Match irregular verbs in bold from the video with the present form in the box.

> be (x2)   fly   go   have   hear   see

1 I **heard** you **were** here.
2 I **went** to Paris yesterday.
3 I **had** some business meetings there.
4 I **flew** here this morning.
5 I **saw** a presentation.
6 It **was** very good.

C Make sentences about your life with three verbs from Exercise 5B. Read your sentences to your partner.

*I **went** to Hamburg last week.*   *I **had** lunch with clients yesterday.*
*I **saw** a good film at the cinema last weekend.*

5.4 Work skills: Socialising with clients

Speaking

SOCIALISING WITH CLIENTS

Starting a conversation topic
How are you? Very well, thanks.
When did you arrive? I flew here [yesterday / today]. (And you?)
Where are you staying? At the [Mason Park Hotel / the Grand].

Asking for an opinion
What do you think of the trade fair?
Do you like the hotel?

Giving an opinion
I think there are some [very good presentations / great new products].
It was [interesting / a bit boring].
I like some of the [exhibitors' stands / talks].
It's [comfortable / nice] and it's [near the park / quiet].

Agreeing
That's right. / You're right.
Yes, I agree. / Me too.

Disagreeing politely
Yes, but it isn't [near the city centre / cheap].
You're right, but it's [expensive / easy to get there by taxi].

Extra activities

6A Work in pairs. Match the questions (1–5) with the answers (a–e).
1 Did you see the football last night?
2 What do you think of the city centre?
3 What do you think of the hotel room?
4 What do you think of the conference?
5 Do you like the food?

a It's a bit small but it's comfortable.
b Yes, it was a very boring game.
c It's very beautiful but there's a lot of traffic.
d It's delicious! I love it!
e It's very interesting. There are some good stands.

B Think of another response to each question in Exercise 6A. Practise asking and answering the questions.

7 Complete the dialogue with the sentences (a–g) in the box.

a Do you like this hotel?
b Did you see the football match on TV last night?
c Yes, it's beautiful but there's a lot of traffic.
d What do you think of the local food?
e That's right. It's very convenient.
f It was very good. The local team won. Football is popular here.
g I think it's perfect. I like cold sunny days.

1 _____?
— What do you think of the city?
— It's very beautiful. Do you like it?
2 _____
— Yes, you're right.
3 _____
— Yes, I think it's comfortable and it's near the airport.
4 _____
— The weather is nice today.
5 _____
— Me too.
— No, I didn't have time. Was it good?
6 _____
— That's right.
7 _____
— It's delicious. Did you enjoy your meal at the hotel?
— Yes, the food's very good here.

8 Work in pairs. Read your information and prepare a dialogue. Use some ideas from the box to help you. Roleplay the situation.

sport   the city   the food
the visitor's hotel
the weather today

Student A: You have a foreign client visiting your company today. Take the visitor to the canteen for lunch. Make small talk while you have lunch.

Student B: You are a foreign client visiting student A's company. Go to the canteen for lunch together. Make small talk while you have lunch.

Self-assessment — I can give opinions on familiar topics using simple language.

BUSINESS WORKSHOP

The conference

Lesson outcome: Learners can talk and write about plans for future events in a simple way.

Introduction

1 Look at the information on a company's website. What is Hopkins Financial Services organising?

HOPKINS Financial Services
Annual Sales Conference 27 and 28 May
This year's sales conference is at the Trent Hotel and Conference Centre in Nottingham on 27 and 28 May. Save the dates!

Speaking

2 Work in pairs. You are going to discuss plans for a conference.

Student A: You work for Hopkins Financial Services. Look at the notes below.
- Phone Trent Conference Centre and confirm these details.
- Introduce yourself when Student B answers the phone.
- Discuss the conference details.

Hello this is [your name] at Hopkins Financial Services. I'm calling about our sales conference on 27 and 28 of May.

Event	Annual sales conference
Dates	27 and 28 May Start time 9 o'clock and finish time 5 o'clock on 27 May Start 9 o'clock and finish at 1 o'clock on 28 May *We're going to start the conference at 9 o'clock on 27 May.*
Participants	About 108–116 people / going to / attend will confirm the number next week
Hotel guests	Between forty-five and fifty people / going to / stay at the hotel on nights of 26 and 27 will confirm the names and number next week
Catering	You / going to / have the morning break at 10.30 a.m. / buffet lunch at 1.00 p.m. and the afternoon break at 3.00 p.m. on 27 May. No lunch or afternoon coffee break on 28th – finish conference at 1 p.m.
Meeting rooms	going to / need a large conference room for about 120 people and four smaller rooms for about thirty people
Equipment	What equipment / there / in the meeting rooms?

Student B: You work at the Trent Hotel and Conference Centre. Look at page 122.

Writing

3A Complete the email to the sales staff at Hopkins Financial Services with the phrases in the box.

> are going to have   best regards   is going to take
> like to invite   look forward   will send

Subject: Annual Sales Conference 27 and 28 May

Hello everyone,
This year's sales conference ¹_____ place on the 27 and 28 May at the Trent Hotel and Conference Centre in Nottingham.
We ²_____ one and a half days to present our sales strategies for the year.
I ³_____ you the full programme soon.
We would also ⁴_____ you to join us for dinner at the hotel restaurant at 7 p.m. on 27 May.
We ⁵_____ to seeing you all in Nottingham.
⁶_____,

B Write a short email to reply to the dinner invitation in Exercise 3A.

Speaking

4A What do you think are interesting topics to talk about at a conference dinner with colleagues?

B Work in groups. You are at the Hopkins sales conference dinner. Read your role cards.

Student A: Look at your information. Talk to your colleagues at dinner.

> What do you think of ... ?   Do you like ... ?

Topic	You think
Conference	There are some interesting sales presentations. The meeting rooms are a bit small.
Hotel	You're a guest in the hotel. You like your room – it's big and comfortable.
The city	You don't know Nottingham – this is your first visit.
The dinner	The food is very good. It's a good opportunity to meet colleagues from other places.

Student B: Look at page 120.
Student C: Look at page 124.

Self-assessment: I can talk and write about plans for future events in a simple way.

Products 6

> What's your favourite product and why?

Unit overview

6.1 Future products
Lesson outcome: Learners can use *will, won't* and *might* to speculate about the future.

Vocabulary: Technology and the environment
Communicative grammar: Speculating about the future
Video: Industry futures
Task: Talking about the future

6.2 A problem with an order
Lesson outcome: Learners can make and respond to a complaint.

Listening: A problem with an order
Vocabulary: Helping with a problem
Speaking: Phoning and answering as customer services

6.3 The production process
Lesson outcome: Learners can write a short description of a production process.

Reading: Environment and ethics
Communicative grammar: Describing production
Writing: A description for a company website

6.4 Work skills: Placing an order
Lesson outcome: Learners can place a simple order.

Video: How many do you want to order?
Speaking: Placing an order

6.5 Business workshop: Buy natural
Lesson outcome: Learners can make and respond to simple orders and complaints, and make simple predictions about the future.

Reading: A company website about ethical products
Speaking: Placing an order; making a complaint about an order

Review 6: p.92
Pronunciation: 6.2 /ɑː/ and /ʌ/
6.3 /uː/ and /ʊ/ p.99
Grammar reference: 6.1 Speculating about the future
6.3 Describing production p.109

6.1 ▶ Future products

Lesson outcome — Learners can use *will*, *won't* and *might* to speculate about the future.

Lead-in

1 How are the products that you buy or use different from ten years ago?
I use lots of apps on my mobile phone.
My smart TV has an internet connection.

Vocabulary — Technology and the environment

2A How do you say the words in the box? Complete the sentences with the words.

electric energy environment machines plastic recycle pollution technology

1 Gas and electricity are two common types of _____ .
2 The air in this city is full of _____ .
3 Many people are buying _____ cars today.
4 The land, water and air that people, animals and plants live in is the _____ .
5 All _____ need to use power, usually electricity.
6 Digital _____ is changing how we live and work.
7 We _____ paper in our office. It's good for the environment.
8 There is a lot of _____ in the sea and it's bad for marine life.

B 🔊 6.01 Listen and check your answers to Exercise 2A.

3 Discuss the questions.

1 What machines and technology do you use for your job?
2 What do you usually recycle at work and at home?
3 How popular are electric cars in your country?
4 Is air pollution sometimes a problem where you live? Why?

4A Read the article about products of the future. Match the pictures (A–C) with the correct part of the article (1–3).

B Which jobs do you think will/might disappear in the future? Why?

T Extra activities

Products of the future

Technology and the environment are changing the products we use every day. We talked to some experts about the products of the future.

1 ____
Paul Kumar, Product Designer
Everyone **will use** their mobiles to pay for things. I **don't think** we **will need** cash and bank cards soon. But we **will need** better online security.

2 ____
Andrew Winter, Green Business Consultant
Consumers want to help the environment. I **think** many products we buy **will change**. One day we **might not see** plastic bags, packaging and water bottles in supermarkets. I **think there will be** more electric cars soon. And companies **will use** electric trucks and drones to deliver our products.

3 ____
Mia Schröder, Digital Engineer
Smart machines **will have** a big impact on our lives. Today we use LED lights and soon we **might use** technology to save energy in our homes. I **think** we **will buy** more robots for our homes. Robots **will do** more jobs in factories as well. Many jobs we do today **won't exist** in future.

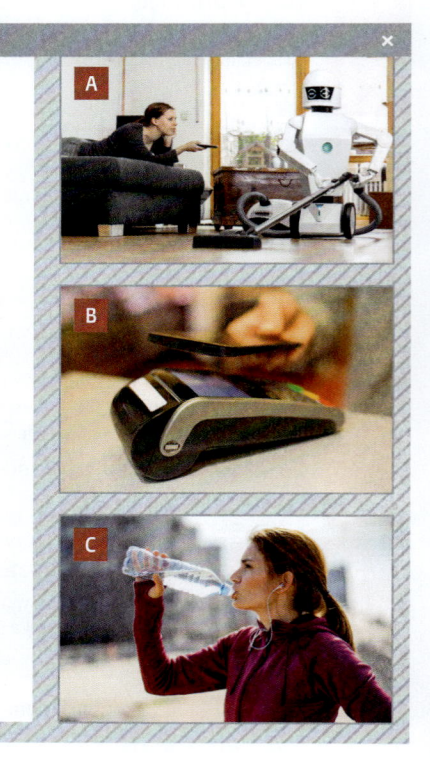

6.1 Future products

Communicative grammar

SPECULATING ABOUT THE FUTURE → Grammar reference: page 109

Certain	Impossible
Everyone **will use** their mobiles to pay for things.	I **don't think** we **will need** cash.
I **think** we **will buy** more robots for our homes.	Many jobs we do today **won't exist** in future.
I **think there will be** more electric cars.	**Possible**
	We **might use** technology to save energy.
	We **might not see** plastic bags in supermarkets.

5A Use *will/'ll*, *won't*, *might* or *might not* to complete the sentences with your ideas.

In the next five years ...

My company
1 There _____ more competition. (be)
2 There _____ more staff. (be)
3 We _____ to a new location. (move)

My job
4 I _____ the same job. (have)
5 A robot _____ my job. (do)
6 I _____ from home. (work)

Products/services I use/buy
7 I _____ an electric car. (buy)
8 I _____ smart technology at home. (use)
9 I _____ more things. (recycle)

B Compare your ideas with a partner.

A: There will be more competition in our industry. **B:** I don't think there will.

VIDEO

6A ▶ 6.1.1 Watch the video. Which speaker (Leona, Steve, Kate or Lisa) talks about these things? Sometimes more than one answer is possible.

Apps	
Electric	
Mobile phones	
Packaging	Leona

Pollution/Waste	
Renting/Sharing	
Robots	
Smart technology	

B Work in pairs. Complete the sentences with a word from the box. Watch the video again and check.

cars   cash   colour   energy
electric   food   packaging
products   recycled   rent
room   share

Speaker 1: _____
There will be more online shopping. People will still want to touch and feel ¹_____ .
²_____ will become less popular. There will be less ³_____ on products.

Speaker 2: _____
In the next five to ten years ⁴_____ cars and motorbikes will become very popular. Many people will choose to ⁵_____ cars. There might be driverless ⁶_____ in five to ten years.

Speaker 3: _____
Clothes will change ⁷_____ and size in the future. Manufacturers will use ⁸_____ materials. People won't buy many clothes. We might ⁹_____ clothes instead!

Speaker 4: _____
Hotel guests will open the door to their ¹⁰_____ with an app. Robots might deliver ¹¹_____ to their rooms. Smart technology will also help hotels to save ¹²_____ .

C Work in pairs. Write the name of each speaker 1–4. Do you agree with their ideas?

▶ TASK

7A Complete each sentence about the future of products, technology and the environment. Then write four sentences of your own using *will*, *won't*, *might* or *might not*.

I think there will _____ .   I don't think there will _____ .
There might/might not _____ .   People will/won't _____ .

B Work in pairs or groups. Discuss your ideas about the future.

Self-assessment

I can use *will*, *won't* and *might* to speculate about the future.

6.2 A problem with an order

Lesson outcome — Learners can make and respond to a complaint.

Lead-in

1A How do you contact customer services: by phone, email or chat box? When and why do you contact them?

B Match the customer problems (1–5) with the customer services solutions (a–e).

Problems
1. These laptops are the wrong model.
2. This chair is blue. I wanted a black one.
3. The machine isn't working.
4. We want to return this old photocopier.
5. There's a mistake on this invoice.

Solutions
a. We'll send a technician.
b. We'll change them.
c. We'll send a truck.
d. We'll correct it.
e. We'll change it.

Listening — A problem with an order

2 🔊 6.02 Listen to a customer phoning customer services. Choose the option in italics to complete the problem with the order.

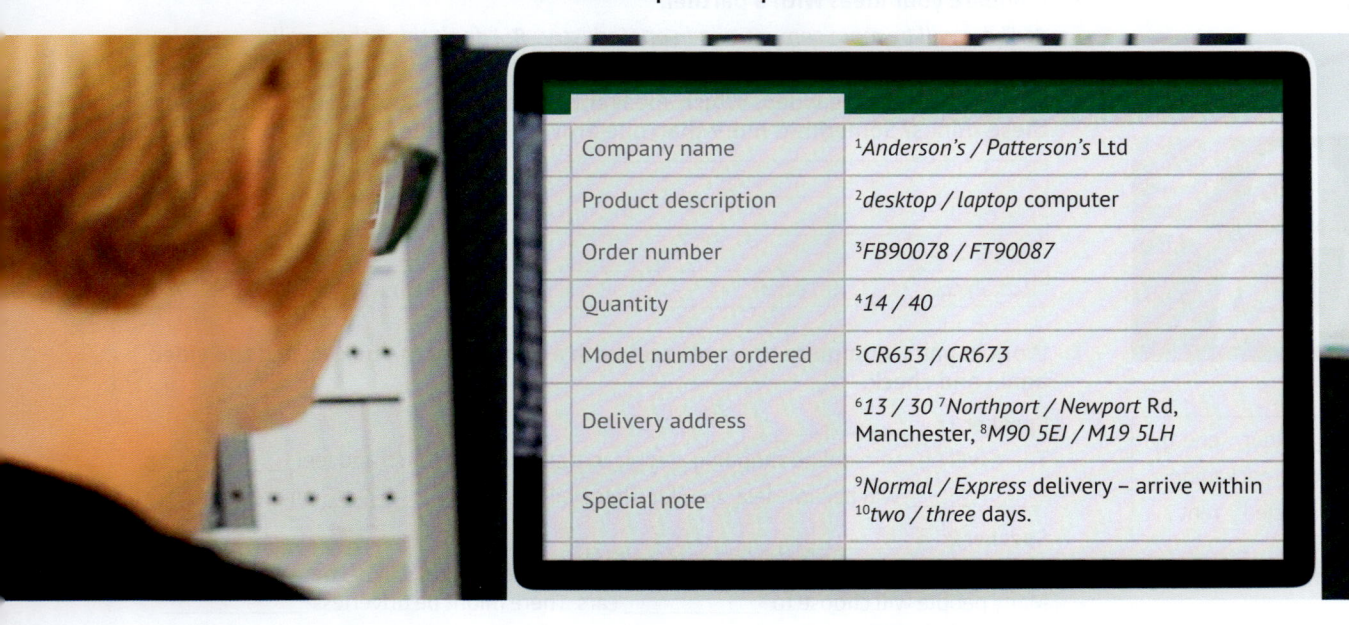

Company name	[1]*Anderson's / Patterson's* Ltd
Product description	[2]*desktop / laptop* computer
Order number	[3]*FB90078 / FT90087*
Quantity	[4]*14 / 40*
Model number ordered	[5]*CR653 / CR673*
Delivery address	[6]*13 / 30* [7]*Northport / Newport* Rd, Manchester, [8]*M90 5EJ / M19 5LH*
Special note	[9]*Normal / Express* delivery – arrive within [10]*two / three* days.

Vocabulary — Helping with a problem

3 Listen again and complete the phrases from the phone call with one or two words.

1. How can _____ _____ you?
2. There's a _____ _____ the laptops you delivered.
3. I'm _____ _____ hear that.
4. _____ _____ have your order number, please?
5. I'm very _____ _____ the mistake.
6. We'll _____ those for you.
7. Can I just _____ your delivery address?
8. It _____ take three to four days.
9. I _____ this is important for you.
10. I'll _____ _____ my manager.
11. Can I help _____ _____ anything else?
12. You're very _____ . Goodbye.

➔ page 99 See Pronunciation bank: /ɑː/ and /ʌ/

6.2 A problem with an order

4A Complete the dialogue with the client's responses in the box.

> Is there anything you can do about it?
> Thank you for your help.
> There's a problem with the photocopier.
> We need it as soon as possible.
> When will the technician get here?

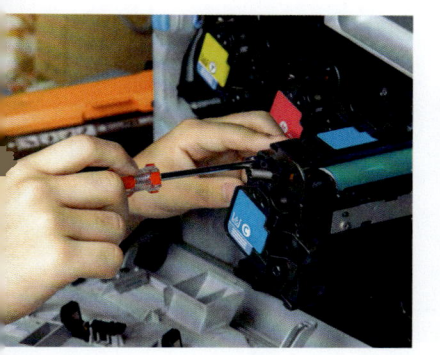

A: Good morning, customer services. Diane speaking. How can I help you?
B: Good morning. ¹_____. It's not working.
A: I'm sorry to hear that. We'll send a technician.
B: ²_____
A: On Friday, but it might be after three o'clock. He's very busy.
B: Oh, no! ³_____
A: I'm sorry about that, but he's very busy.
B: We can't print without it. ⁴_____. We have deadlines to meet.
A: I understand. I'll tell them it's urgent. I'll try and send someone in the morning.
B: ⁵_____
A: You're very welcome. Goodbye.

B Work in pairs. Practise the conversation in Exercise 4A.

Speaking

5 Work in pairs. Take turns to phone customer services. Use expressions from Exercises 3 and 4.
Student A: Look at the information below. **Student B:** Look at page 121.

Phone call 1: You are the client

Your order number: HY00634GC
Product: Black computer chairs
Product number: AY35CB
Quantity: 15

You ordered fifteen black computer chairs but you received fourteen white computer chairs (product number AY26CW) yesterday. You want to change the chairs.

- Phone customer services. *Good morning, I'm …*
- Explain the problem. *There's a problem with …*
- Ask when they can change the chairs. *When will … ?*
- You need delivery tomorrow. You have staff without chairs. *We need …*

Phone call 2: You are the Customer Services Agent

All your technicians are very busy and some are on holiday. They might take two days to visit the client. If a customer says it's urgent, you can send one within twenty-four hours.

- Answer phone call. *Customer Services, …*
- Ask about the problem. *How can I …*
- Say what you will do. *We'll …*
- Be polite. *I'm sorry …*
- Ask if they need anything more. / End the call. *Can I help you with …*

Self-assessment: I can make and respond to a complaint.

6.3 The production process

Lesson outcome — Learners can write a short description of a production process.

Lead-in **1** Look at the supply chain for cotton clothes. Complete the infographic with the words in the box.

> clothes manufacturer   ~~cotton farmer~~   cotton supplier
> customer   distribution centre   retail store

1 _cotton farmer_   2 _____   3 _____
4 _____   5 _____   6 _____

Reading **2A** Read the text. Why do you think the company describes the supply chain?

B Read the text again and answer the questions.
1 Where is the cotton from?
2 Who designs the T-shirts?
3 Where are the T-shirts produced?
4 What is special about the packaging?

C Match the words in the box with their verb forms in bold in the text.

> design   grow   make (x2)   pay   produce   sell   use

Our story: environment and ethics

You know our T-shirts feel great and look good on you. But do you know how we make them? One hundred percent of our cotton **is grown** on organic farms in India. The farmers **are paid** a fair price for their cotton. We work hard to protect the environment and be ethical.

Our T-shirts **are designed** by our creative team. They **are made** in Morocco and **are produced** to the highest standards. No dangerous chemicals **are used** in the process. And the packaging **is made** from recycled materials. Our popular T-shirts **are sold** all over the world. Want to know more about our supply chain?

Click here

6.3 The production process

Communicative grammar

> **DESCRIBING PRODUCTION** → Grammar reference: page 110
>
> **Present Simple Passive**
>
> **Regular forms**
> Our T-shirts **are designed by** our creative team.
> No dangerous chemicals **are used** in the process.
> They **are produced** to the highest standard.
>
> **Irregular forms**
> Our cotton **is grown** on organic farms in India.
> The farmers **are paid** a fair price.
> They **are made in** Morocco.
> Our packaging **is made from** recycled materials.
> Our T-shirts **are sold** all over the world.

→ **page 100** See Pronunciation bank: /uː/ and /ʊ/

3 Use the Present Simple Passive to complete the sentences about some ethical products.
1. This denim jacket _____ (make) from sixty percent organic cotton.
2. The workers in our shoe factory _____ (pay) a fair wage.
3. No animal products _____ (use) to make our products.
4. All our fruit _____ (grow) on organic farms.
5. This chair _____ (design) to be recycled.
6. These eco-friendly tablet sleeves _____ (sell) in three colours.

4 Rewrite the sentences in the Present Simple Passive.
1. We make these mobile phone covers from recycled plastic.
   These mobile phone covers _____ from recycled plastic.
2. We do not use chemicals to produce our organic coffee.
   No chemicals _____ to produce our organic coffee.
3. We produce our chocolate from local beans grown on the island.
   Our chocolate _____ from local beans grown on the island.
4. We give ten percent of our profits to children's charities.
   Ten percent of our profits _____ to children's charities.
5. Local farmers deliver the organic meat to your door.
   The organic meat _____ to your door by local farmers.
6. We buy ninety-five percent of our tea from ethical suppliers.
   Ninety-five percent of our tea _____ from ethical suppliers.

Extra activities

Writing

5 Write a description of direct trade coffee for a company website. Use Present Simple active and passive forms. Use the pictures and phrases to help you.

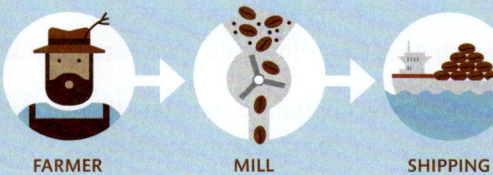

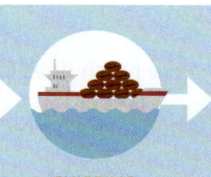

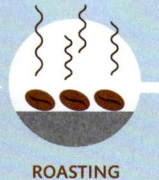

OUR DIRECT TRADE COFFEE

FARMER → MILL → SHIPPING → ROASTING → DELIVERED TO YOU

1. We / buy / all our coffee direct / farmers / Colombia
2. We / visit / farms / every year
3. No dangerous chemicals / use / produce your coffee
4. We / use / quality beans / our speciality coffee
5. The farmers / pay / guaranteed minimum price / their coffee beans
6. The beans / deliver to / mill / then / ship to / our headquarters
7. We / roast and pack / the beans here
8. We only / sell / our fresh coffee directly / you

We buy all our coffee direct from farmers in Colombia. We visit …

Self-assessment
I can write a short description of a production process.

6.4 WORK SKILLS
Placing an order

Lesson outcome — Learners can place a simple order.

Lead-in **1** Look at the information from a company's website. Match the words in the box with extracts 1–4.

> delivery date   payment terms   price   quantity

1 We offer a ten percent discount on orders of over 100 shirts.

2 WE HAVE MORE THAN FIFTY DIFFERENT DESIGNS IN STOCK.

3 You'll receive the items two days after you make your order.

4 Bank transfers are accepted.

VIDEO **2** ▶ 6.4.1 Eduardo, the owner of a fashion retailer, is placing an order with Maria, Sales Manager for a clothes manufacturer. Watch the video. Number the points 1–6 in the order they talk about them.

a payment terms ____   c delivery date ____   e quantity ____
b price ____   d discount ____   f sizes ____

3A Watch the video again and complete Eduardo's notes.

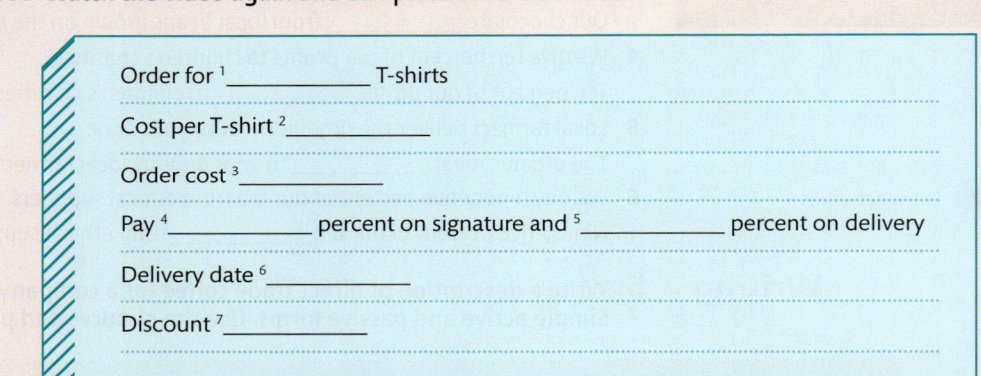

> Order for ¹_____ T-shirts
> Cost per T-shirt ²_____
> Order cost ³_____
> Pay ⁴_____ percent on signature and ⁵_____ percent on delivery
> Delivery date ⁶_____
> Discount ⁷_____

B How much does Eduardo's order cost with the discount?

4 Choose the correct option to complete the phrases from the video.
1 Could we talk about *price / delivery* now?
2 *How many / What type of* T-shirts do you want to order?
3 Can you give us a *good / lower* price?
4 *How about / Can you give us* €2 per T-shirt?
5 *I'm sure / I'm afraid* I can't agree to that.
6 *Could we pay / Shall we pay* twenty-five percent on signature and seventy-five percent on delivery?
7 *When / Where* can you deliver the order?
8 *You need to / Can you* deliver them by 17 March?
9 *Why not / Is there a* discount?
10 What do you *think / say*?
11 I think that's *OK / possible*.
12 I think we *can / need to* do that.

6.4 Work skills: Placing an order

Speaking

> **PLACING AN ORDER**
>
> **Ordering products**
> I'd / We'd like [1,000 small T-shirts / 500 jackets / 25 boxes].
> The price is [€2.50 / £5 / $6] per [T-shirt / jacket / box].
> We'll pay by bank transfer.
> I'll confirm my order by email.
>
> **Asking questions**
> How many [T-shirts / laptops / boxes] do you want to order?
> Could we talk about price now?
> Can you give us a lower price?
> How about [€2 a T-shirt / 5 April / four percent]? (What do you think?)
> Could we pay twenty-five percent on signature and seventy-five percent on delivery?
> Can you deliver them [by 15 March / Thursday]?
> When can you deliver the order?
> Does delivery (usually) take [two / four / six] weeks?
> Is there a discount?
>
> | **Agreeing** | **Saying no** |
> |---|---|
> | I think that's OK. / We can do that. | I'm afraid I can't agree to that. |
> | Yes, that's right. | Sorry, but that's not possible. |
> | That's fine. | I'm afraid for new clients it's [thirty / fifty / sixty] percent (on delivery). |

T Extra activities

5 Work in pairs. Read your information. Roleplay the situation.

Student A: You are the Buyer for a children's clothing company. You want to make an order with Student B. Look at page 121.

Student B: You are the Sales Manager for a clothes manufacturer. Student A wants to make an order with you. Look at page 123.

Student A
- Ask if you can discuss the price.
- Tell Student B how many jumpers you want.
- Ask for a lower price per jumper.
- Check the total price for the jumpers.
- Suggest the payment conditions.
- Suggest a delivery date.
- Explain that you need them on 8 July. Ask for a discount on the total price. Explain how you will pay and confirm the order.

Student B
- Agree. Ask how many jumpers Student A wants to buy.
- Tell Student A the price for that number of jumpers.
- Explain your discount policy.
- Confirm or correct the total price.
- Give your payment conditions.
- Answer.
- Answer.

Self-assessment I can place a simple order.

BUSINESS WORKSHOP

Buy natural

Lesson outcome: Learners can make and respond to simple orders and complaints, and make simple predictions about the future.

Introduction

1 Read the ethical company webpage. Answer the questions.
1. What products does Natural sell?
2. What ingredients does the company use?
3. What packaging does it use?
4. What does the company give money to?

Our Natural promise

We believe in being natural. We believe in natural ingredients. We want to protect your skin and hair. We promise that all our beauty products are made from plants and organic ingredients. Our products are not tested on animals. We do not use any animal products in our shampoos, shower gels, hair conditioners and face creams. No dangerous chemicals are used. All our packaging, bottles and boxes are made from recycled paper and plastic. Please remember to recycle the packaging. We give money to nature projects and environmental organisations.

Click here for more information.

Speaking
Placing an order

2 Work in pairs. Read your information.

Student A: You are a retailer. You want to order Natural's products for your shops. Read the information below and prepare for the roleplay. Then make your order.
- You want 400 bottles of Natural shampoo and 400 bottles of shower gel.
- Agree the price, delivery date and payment terms.

	You would like	You can accept
Price	$250 per 100 units	$250 to $300 per 100 units
Delivery date	seventy-two hours (three days) from now	Up to five days from now
Payment	Payment by bank transfer when the order is delivered.	Twenty-five percent when the contract is signed and seventy-five percent by bank transfer when the order is delivered.

Student B: You are the Sales Manager at Natural. Look at page 120.

Speaking
A problem with an order

3A Read the email about the delivery from Natural. What is the problem?

They delivered 200 bottles of shampoo, 200 bottles of hair conditioner and 400 bottles of shower gel. Could you phone customer services at Natural about this?

B Work in pairs. You are going to have a conversation.

Student A: You are the customer. Read your information below. Phone Student B about the problem.
Student B: You are the Customer Services Agent at Natural. Look at page 126.

Your order number: JB88051XT
Products: Natural shampoo and shower gel
Quantity: 400 bottles of shampoo and 400 bottles of shower gel

Problem: You ordered 400 bottles of shampoo but received 200 of shampoo and 200 of hair conditioner. This is wrong. You want to change the hair conditioner for shampoo.

Phone customer services.
Good morning, I'm phoning from (company name).
Explain the problem.
There's a problem with …
Ask when they can change the products.
When will you …
You need delivery tomorrow.
We need them tomorrow.

4A What do you think will happen to the products in the box in future? Write three or four sentences.

> beauty products   cleaning products
> meat   vegan products

There might be more organic meat.
I don't think people will pay more for organic products.

B Work in pairs. Compare your ideas.

Self-assessment: I can make and respond to simple orders and complaints, and make simple predictions about the future.

Competition

7

> Is your business winning?

Unit overview

7.1 **Should I upgrade?**
Lesson outcome: Learners can compare a product with other products or an older version.

Vocabulary: Product qualities
Listening: Talking about using a product
Communicative grammar: Comparing (1): comparatives
Video: Comparing sports cars
Task: Comparing two models

7.2 **Services**
Lesson outcome: Learners can explain the cost of a service.

Vocabulary: Fees
Listening: Comparing recruitment agencies
Writing: An advertisement for services

7.3 **The best providers**
Lesson outcome: Learners can compare services.

Reading: An email comparing services
Communicative grammar: Comparing (2): superlatives
Writing: An email summarising survey results

7.4 **Work skills:** Presentations
Lesson outcome: Learners can make a simple presentation about their company and/or product/service.

Video: Our products and services
Speaking: Presenting

7.5 **Business workshop:** The big contract
Lesson outcome: Learners can make comparisons of products, present information and write a simple recommendation and summary email.

Reading: An email about a trade show
Speaking: Giving presentations
Writing: A summary email giving a recommendation

Review 7: p.93 | Pronunciation: 7.2 /əʊ/ and /aʊ/ 7.3 /p/, /b/, /f/ and /v/ p.100 | Grammar reference: 7.1 Comparing (1) 7.3 Comparing (2) p.111

7.1 Should I upgrade?

Lesson outcome — Learners can compare a product with other products or an older version.

Lead-in

1 Choose a product from the box and use the questions to make some notes. Tell your partner about it.

| a car   a phone   a television   a watch |

What brand is it? Why do you like it? What is special about it?

Vocabulary

Product qualities

2 Match the phrases in the box with their descriptions (a–h).

| design   product life |
| features   speed |
| unique selling point (USP) |
| user experience |
| value for money   weight |

a how fast it is
b how heavy it is
c how long a product works
d how a product looks or works
e the useful things that the product has (e.g. camera) or the things it can do (e.g. talk)
f something that makes the product different to others
g what it feels like or how easy it is to use the product
h the price of the product vs. the product performance/features

3A Read the advert about the Waiwex TP Pro. Which of the qualities in Exercise 2A does it mention?

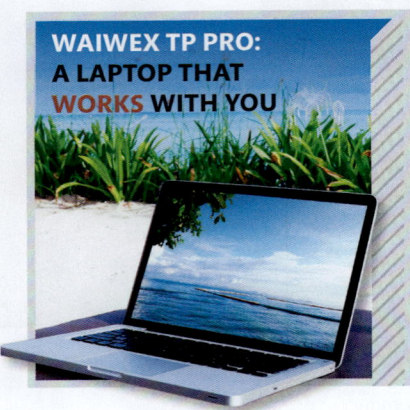

WAIWEX TP PRO: A LAPTOP THAT WORKS WITH YOU

WORK ON THE GO
The TP Pro is **lighter than** other models so you can take it with you wherever you go.
It has a **longer** battery life **than** any other laptop so you can work without a power lead for up to twelve hours while you travel.

WORK BIGGER, WORK FASTER
The TP Pro has a **larger** memory **than** our older models and files and programs load three times faster.

WORK SAFER
Our security software partners PRO-TEC offer a discount on their software when you buy the new TP Pro. Their advanced security software features keep your files and data **more secure than** ever.

B Read the advert again. Are the statements *true* (T) or *false* (F)?

1 The new TP Pro is easy to carry.
2 The power lead is important when you travel for eight hours.
3 The TP Pro can hold three times more files than previous models.
4 It costs more money for the security software.

4 Discuss the questions with a partner.
1 What laptop do you use for work/study?
2 Do you like it? What are its strengths/weaknesses?

T Extra activities

Listening

5A 🔊 7.01 Listen to Misako and Karim talk about using the TP Pro laptop. Tick (✓) the things they talk about.

| battery life   camera   memory   how it looks   operating system   security software   speed |

B Listen again. Tick (✓) each speaker's opinions.

	Karim thinks the TP Pro is		Misako thinks the TP Pro is	
	Good	Bad	Good	Bad
Speed				
Battery				
Size and weight				
Security				

7.1 Should I upgrade?

Communicative grammar

COMPARING (1): COMPARATIVES
➡ Grammar reference: page 111

Short adjectives
The battery life is **longer** on this model.
This phone is **heavier than** other models.
My new TV is **bigger**.

Long adjectives
This model has a **more powerful** battery.
The new model is **more expensive than** the old model.

Irregular adjectives
good – **better**, bad – **worse**

6 Put the words in the correct order to make sentences.
1 goes / others / this model / than / faster
2 's / than / my last one / my phone / bigger
3 lighter / my new laptop / is
4 is / the new car / more spacious / than the / old car
5 more expensive / than / the standard car / the GTI model is
6 than / more advanced / the features / are / for other TVs

7 Choose the correct option.
1 It's *better / worse* than my old laptop. I like it a lot.
2 The battery on this phone is *better / worse* than my old phone. It dies after just four hours.
3 This model is *more cheap / cheaper* than the new model.
4 This one's *bigger / biger* than my old laptop.

8 Complete the sentences about two cars with the correct form of the words in brackets.
1 The Morgan Plus Six model is _____ (new) than the Morgan Plus 4.
2 The Morgan Plus 4 has a _____ (powerful) engine than the Plus Six model.
3 The Morgan Plus 4 goes _____ (fast) than the Morgan Plus Six.
4 The Morgan Plus Six is _____ (comfortable) for tall drivers.
5 The Morgan Plus 4 is _____ (heavy) than the Morgan Plus Six.
6 The Morgan Plus 4 has _____ (big) wheels than the Morgan Plus Six.
7 The Morgan Plus 4 is _____ (cheap) than the Morgan Plus Six.
8 The Morgan 3 Wheeler is _____ (small) than the Plus 4.

T Extra activities

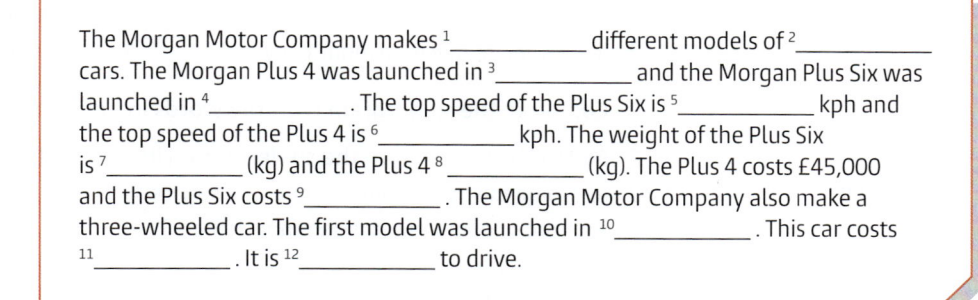

VIDEO

▶ The Morgan Plus 4
▶ The Morgan Plus Six 

9 ▶ 7.1.1 Watch the video. Are the sentences in Exercise 8 *true* (T) or *false* (F)?

10 Watch the video again and complete the text.

The Morgan Motor Company makes ¹_____ different models of ²_____ cars. The Morgan Plus 4 was launched in ³_____ and the Morgan Plus Six was launched in ⁴_____. The top speed of the Plus Six is ⁵_____ kph and the top speed of the Plus 4 is ⁶_____ kph. The weight of the Plus Six is ⁷_____ (kg) and the Plus 4 ⁸_____ (kg). The Plus 4 costs £45,000 and the Plus Six costs ⁹_____. The Morgan Motor Company also make a three-wheeled car. The first model was launched in ¹⁰_____. This car costs ¹¹_____. It is ¹²_____ to drive.

11 Work in pairs.
Student A: Look at page 126. Student B: Look at page 124.

➤ **TASK**

Self-assessment I can compare a product with other products or an older version.

69

7.2 Services

Lesson outcome: Learners can explain the cost of a service.

Lead-in **1** Work in pairs. Which of these services or agencies do you or your company use?

> advertising cleaning courier financial IT
> marketing recruitment tax training travel

Vocabulary Fees

2A Read the adverts for three companies. Which services from Exercise 1 do they offer?

B Choose a name for each company (1–3).
Best Clean UK   Office Professionals   Cox & Co. Worldwide

A _____

We are a UK recruitment agency with a wide range of candidates for every job. For more details, click here.

There is a **fixed fee** of just 399 GBP for our standard service. The **fee includes**:

- advertisements in local newspapers and recruitment websites.
- a high number of qualified and experienced candidates for your interview.

For an **additional fee**, we can also interview candidates and complete full background checks. Your company can **pay this fee** after successful recruitment.

B _____

We offer a wide range of cleaning services at great prices. We clean offices, warehouses, factories and private houses. For our standard service, we offer contracts with a **monthly** or **annual fee***. Our staff are friendly, experienced and professional.

*Please note, there is an **administration fee** for your first contract.

C _____

We offer a wide range of travel services including holidays, business travel or just flights and hotels, anywhere in the world. For group bookings, we can also offer discounts for tourist attractions. We do not **charge a fee** for online reservations*.

Please note: there is a **cancellation fee** on all reservations. This is charged for cancellations 7 days after reservation.

*Individual flight bookings are not included. Airlines may charge **booking fees**.

C Read the adverts again. Answer the questions.

Which company…

1. gives you a discount for large bookings?
2. finds out information about people?
3. allows you to pay each month or year?
4. will create an advertisement for you?
5. will come to your workplace?
6. allows you to book online?

3A Complete the spidergram with the words in bold from the adverts.

Spidergram:
1. (the) **fee** _____
2. _____ a/the **fee**
3. _additional_ _____, monthly or _____ **fee**, _____, _____

B Match the words from the spidergram with the explanations below.

1. ask someone to pay some money for a service (_____ a fee)
2. an amount of money that does not change (_____ fee)
3. when you pay every month (_____ fee)
4. some extra money (_____ fee)
5. the money you pay for booking something (e.g a hotel room) that you don't want (_____ fee)
6. you pay a fee and you get these things (the fee _____)
7. the fee you pay for the work of creating new documents etc., (e.g. contracts) (_____ fee)
8. you pay the company to cover the work of arranging tickets (_____ fee)

➔ **page 100** See Pronunciation bank: /əʊ/ and /aʊ/

7.2 Services

C Complete the sentences with the correct form of the words in Exercise 3A.
1 The cleaning company _____ a fee of £20 an hour.
2 The price is $250. There is a(n)_____ fee of $4 for delivery.
3 You can rent a bike for 24 hours for a(n)_____ fee of €20.
4 The fee for the training _____ all training materials.
5 We can arrange a(n) _____ fee for our catering services, paid on the first of each month.
6 There is no _____ fee if you inform us you are not coming three days before the training.
7 All hotel reservations include a standard _____ fee of £3.50.
8 Johnson Lawyers will charge a(n) _____ fee of £100 for rent agreements.

Listening Comparing recruitment agencies

4A Work in pairs. Which services are important for a recruitment company to offer? Why?

B 🔊 7.02 Tom and Ellie are discussing two recruitment agencies. Which agency do they choose? Why?

C Listen again and complete the gaps in the webpages.

▼ All Recruit	≡ Menu 🔍 Search
Speciality areas	advertising, marketing, sales
offices	¹_____ , Manchester
services	• online advertising • recruitment for permanent and temporary roles • ²_____ -month guarantee on candidates • background checks on candidates • search of ⁴_____ networking sites • candidate ⁵_____ with expert consultants
fees	• fee between ⁶_____ of candidate's first annual salary

▼ Jones Recruitment	≡ Menu 🔍 Search
Speciality areas	advertising, marketing, media, sales, television
offices	Brighton, Bristol, Belfast, Glasgow, Reading, Manchester
services	• online advertising • recruitment for permanent and temporary roles • ³_____ -month guarantee on candidates • background checks on candidates
fees	• fixed fee of ⁷£ _____ for **standard service** (the fee includes advertising and selection of CVs) • ⁸_____ fee for background checks

D Look at the webpages in Exercise 4C. Are the sentences *true* (T) or *false* (F)?
1 Jones Recruitment have a wider range of speciality areas.
2 All Recruit has more offices than Jones Recruitment.
3 Jones Recruitment advertise temporary jobs.
4 The standard service at Jones Recruitment includes interviews with candidates.
5 All Recruit use people with special knowledge to interview candidates.

Writing

5 Write an advertisement for the services of a courier agency. Use the information in the table below to answer the questions. Write full sentences.
1 What types of delivery do you offer? *We offer … We charge …*
2 Do you charge a fixed fee? What for? What does the fixed fee include? *We charge … Our fixed fee …*
3 What fee do you charge for next-day delivery of items between 1kg and 5kg? *We charge …*
4 Do you offer contracts? What for? *We also offer …*
5 What do you charge additional fees for? *There is …*

AP Couriers			
Where they deliver	Services	Delivery/Fees (1kg–5kg parcels) (includes collection and recorded delivery)	Additional fees
Local / National	Parcels & large/ heavy items	Same day – all items £22 Next day – £10–20 2 days – from £3, 3–7 days – from £2 Daily courier service contracts (pay monthly or yearly)	Contract agreements for daily courier service (administration) Items over 5kg Cancellation of orders

Self-assessment I can explain the cost of a service.

7.3 The best providers

Lesson outcome: Learners can compare services.

Lead-in

1A Do you choose service providers for your company, your home or yourself? Tell your partner about services you choose.

> energy provider   internet provider   mobile phone contract
> office cleaning service   printer/photocopier contract

B What is important for you when choosing a service provider? Put the things in the box in order of importance (1 = very important, 6 = not important).

> ☐ easy to access   ☐ good service
> ☐ value for money   ☐ staff knowledge
> ☐ quality of communication   ☐ friendly staff

Reading

2 First Serve provide home and car insurance. They asked Market Watch, a market research company, to compare their services to other insurance providers. Read the email and tick (✓) the correct boxes.

	Good performance	Bad performance
Service reliability		
Staff knowledge		
Satisfied customers (40–50 yrs)		
Time to answer calls		
Problem solving		
Value		

✉ **Market research results**

K. Ferner
Kelly.Ferner@marketwatch.com

📎 Jan Survey Results

Dear Mia,

Please find attached the customer satisfaction report you asked us to complete.

We compared First Serve to six other insurance providers to see who was **the most reliable** and and who had **the most satisfied** customers.

Here is a summary of the findings:

Strengths

First Serve has:
- **the highest number** of successful claims.
- **the most knowledgeable** staff.
- **the best** value for money.

Areas of improvement

First Serve has:
- **the biggest** delay in answering calls.
- **the worst** record for solving problems quickly.
- **the lowest** number of satisfied customers in the 40–50 age group.

If you have any questions, please let me know.

Best regards,

Kelly Ferner
Market Researcher

3 Match the phrases (1–4) with phrases with the same meaning (a–d).

1 Please find attached …
2 Please find a summary below.
3 If you have any questions, please let me know.
4 Best regards,

a Contact me if you need anything else.
b See the attached document.
c Kind regards,
d See the outline below.

T Extra activities

7.3 The best providers

Communicative grammar

> **COMPARING (2): SUPERLATIVES** → Grammar reference: page 111
>
> **Short adjectives**
> First Serve have **the highest** number of successful claims.
> They have **the friendliest** team.
> They had **the biggest** delay in answering calls.
>
> **Long adjectives**
> They had **the most satisfied** customers.
> They have **the most knowledgeable** staff.
>
> **Irregular adjectives**
> good – better – the best
> bad – worse – the worst

4A Complete the sentences with *the* and the correct form of the words in brackets.
1. We have _____the shortest_____ delivery times. (short)
2. Our products are _____ on the market. (cheap)
3. We have _____ service. (reliable)
4. Our staff are _____ in the industry. (knowledgeable)
5. We have _____ staff in our stores. (friendly)
6. We have _____ product range in store. (wide)
7. We have _____ number of satisfied customers. (high)
8. Our products are _____ value for money. (good)

B Rewrite the words in bold in the superlative form.

> M. Deserio <Mia.Deserio@firstcall.com> 📎 Attachment ✉ <
> **Market research results**
>
> Dear All,
>
> Here are the results from our survey to find out what customers think about our insurance services.
>
> Our service is ¹**reliable** and we offer ²**good** value for money. We also have ³**knowledgeable** staff.
>
> However, we have ⁴**a low** number of satisfied customers in the 40-50 age group, our record for solving problems is ⁵**bad** and we have ⁶**big** delays in answering calls.
>
> So overall, we're doing well in some areas, but there are things we can improve.
>
> Best regards,
>
> Mia

T Extra activities

Writing

5 You are a Market Researcher at Market Watch. Travel Care, a business travel agent, wants you to compare its customer experience to other business travel companies. Use the information in the table to write an email summarising your survey results.

	Travel Care	Travel Forward	The World Traveller
Staff knowledge	★★★★★	★★★★	★★★
Staff friendliness	★★★★★	★★★★	★★★★
Price and discounts	★★	★★★	★★★
Value for money	★★	★★★	★★★
Customer service	★★★★★	★★★★	★★

★★★★★ very good ★★★★ good ★★★ satisfactory ★★ needs to improve ★ bad

→ page 100 See Pronunciation bank: /p/, /b/, /f/ and /v/

Self-assessment I can compare services. 🙂 ☹

7.4 WORK SKILLS
Presentations

Lesson outcome — Learners can make a simple presentation about their company and/or a product/service.

Lead-in 1A Do you give presentations in your company or studies? How do you feel about this?

B Work with a partner. What information would you tell potential customers in a company presentation? Use ideas from the box or your own ideas.

> company history   location   prices   products/services
> quality   unique selling point   other

C Put the stages of a company presentation (a–f) in the correct order.
a Questions   ____
b Your name and your company's name   ____
c Information about other products/services   ____
d Company history/background   ____
e Information about main product/service   ____
f Aim of the presentation   ____

VIDEO 2A ▶ 7.4.1 Watch a presentation on a company and their products and services. Answer the questions.
1 What is the aim of the presentation?
2 What product or service is the presenter selling?
3 Were the stages of the presentation in the same order as in Exercise 1C?

B Watch the presentation again. Are the statements *true* (T) or *false* (F)?
1 Web Trade Builder started in 2004.
2 They are the largest e-commerce company in Europe.
3 They have offices in three countries.
4 They sell services to over 20,000 companies.
5 They create payment services for online shops.
6 They can build websites for other companies.
7 Their credit card payment system doesn't work in all countries.
8 The payment system can store customer details.

3 Watch the video again. Choose the correct word.
1 So, good *morning / afternoon*.
2 The *aim / plan* of today's presentation is to *sell / introduce* our company and services.
3 First, I'll *tell / inform* you a bit more about the company's history.
4 *First / Finally*, we'll have a question and answer session at the end.
5 So let's *move on / start* with more information about the company.
6 We are the *biggest / best* provider of e-commerce services in Europe.
7 We're *based / located* in Birmingham, in the UK.
8 So let's *start / move* on to our products and services.
9 We can *build / develop* a complete website.
10 We *will / can* design a system that allows your customers to pay faster.
11 OK. So that's the *finish / end* of my presentation.
12 Does anyone have any *questions / comments*?

7.4 Work skills: Presentations

Speaking

> **PRESENTING**
>
> **Introduction**
> So, good morning everyone. I'm … , Sales Director at …
> Thank you for attending this presentation.
> The aim of today's presentation is to …
>
> **Changing topic**
> So,/OK, …
> Let's start with …
> Let's move on to …
> Now let's talk about …
>
> **Giving the agenda**
> First/Then/Finally
> I'll tell you about …
> I'll explain …
> I'll talk about …
>
> **Introducing the company**
> We are the … provider of …
> We're based in …
> We have offices in …
> We provide a range …
>
> **Explaining what you offer**
> We can / We'll start fixing your car immediately.

T Extra activities

4 You work for Force Sport Cars. Use the notes to create a short presentation about the company and its products for an international car show.

COMPANY HISTORY
- Factory and head office – Spa, Belgium
- Force Sport started in 1987
- Fixed engines for motor-racing teams
- Launched own small sports car in 1992 for public roads

MAIN PRODUCTS
- Hand-built engines for motor-racing cars and motorcycles
- In our industry, our high-performance engines are the most reliable, quickest to build, lightest and last the longest
- Customer reviews – the best car for new racing teams

SERVICES
- Fix your motorsports cars and motorcycles
- Ship to us
- Replace engines and other parts with our quality products
- Team have over 30 years' experience / best in industry
- Make new engines and parts to meet customer requirements

5 Now imagine you are presenting your company and its products/services at a trade show. Use the questions to prepare a short presentation.

Company history
1 When did your company start? Where are you based? How many employees do you have at your main office / across the world? Why is your product/service good?

Products/Services
2 How can you help the customer? What are the main products/services that you provide? What other products/services do you provide? What do customers say about your products/services? When can you deliver the product/service?

B Work in small groups. Take turns to present your product/service. After each presentation, ask the presenter some questions.

How long does it take to build your product?

Self-assessment I can make a simple presentation about a company and/or a product/service.

75

BUSINESS WORKSHOP

The big contract

Lesson outcome: Learners can make comparisons of products, present information and write a simple recommendation and summary email.

Introduction

1 Look at the information about the International Cruise Show and read the email. Why is Hugo from Sunset Luxury Cruises going to the show?

THE INTERNATIONAL CRUISE SHOW

The international cruise show brings together cruise ship builders, cruise operators and other tour companies to show what's new in the industry.

---

to: Hugo.Vasquez@sunset. **from** David.Golden@sunset

Hi Hugo,

As we discussed yesterday, I'd like you to look at the new cruise ships at the International Cruise Show next week. We need to buy a new ship for our Caribbean tours, to meet increasing customer demand.

Can you look at the options and write an analysis that recommends a ship?

Thanks,
David

Presentations

2 Work in two groups.

Group A: You work for Seven Seas Ships. Look at page 123 and read the information. Complete the table with details about your ship.

Group B: You work for Saffron Ship Company. Look at page 125 and read the information. Complete the table with details about your ship.

Company	Seven Seas Ships	Saffron Ship Company	Delta Luxury Ships
Ship	The River Queen	The Star Sailor	The Cruise Star
Size			200 x 30 m
Decks			4
Rooms			110
Features			5 bars, 3 restaurants, 3 swimming pools
Build/Delivery time			1 year 2 months
Estimated cost			$5.25 million

3A Work with a partner from the other group. Present your information from Exercise 2.

B Listen to your partner's presentation. Complete the table in Exercise 2.

4 Work in pairs. You work for Sunset Luxury Cruises. Use the information in the table in Exercise 2 to compare the three ships and decide which one is best for your company.

Sunset Luxury Cruises want:

- the new ship to be ready in less than one year.
- to spend less than $5 million.
- to have 100 rooms or more.
- to have two bars and two restaurants or more.
- to have three swimming pools or more.

Writing

5A Decide if the phrases are from the beginning (B), middle (M) or end (E) of an email.

1 If you have any questions, please let me know.
2 *The Star Sailor* is the biggest ship.
3 *The River Queen* is cheaper but smaller than the other ships.
4 Please find attached the analysis of …
5 Can we arrange a meeting to discuss the options?
6 Here is a summary of the findings.

B You are Hugo Vasquez from Sunset Luxury Cruises. Write a summary email to your manager to explain which ship you recommend.

Hi David,
Please find attached the analysis of …

Self-assessment: I can make comparisons of products, present information and write a simple recommendation and summary email.

Jobs 8

> What are you good at?

Unit overview

8.1	**Work experience**	**Vocabulary:** Skills and personal qualities
	Lesson outcome: Learners can talk about their previous work experience.	**Communicative grammar:** Talking about experience
		Video: Skills and experience
		Task: Asking and answering interview questions

8.2	**The best person for the job**	**Vocabulary:** Job requirements
	Lesson outcome: Learners can compare people's skills and experience and choose the best person for a job.	**Listening:** Choosing job candidates
		Speaking: Describing and comparing candidates

8.3	**Professional profiles**	**Reading:** A professional profile
	Lesson outcome: Learners can write a simple profile for a professional website.	**Communicative grammar:** Talking about experiences and completed past events
		Writing: An employee profile

| 8.4 | **Work skills:** A job interview | **Video:** The job interview |
| | **Lesson outcome:** Learners can ask and answer simple questions in a job interview. | **Speaking:** Job interviews |

| 8.5 | **Business workshop:** The interviewer and the candidate | **Speaking:** Interview questions; choosing the best candidate for the job |
| | **Lesson outcome:** Learners can ask and answer simple questions in a job interview. | |

Review 8: p.94 | **Pronunciation:** 8.2 The vowel /ɒ/ The letter 'o' as /ɒ/, /əʊ/ and /ʌ/ 8.3 Silent letters p.101 | **Grammar reference:** 8.1 Talking about experiences 8.3 Talking about experiences and completed past events p.111

8.1 Work experience

Lesson outcome — Learners can talk about their previous work experience.

Lead-in

1 Think of someone you like working with. Say why you like working with him/her.

> calm   hard-working   friendly   funny   intelligent   organised   polite   reliable

I like working with my manager. She's organised and helpful.

Vocabulary — **Skills and personal qualities**

2 Read the blog post from a job website and answer the questions.
   1 Who did the blog writer interview? Why?
   2 What two things are good to talk about at a job interview?
   3 What can people with no work experience do at an interview?

What employers want

We interviewed 100 employers about the skills and qualities they want when recruiting employees. Here are the top eight:

1	good communication skills	5	IT skills
2	organised	6	motivated
3	team worker	7	hard-working
4	analytical	8	language skills

They also say it's important that employees are reliable, know about the company's products and have a friendly personality.

Top Tip!

Next time you have a job interview, prepare to talk about real-life examples of the skills and personal qualities that are important for the job. For example, 'I'm very analytical. I'**ve analysed** sales data and **written** sales reports.' Or 'I'm a team worker. I'**ve worked** in international teams to solve problems on projects.' Or 'I'm very organised. I'**ve never missed** an important deadline.'

If you **haven't had** any work experience, give other examples from your life, interests and studies. For example, 'I have excellent communication skills. I'**ve written** blogs for a website.' Or 'I'm a good communicator and team worker. I'**ve given** many team presentations in my university classes.'

---

3 Complete the table with the skills/qualities (1–8) in the blog post.

What employers want	Examples
1 _____	complete tasks on time, meet deadlines
2 _____	express ideas well when speaking and writing, listen to others
3 _____	work with other people on projects
4 _____	assess information, analyse data, solve problems
5 _____	speak German, English and Spanish
6 _____	use Microsoft Word and Excel
7 _____	have a positive 'can-do' attitude to work
8 _____	make a lot of effort to do a good job

4 Match the correct skill/quality (1–8) in the blog post with the sentences (a–h).
   a I do a lot of work when I'm at the office.
   b I can work with many different software programs.
   c I try to solve problems in a logical way.
   d I know how to give a clear presentation and explain my ideas.
   e I'm good at planning things.
   f I can read emails in Portuguese.
   g I really want to achieve success in my work.
   h I work well with colleagues in my department.

Extra activities

5 Look at page 124. Complete the questionnaire with your own examples.

8.1 Work experience

Communicative grammar

TALKING ABOUT EXPERIENCES → Grammar reference: page 111

+ I've written sales reports.
  You've worked in international teams.
  She's given many presentations.

− I've never missed an important deadline.
  You haven't had any work experience.
  He hasn't had much experience in sales.

? Have you ever written blogs? Yes, I have. / No, I haven't.
  Has she worked on international projects? Yes, she has. / No, she hasn't.

6 Complete the sentences with the correct form of the verbs in brackets.

They ¹_____ (work) in over ten countries. He ²_____ (not have) much experience in the UK, and she ³_____ (not write) any reports in English.

I ⁴_____ (give) lots of sales presentations with this software, and you have ⁵_____ (use) a similar program. However, I ⁶_____ (never present) in a large organisation.

7A Put the words in the correct order to make questions.
1 ever / a team / managed / you / Have / ? _____
2 for / many / have / companies / you / How / worked / ? _____
3 or region / you / Have / lived in / another country / ever / ? _____
4 you / in an international / Have / team before / worked / ? _____
5 Have / in English / ever / written emails / you / ? _____
6 for / Where / travelled / have / work / you / ? _____

B Match the answers (a–f) with the questions (1–6) in Exercise 7A.
a No, I haven't. I've only lived in this country.
b I've worked for three different companies since university.
c I've travelled a lot around Germany and visited our Paris office.
d Yes, I have. I manage a team in my current job.
e Yes, I have. Our company has lots of European and Japanese employees.
f Yes, I have. I write them for our UK sales team.

T Extra activities

VIDEO

8A ▶ 8.1.1 Watch the start of the video. What type of companies do the two speakers work for?

B Watch the complete video. What skills and personal qualities does each person need? Write James (J), Polly (P) or Dan (D) next to the words in the box.

analytical skills   communication skills   decisive   organised
positive attitude   reliable   team worker   write well

C Watch the interview again. Complete the notes.

James has worked for ¹_____ companies as a ²_____ and an editor. He's also ³_____ his own company. James was an English teacher in Malta for ⁴_____ years. He also worked in Valencia, Spain, from ⁵_____ to _____ . He worked in Singapore as an editor for ⁶_____ months.

Polly has worked in Amsterdam, Eindhoven, ⁷_____ and Paris. In Paris, she spent ⁸_____ months working on a ⁹_____ project.

Dan set up the advertising agency ¹⁰_____ years ago. He worked for ¹¹_____ large businesses before Creature. The team at Creature are very ¹²_____ .

9 Work in pairs. Ask and answer the questions in Exercise 7A.

> Yes, I have. I've written emails to suppliers in China.

> No, I've never been to another country for work but I've been to lots of places on holiday.

▶ TASK

Self-assessment I can talk about my previous work experience.

8.2 The best person for the job

Lesson outcome — Learners can compare people's skills and experience and choose the best person for a job.

Lead-in 1 Look at the job advertisements. Where do companies usually advertise vacancies?

We have these vacancies. If you are interested, please click the link below.

GF Hospitality	**Sales Consultant** — GF Hospitality Group, London	View Job ❯
Townsends Logistics	**Sales Assistant** — Townsends Logistics, Birmingham	View Job ❯
Middleton Pharmaceuticals	**Sales Executive** — Middleton Pharmaceuticals, Coventry	View Job ❯
Danotex	**Sales Manager** — Danotex Chemicals, Birmingham	View Job ❯

Vocabulary — Job requirements

2A Read the email from Dan Baker to Elsa Hernández at Danotex Chemicals. What does Dan want Elsa to do?

From: Dan Baker
To: Elsa Hernández
Subject: Sales Manager Vacancy

Hello Elsa,

Here's a list of the skills and experience we need for the Sales Manager **vacancy**. Can you put these details in the job **advertisement**?

Essential skills and experience

- has Sales Manager or Sales Representative experience
- has managed staff
- has worked in chemical or related industry
- has excellent communication and negotiation skills
- is a team worker

Useful skills and experience

- has a **degree** in business administration or a similar university **qualification**
- can speak languages, especially German
- has experience in international sales

Can you **choose** the best **candidates** for me to interview? Let's talk on the phone after you speak to them.

Best wishes,

Dan Baker

Assistant Sales Director

Danotex Chemicals

B What is the difference between 'essential' and 'useful' skills?

8.2 The best person for the job

3 Choose the correct option, a, b or c.
1. We have two _____ in our production department at the moment.
   a advertisements   b qualifications   c vacancies
2. There are a lot of _____ for IT jobs on this website.
   a advertisements   b qualifications   c vacancies
3. We need staff with _____ in science, engineering and technology.
   a advertisements   b qualifications   c vacancies
4. Language skills are _____ for the job, but not essential.
   a excellent   b similar   c useful
5. It's important to _____ the best person for the job.
   a need   b choose   c manage
6. There are ten _____ for this new job.
   a candidates   b degrees   c vacancies
7. Why did you study for a _____ in economics?
   a candidate   b experience   c degree
8. You need strong analytical skills. They are _____ in this job.
   a excellent   b essential   c similar

T Extra activities

Listening   Choosing job candidates

4A 🔊 8.01 Listen to Dan's conversation with Elsa. Who is going to interview the candidates?

B Listen again and complete the profile for each candidate.

	Vicki Grant	Sam Gowan	Isaac Lange
Impression of candidate	Very friendly, good ¹_____ skills.	Knows a lot about our company, good ⁴_____ skills.	Good team worker, has a ⁷_____ personality.
Essential	²_____ years' experience in sales, manages a team of twelve staff.	Three years' experience in sales, manages a team of ⁵_____ staff.	⁸_____ years' experience in sales, manages a team of twenty staff.
Useful	Works in pharmaceutical industry, degree in chemistry, speaks ³_____ .	Works for a ⁶_____ chemical company, has business degree, has worked in Germany, excellent German.	Works for paint manufacturer, has travelled for work, ⁹_____ German.

→ page 101 See Pronunciation bank: 8.2 The vowel /ɒ/. The letter 'o' as /ɒ/, /əʊ/ and /ʌ/

5 Look at the information about the candidates in 4B. Complete true sentences with the positive or negative form of the verbs in brackets.
1. Vicki _hasn't worked_ (work) in the chemical industry.
2. She _____ (study) German, but she _____ (study) French.
3. Sam _____ (live) and _____ (work) in another country.
4. Sam _____ (work) for a bigger company than Danotex.
5. Isaac _____ (have) the most experience as a sales manager.
6. Issac _____ (travel) for work.
7. Vicki and Sam _____ (go) to university but Isaac _____ .
8. Sam _____ (work) in the chemical industry but Vicki and Isaac _____ .

Speaking

6A Describe each candidate's experience.

Vicki has a degree in chemistry. She has worked in pharmaceutical industry and has managed a team. She can speak …

B Work in pairs. Compare your sentences from Exercise 6A. Who do you think is the best candidate for the job? Why?

I think Sam is the best candidate. He's worked in Germany and he's had experience in the chemical industry.

Self-assessment
I can compare people's skills and experience and choose the best person for a job.

8.3 Professional profiles

Lesson outcome — Learners can write a simple profile for a professional website.

Lead-in 1 Which of these photos would be best for 1) a social media website, 2) a professional website? Why?

A   B   C

Reading 2 Label the online parts of the online profile with the words and phrases in the box.

Current job | ~~Full name~~ | Job title | Location | Past positions | Qualifications | Skills summary

1 _Full name_

Home   Groups   Inbox

Elsa Hernández Garcia
Human Resources Manager — 2 _____
Birmingham, UK

3 _____

Motivated, organised and creative HR Manager. I **have worked** in large organisations across different industries. I am friendly, a team worker and have excellent communication skills.
I **have designed** HR strategies, **organised** staff recruitment and **managed** HR teams for companies. I **have** also **worked** on projects with other departments and **planned** training programmes.
Specialties and interests: HR Strategy • Recruitment • Talent Management • Employee Relations

4 _____

Experience

5 _____

Human Resources Manager
Danotex Chemicals
Birmingham, UK
Feb 2019–present date

I am responsible for HR operations across the UK. I design HR strategy, organise recruitment and staff-training programmes. I work on projects with other department managers.

HR Officer
CUG Engineering Group
Leicester, UK
Jan 2016–Feb 2019

I **worked** for CUG Engineering **for three years**. I **was** responsible for recruitment in the UK. I **designed** the company's internship programme **in 2017** and **trained** interns. I **managed** a small HR team.

6 _____

Recruitment Specialist
Oscar Lane Recruitment International
London, UK
Sept 2013–Dec 2015

I **was** responsible for recruiting across Europe. I **advertised** vacancies and **interviewed** and **recruited** candidates for our clients.

Education

Master's in Human Resources Management
Filton Business School
2015–2018

BA (Hons) Degree in Psychology
Drumford University
2009–2012

7 _____

8.3 Professional profiles

> **TALKING ABOUT EXPERIENCES AND COMPLETED PAST EVENTS** → Grammar reference: page 113
>
> **+ Experiences**
> I **have worked** in large organisations across different industries.
> I **have organised** staff recruitment for companies.
>
> **+ Completed past events**
> I **worked** for CUG Engineering **for three years**.
> I **designed** the company's internship programme **last year**.

→ **page 101** See Pronunciation bank: Silent letters

3 Choose the correct option to complete the sentences.
1 She *has worked / worked* for several companies in this industry. She *has started / started* working for this company two years ago.
2 He *has been / was* a Project Manager with Danotex Chemicals from 2017 to 2020. He *had / has had* a lot of management experience.
3 I *have studied / studied* web design in 2018. I *have designed / designed* e-commerce websites for over fifty corporate clients.
4 She *has been / went* to Germany on business many times. She *has been / went* there again last month to visit clients.
5 I *have managed / managed* many international teams in my career. I *have worked / worked* on a difficult project last year.

4 Complete the sentences with the correct form of the verbs in brackets.
1 She _____ (finish) her degree two years ago. Then she _____ (spend) a year working in France.
2 I _____ (write) marketing materials for different companies. In 2018 I _____ (start) my own marketing blog.
3 Susan _____ (work) on many projects. She _____ (produce) many creative solutions on the last project.
4 He _____ (organise) several events. Last year he _____ (help) to prepare the annual sales conference.

T Extra activities

5 Complete the parts of a profile with the correct form of the verbs in brackets.

I am a confident, experienced Retail Sales Manager with excellent customer service skills.
I ¹_____ (work) for several companies in the retail industry. I ²_____ (manage) and ³_____ (motivate) large teams of sales staff. I ⁴_____ (train) staff to give excellent customer service.

From 2016 to 2019 I ⁵_____ (be) the Assistant Manager in a large department store. I ⁶_____ (interview) and ⁷_____ (recruit) sales staff during the time I was there. I also ⁸_____ (help) staff when they ⁹_____ (have) questions and problems. I ¹⁰_____ (prepare) training sessions. I ¹¹_____ (analyse) sales data and ¹²_____ (write) monthly reports.

Writing

6 Choose an option. Either: Imagine yourself in five years' time. Use the form below to write a profile. You can invent information. Or: Imagine you are Jay Peters. Look at page 127.

Your photo	FULL NAME _____ JOB TITLE (you have or want) _____ LOCATION _____ EXPERIENCE (current job) _____ EXPERIENCE (past positions) _____ EDUCATION _____

Self-assessment I can write a simple profile for a professional website.

8.4 WORK SKILLS
A job interview

Lesson outcome — Learners can ask and answer simple questions in a job interview.

Lead-in 1 Look at the job advert. What skills, personal qualities and experience does the employer want?

> **Assistant Customer Services Manager**
>
> We need an enthusiastic and motivated Assistant Customer Services Manager with excellent communication skills. You will be responsible for a team of Customer Service Reps for a major bank. We work across multiple channels – email, live chat, telephone and social media. The ideal candidate will have at least two years' customer service experience.

VIDEO 2 ▶ 8.4.1 Watch the beginning of the video. What is Angela's current job?

3A Watch the video. Are the sentences *true* (T) or *false* (F)?
1. Angela's first job was as a Personal Assistant (PA).
2. She has a lot of experience of dealing with customers.
3. She says speaking is the most important communication skill.
4. Problem-solving skills are a part of her job every day.
5. She deals with customers using social media.
6. She says her job can sometimes be stressful when customers are bored.
7. She wants to work for the bank because it has an excellent reputation for social media.
8. She'd like to do more staff training in the future.

B Correct the wrong words in the sentences in Exercise 3A.

4A Watch again. Complete the interview questions with the words in the box.

| had   helped   leave   questions   see   strengths   tell   want |

1. Can you _____ me about your work experience?
2. What are your main _____ ?
3. How have you _____ to motivate staff?
4. Have you ever _____ any problems with difficult people in your teams?
5. Why do you _____ to work for our company?
6. Why do you want to _____ your current job?
7. Where do you _____ yourself in five years?
8. Do you have any _____ for me?

B Work in pairs. Match the answers (a–h) with the questions (1–8) in Exercise 4A. What other answers can you give to the questions?

a Your company has an excellent reputation for customer service.
b I'd like to develop my skills and do more staff training.
c I work as a team leader in customer services.
d I have excellent communication skills.
e I've always set goals with my staff and when they meet the goals, we celebrate.
f Yes, I do. What training opportunities are there with this job?
g I enjoy my work and I've learnt a lot but your organisation offers more opportunities.
h Yes, there have sometimes been problems between team members.

8.4 Work skills: A job interview

Speaking

> **JOB INTERVIEWS**
>
> **Talking about work experience**
> Can you tell me about your work experience?
> I work as a /an [team leader / Manager / Assistant] in [customer services / Sales / Marketing].
> I started as a /an [Shop Assistant / Junior Designer / Admin Assistant].
> Then I moved into [customer services / Banking / Engineering].
> I have a lot of experience dealing with [customers / suppliers / difficult staff].
>
> **Talking about skills and personal qualities**
> What are your main strengths?
> How have you helped to motivate staff?
> Have you ever organised training sessions?
> Have you ever had problems with difficult people?
> I'm good at [motivating a team / training staff / managing projects].
> I have excellent/good [communication skills / IT skills / presentation skills].
> I've always [set goals with staff / listened to staff / given staff targets].
> I've done a lot of staff training and given presentations.
> I've [learnt a lot / always worked hard / enjoyed challenges].
>
> **Talking about the company**
> Why do you want to work for our company?
> Your [company / bank] has an excellent reputation for [customer service / career development].
> Your organisation offers [more opportunities / career development / interesting challenges].
> Do you have any questions for me?
> What training opportunities are there with this job?

T Extra activities

5 You are going to roleplay two job interviews.
Student A: Look at page 124.
Student B: Look at page 126.
Read your information. Use the phrases in the box to help you and add any extra ideas you want.

Interviewer / **Job candidate**

- Ask about work experience. → Answer.
- Ask about main strengths. → Answer.
- Ask about helping to motivate staff. → Answer.
- Ask why he/she wants to join the company. → Answer.
- Ask why he/she wants to leave his/her current job. → Answer.
- Ask him/her his/her thoughts on his/her future in five years. → Answer.
- Invite the job candidate to ask questions. → Ask the interviewer some questions.

Self-assessment I can ask and answer simple questions in a job interview.

BUSINESS WORKSHOP

The interviewer and the candidate

Lesson outcome: Learners can ask and answer simple questions in a job interview.

Introduction

1 Complete the job advertisement with the headings in the box.

> Your role and responsibilities   About our company   Your skills and experience

Operations Manager

a _____
We are a global transport and logistics company with over 64,000 employees at 1,200 locations in over 90 countries.

b _____
We have a great opportunity for an Operations Manager for the northern UK region. You will manage transport services for our customers. Our contracts include the delivery of food and drink to thousands of cafés, hotels and restaurants in the region.

c _____
- degree or equivalent
- previous experience of managing transport operations essential
- previous experience of dealing with clients
- can use Microsoft Word, Excel and PowerPoint
- can manage and motivate a team of managers and staff
- good problem-solving skills
- can meet project deadlines

Speaking

2 Look at the words in the box. Which of these skills and personal qualities are essential for the job in Exercise 1? Which are useful? Why?

It's essential to have good IT skills. The Operations Manager will use software programs.

> analytical   communication skills   hard-working   IT skills
> language skills   motivated   organised   team worker

3 Match the halves of the interview questions.

1 Can you tell me about   a current job?
2 What are your   b in our company?
3 Why do you want to work   c your work experience?
4 Why do you want to leave your d main strengths?
5 Where do you see yourself   e in five years?

4 Complete the interview questions with the Present Perfect Simple form of the words in brackets.

1 _____ (you/ever/work) with clients in this industry?
2 _____ (you/manage) a large team of staff?
3 _____ (you/ever/deal with) difficult customers?
4 _____ (you/use) Microsoft software?
5 _____ (you/ever/work) on projects with deadlines?

Roleplay

5 You are candidates for the job in Exercise 1. Read and complete your information.
Student A: Look at page 120. **Student B:** Look at page 125.
Student C: Look at page 127. **Student D:** Look at page 123.

6 Take turns being the interviewer and the candidate. Use the questions from Exercises 3 and 4 in your interview.
Student A: Interview Student C. **Student B:** Interview Student D.
Student C: Interview Student B. **Student D:** Interview Student A.

7A Work in pairs. Tell each other about the candidate you interviewed.

B Compare the candidates. Who is the best candidate for the job? Why?
I think she is the best candidate. She's had more experience in the transport industry.

Self-assessment: I can ask and answer simple questions in a job interview.

1 REVIEW

Vocabulary

1 Choose the correct words to complete the texts.

I'm a Sales Manager. I have a team of ten people. We always ¹*have / make* a meeting on Monday morning. The sales team usually ²*do / go to* meetings with their customers on Tuesdays, Wednesdays and Thursdays. Everyone works in the office on Fridays. We ³*write / call* customers by phone, process orders and ⁴*do / go to* research about the competition. I sometimes ⁵*start / analyse* sales data and ⁶*call / write* reports for my manager.

I'm an Office Assistant. I usually ⁷*have / answer* the phone, and I sometimes ⁸*do / make* calls. I call hotels and restaurants and plan business travel for the sales team. I never ⁹*travel / process* for work because my job is here, in the office. I sometimes ¹⁰*go to / write* meetings. I ¹¹*travel / start* work at 8.30 a.m. in the morning and ¹²*finish / call* work at 5.30 p.m.

2 Complete the dialogue with the words in the box.

| available | book | calculate | fine |
| have | how about | meet | send out |

A: We need to ¹_____ a budget meeting.
B: Are you ²_____ on Friday?
A: Yes. ³_____ Friday afternoon?
B: Friday afternoon is good. Shall we ⁴_____ in your office?
A: Yes, that's ⁵_____ .
B: I need to ⁶_____ the production costs before the meeting.
A: OK. And I need to ⁷_____ the agenda and ⁸_____ a meeting room.

Grammar

3 Put the words in the correct order to make sentences.

1 always / He / starts / at / work / o'clock / eight / .
_____
2 work / for / I / other / often / travel to / countries / .
_____
3 Fridays / We / on / usually / meetings / have / .
_____
4 with me / They / work / sometimes / on projects / .
_____
5 excellent, / Her / is / English / she / but / studies / never / !
_____
6 meetings / We / go / often / to / customers / with / .
_____

4 Complete the sentences with the correct form of the verb.

1 Jon _____ (be) a Sales Assistant.
2 I _____ (not be) a Finance Officer.
3 They _____ (not finish) work before seven o'clock.
4 Jo and I _____ (work) in an office.
5 We _____ (start) work at nine o'clock.
6 I _____ (travel) for work a lot.
7 Hal _____ (not be) a Sales Manager.
8 They _____ (be) Admin Assistants.

5A Choose the correct word to complete the sentences.

1 What *are / do* their working hours?
2 How long *is / does* your lunch break?
3 How *are / do* you get to work?
4 *Is / Does* there a canteen?
5 *Are / Do* you go to the gym?
6 *Is / Does* your work space have a window?

B Write questions.

1 Where / their office / ?
_____
2 Why / Helena need a computer / ?
_____
3 Who / book meeting rooms / ?
_____
4 When / your meetings / ?
_____
5 Who / manage the sales team / ?
_____
6 How / he get to work / ?
_____

Functional language

6 Complete the dialogues with the phrases (a–f).

a He analyses sales data
b This is Josh from Boston
c Nice to meet you, too
d and work with the local sales teams
e I work in IT
f What do you do

A: ¹____ ?
B: I'm a Project Manager. I visit the markets ²____ .
A: Which department do you work in?
B: ³____ .
A: ⁴____ . He's a Sales Rep.
B: Nice to meet you.
A: ⁵____ .

A: Do you know Leo? He's in sales. ⁶____ .
B: Nice to meet you, Leo.

87

2 REVIEW

Vocabulary

1 Choose the correct word to complete the sentences.
1 The transport company don't make *deliveries / orders / suppliers* on Sundays.
2 Customers can *deliver / order / supply* their food on our website or app.
3 Our company *deliveries / order / supplies* printers and other office equipment.
4 They *delivered / ordered / supplied* the products to our warehouse yesterday.
5 We work with hundreds of *delivers / orders / suppliers* in twenty-five different countries.
6 The supermarket placed a big *delivery / order / supply* for fresh bananas.

2A Put the words in the correct order to make questions.
1 can / help / you / How / I / ?
_____
2 office desks / I'd / order / like to / some / .
_____
3 product reference number / have / you / the / Do / ?
_____
4 small boxes / do / How / need / you / many / ?
_____
5 are / much / large boxes / How / the / ?
_____
6 delivery / much / cost / does / How / ?
_____
7 deliver / morning / you / by Monday / Can / ?
_____

B Match the questions (1–7) in Exercise 2A with the responses (a–g).
a One euro each, or ten for €8.50. ____
b I'd like to order 5,000, please. ____
c Yes, I have it here. It's JX12045GE. ____
d I'd like to order some of your boxes. ____
e I'm very sorry, we can't deliver until Tuesday. ____
f It's free of charge for orders over €100.00. ____
g Yes, of course. How many would you like? ____

Grammar

3 Complete the sentences with *much* or *many*.
1 We don't have _____ orders today.
2 How _____ time do we have for the meeting?
3 Do you have _____ work this week?
4 How _____ does this smartphone cost?
5 Do you have _____ customers in this country?
6 How _____ people are in the office today?
7 We don't get _____ deliveries at the weekend.
8 The store doesn't have _____ fresh food on Friday.

4 Choose the correct option.
1 We are expecting _____ deliveries this morning.
  a a   b any   c some
2 She has _____ of meetings this week.
  a a lot   b any   c some
3 We don't have _____ suppliers in that country.
  a a   b any   c some
4 I have _____ important work to finish.
  a a   b any   c some
5 He doesn't have _____ time to visit the client today.
  a any   b a lot   c some
6 They sell _____ of food to the European market.
  a a lot   b any   c some

5 Complete the sentences with the correct form of *there is/there are*.
1 _____ any paper in the photocopier?
2 _____ a lot of people in the canteen.
3 _____ any coffee. Can you buy some?
4 _____ any cold water in the fridge?
5 _____ many deliveries today.
6 _____ a problem in the warehouse.
7 _____ any refunds on orders?
8 _____ much time to prepare the order.

Functional language

6A Complete the sentences for making agreements about a service.
1 How _____ offices are _____ ? ____
2 How _____ days _____ you need a cleaner? ____
3 What _____ you want the designer to do? ____
4 How _____ time does the engineer need? ____
5 What time _____ you want the consultant to come? ____
6 How _____ is that? ____
7 _____ the price include VAT? ____
8 _____ _____ a place for the equipment? ____
9 When _____ the caterers start? ____

B Who asks questions 1–9 in Exercise 6A, the *Service Representative* (S) or the *Client* (C)? Write S or C for each question.

88

3 REVIEW

Vocabulary

1 Choose the correct words to complete the timeline.

1975 Teenage brothers Jun and Kenji Yamada ¹*move / expand* from Osaka to San Francisco with their parents.

1982 Aged 20 and 22, they ²*hire / start* a tea company and ³*hire / produce* Japanese tea for local restaurants.

1984 They ⁴*open / move* a tea house called Yamada Tea.

1988 Jun leaves the business and ⁵*moves / creates* a different company.

1990 Yamada Tea opens more shops and ⁶*hires / produces* more employees.

1994 Yamada Tea ⁷*expands / starts* its market to Canada.

1998 Kenji ⁸*opens / launches* a new brand: Yamada Coffee.

2 Complete the email with the phrases (a–d).

a please do the following
b We appreciate your cooperation
c To all staff
d Best wishes

New canteen cards

¹_____ ,

Next week, the new canteen opens. In preparation for this, ²_____ :

- Get your new canteen card from Martin (Admin Assistant).
- Use the machine outside the canteen to add money to the card.
- From next Monday, pay in the canteen with your card.

³_____ . Have a great weekend!

⁴_____ ,

Leon Dupuy
Office Manager

Grammar

3 Complete the questions with the correct form of the verbs.

A: When ¹_____ the company ²_____ ?
B: It expanded in 2009.
A: When ³_____ they ⁴_____ to Brazil?
B: They moved in 2018.
A: Who ⁵_____ the company?
B: The Zheng sisters started it.
A: What ⁶_____ Joe ⁷_____ in 2015?
B: He created a different company.
A: ⁸_____ you ⁹_____ new employees?
B: No, I didn't hire new employees.
A: ¹⁰_____ they ¹¹_____ new products often?
B: Yes, they launched new products every month.

4A Complete the sentences with the Past Simple form of the verb in brackets.

1 Pierre _____ (work) in Germany last year.
2 I _____ (hire) two employees last month.
3 We _____ (stay) near the factory.
4 They _____ (study) in the USA in 2016.
5 You _____ (develop) new products in your last job.
6 The factory _____ (produce) cars and trucks from 2010 to 2018.

B Complete the sentences with the Past Simple form of the verbs in the box.

| build   grow   have   not be   not hit   not win |

1 They _____ their customer base from ten to twenty corporate customers.
2 We _____ strong relationships with important clients.
3 There _____ a complaint about the service.
4 Some customers _____ problems with the website.
5 We _____ any new business in Canada.
6 You _____ your target of $10,000.

Functional language

5 Choose the best response to each question (a–c).

1 How did it go generally?
 a We changed to a different factory.
 b Not very well.
 c Improve our design.
2 What went well in particular?
 a We met each deadline.
 b It was OK.
 c We had a problem with quality.
3 What didn't go well?
 a It went well.
 b The teamwork was good.
 c We had a problem with quality.
4 What did you do?
 a We changed to a different designer.
 b The budget was good.
 c We need to improve our design.
5 What was the problem?
 a We had serious problems.
 b We grew the business.
 c We didn't meet the deadline.
6 What do we need to change?
 a We changed to a different material.
 b I think we need to improve our teamwork.
 c We didn't explain the change.

4 REVIEW

Vocabulary

1 Choose the correct word to complete the sentences.

1 When I travel for work, I usually *book / stay at / go by* a flight online.
2 The team *stay at / go by / rent* a hotel near the office.
3 My boss rarely *rents / stays at / goes by* coach when she travels for work.
4 I sometimes *go by / rent / stay at* a car at the airport.
5 Our clients usually *book / stay at / go by* an apartment before they travel.
6 You always *stay at / go by / rent* plane when you travel.

2 Complete the sentences with the words in brackets.

1 Her train was _____ , so she _____ in Paris four hours _____ . (arrived / cancelled / late)
2 My coach _____ from Zurich. I _____ at Basel, but that coach was _____ by thirty minutes. (changed / delayed / departed)
3 Their train to the airport arrived at _____ four. They checked in, went through _____ , and went to _____ seventeen for their flight. (gate / platform / security)
4 The fast train was _____ , so we took the slow train. It _____ at every station, so we _____ about an hour late. (arrived / cancelled / stopped)

Grammar

3 Complete the conversations with *be* and the correct form of the verbs in the boxes.

| fly   meet   stay |

A: When ¹_____ you _____ to Beijing?
B: Next week.
A: ²_____ you _____ customers there?
B: Yes, I ³_____ .
A: Where ⁴_____ you _____ ?
B: In a hotel.

| get   go   meet   visit |

A: ⁵_____ David _____ Stella at the airport?
B: Yes, he ⁶_____ .
A: How ⁷_____ Stella _____ to the hotel?
B: She and David ⁸_____ by bus.
A: ⁹_____ she _____ the factory on Tuesday?
B: Yes, she ¹⁰_____ .

4 Write questions and sentences giving updates.

A: What / you work on right now?
1 _____*What are you working on right now?*_____
A: Is everything OK?
B: Everything / go well here.
2 _____
A: How is work?
B: It / not go well today.
3 _____
A: Gerard / write report?
4 _____
B: No / not be.
5 _____
A: They / give presentation?
6 _____
B: Yes / be.
7 _____
A: What / Lisa do at the moment?
8 _____
B: She / prepare the price list.
9 _____

Functional language

5 Match the sentences with the best responses (a–d).

1 Good morning! Are you ready?
2 Sorry, the connection isn't very good.
3 I'm sharing my screen.
4 Can you repeat that, please?

a Hang up. I'll call you back.
b Yes. I said I'm adding Bill to the call.
c Yes, I'm here.
d Yes, I can see it.

5 Can you see me?
6 You're breaking up.
7 I'm adding Jo to the call.
8 My internet connection is slow. The screen is frozen.

a OK, great.
b Yes, no problem.
c Try turning off your video.
d Then let's have an audio call.

9 Are you there?
10 I can't hear you.
11 Sorry, I can't see you.
12 Try unmuting your microphone.

a My camera isn't working.
b OK, I did that. Can you hear me now?
c Oh, sorry. I was on mute!
d Yes, I'm here.

5 REVIEW

Vocabulary

1 Complete the sentences with the words in the box. There are two extra words you do not need.

> attend   badge   brochures   exhibition   exhibitors
> launch   meet   provide   show   stand

1 We go to this trade _____ every year.
2 We're having the same exhibition _____ this year.
3 _____ come from hundreds of countries.
4 We're designing new _____ to give to visitors.
5 Remember to wear your _____ at all times in the conference centre.
6 We often _____ conferences in Europe for work.
7 The _____ centre was an old train station in the city centre.
8 They want to _____ their new electric car at the motor show in Frankfurt.

2 Choose the correct option to complete the phone conversation.

A: Good morning, Finlay Engineering. ¹*What / How* can I help you?
B: Hello this is Georgios Papadakis at Doyle's Conference Centre. It's ²*about / for* next week's conference. Can I speak to Mr Finlay?
A: ³*I / I'm* sorry, he's not available right now. Can I ⁴*give / take* a message?
B: Yes, please. Can you tell him Georgios Papadakis ⁵*phoned / phoning*?
A: Certainly. Could you ⁶*have / spell* your surname for me, please?
B: Yes, it's P-A-P-A-D-A-K-I-S.
A: And can I ⁷*have / say* your phone number?
B: Yes, it's 690276335.
A: Sorry, could you ⁸*say / tell* that again, please?
B: Sure, it's 690276335.
A: Thank you. ⁹*I'll / I* give him your message.

Grammar

3 Choose the correct option.

1 We _____ to have a stand in the main hall this year.
  a 's going   b isn't going   c 're going
2 They _____ stay in the conference hotel.
  a isn't going   b aren't going to   c 're going
3 When _____ set up the exhibition stand?
  a 's going   b are you going to   c are you going
4 She _____ to send you more brochures soon.
  a 's going   b going   c 're going to
5 I _____ attend the trade fair this year. I'm very busy.
  a 's going   b aren't going to   c 'm not going to
6 How many people _____ attend the exhibition?
  a is going to   b going to   c are going to

4 Use *would like* to make these sentences and questions more formal.

1 I want to speak to the manager.
   _____
2 He wants to join us for the meeting.
   _____
3 We want to order more computers.
   _____
4 A: Do you want to join us at the restaurant?
   B: Yes, I want to.
   _____
5 What time do you want to have lunch?
   _____
6 A: When do you want to see the factory?
   B: I want to see it this afternoon.
   _____

Functional language

5 Put the word in brackets in the correct position to complete the phrases for socialising with clients.

1 What do you think the conference? (of)
   _____
2 Do you your hotel? (like)
   _____
3 Did you the meal? (enjoy)
   _____
4 I think are some very good new products. (there)
   _____
5 The meeting was interesting. (very)
   _____
6 I like some of the stands. (exhibitors')
   _____
7 The hotel is beautiful and near the town centre. (it's)
   _____
8 Yes, but it near our office. (isn't)
   _____
9 You're but it's a very popular product. (right,)
   _____
10 Did you the local music show? (see)
   _____
11 I want to visit the old city. I it's beautiful. (hear)
   _____
12 When you arrive? (did)
   _____

91

6 REVIEW

Vocabulary

1 Choose the correct word to complete the sentences.
1. Many people are buying *electric / energy* cars and motorbikes these days.
2. There is a problem with air *environment / pollution* in our cities today.
3. Our office has bins to *use / recycle* glass and paper.
4. I think *electric / technology*, like smartphones, makes our lives easier.
5. About 22 percent of our country's *energy / plastic* comes from natural gas.
6. This *machine / energy* can work faster than ten people.
7. We all use a lot of *technology / plastic*. It is a problem for our seas and oceans.
8. If we want to protect the *environment / pollution*, we need to make many changes.

2 Choose the correct words to complete the dialogue.
A: Good morning, Customer Services. Ernesto ¹*speaking / talking*. How can I help you?
B: There's a problem ²*with / in* the printer you delivered yesterday. It's not working.
A: I'm sorry to ³*hear / know* that. We'll send a technician.
B: ⁴*When / How* will the technician get here?
A: On Thursday, but it ⁵*can / might* be in the afternoon. They're very busy.
B: We ⁶*can't / might not* wait until Thursday.
A: I'm sorry ⁷*about / for* that but they're very busy.
B: We need it as soon as ⁸*urgent / possible*! Can someone come tomorrow morning, please?
A: I understand. I'll ⁹*talk / say* to my manager. Someone might come in the morning.
B: Thank you ¹⁰*for / with* your help.
A: You're very ¹¹*sorry / welcome*. Goodbye.

Grammar

3 Choose the correct words to complete the sentences. Which verbs are active? Which are passive?
1. We *buy / are bought* all our tea from farms in China.
2. Factory workers *are paid / pay* a fair wage.
3. Most of them *work / are worked* eight hours a day, five days a week.
4. The manager *visits / is visited* the suppliers every year.
5. Our tea *sells / is sold* by specialist shops and online retailers.
6. These swimsuits *are made / make* from recycled plastic.
7. No chemicals *are used / use* in the production process.

4 Put the word in brackets in the correct position in the sentences. Do you agree with the speculations about the future?
1. There be any cash in the future. (might not)
2. I think everyone use their mobiles to pay for things. (will)
3. The weather get hotter in the next few years. (might)
4. Children go to school. They will study by computer at home. (won't)
5. I don't think there be many shops. We will order everything online. (will)
6. There be many jobs in offices. Robots will do our work. (won't)
7. I be in the same job two years from now. (might not)

Functional language

5 Put the phrases in order to make statements and questions about orders.
1. to order / I'd / cotton shirts / 12,000 / like / .
2. many / do you / How / order / white shirts / want to / ?
3. price now / we talk / Can / about / ?
4. a shirt / How / two dollars / about / ?
5. you give / Can / a lower price / us / ?
6. there / a large order / a discount / Is / for / ?
7. pay / bank transfer / by / We'll / .
8. I can't / I'm / to that / afraid / agree / .
9. 25 percent on / we pay / signature / Could / on delivery / and 75 percent / ?
10. afraid / 50 percent on / on delivery / it's / I'm / .
11. can / When / you / this order / deliver / ?
12. you / do / think / What / ?

7 REVIEW

Vocabulary

1 Complete the sentences with the words in the box.

| design | features | life | point |
| speed | user | value | weight |

1 The new DX4 is beautiful. It is a modern car with a classic _____ .
2 The phone has a long product _____ . It never breaks.
3 How many special _____ does the TV have?
4 Consider the _____ of their internet connection when you choose a provider.
5 The design is the product's unique selling _____ .
6 This website is easy to use. It has a nice _____ experience.
7 Expensive brands don't often offer _____ for money.
8 My new laptop is very light. The _____ is less than two kilogrammes.

2 Choose the correct word to complete the sentences.

1 We *charge / pay* a fee to customers for our booking service.
2 The *monthly / fixed* fee will be in 12 payments on the 1st.
3 The fee *includes / pays* all paperwork and background checks.
4 There is a small *administration / cancellation* fee for arranging the contracts.
5 Customers need to *charge / pay* a fee for all money transfers.
6 Please note: *annual / booking* fees apply for all reservations made by telephone.
7 Our specialist doctors offer a number of *fixed / cancellation* fee options for patients.
8 A *cancellation / booking* fee applies seven days before all reservations.

Grammar

3 Complete the sentences with the comparative form of the words in brackets.

1 The Super Drive car is _____ than the Tornado. (expensive)
2 The Tornado is _____ than the Super Drive. (fast)
3 The Tornado has _____ seats. (big)
4 The Super Drive is _____ to drive than the Tornado. (easy)
5 The experience of driving the Super Drive is _____ . (good)
6 The Super Drive is _____ than the Tornado. (safe)
7 The Tornado has a _____ engine than the Super Drive. (noisy)
8 The Tornado is _____ than the Super Drive. (powerful)

4 Complete the sentences with the superlative form of the words in brackets.

1 That company has the _____ customer service. (good)
2 We have the _____ database of candidates. (big)
3 The online store sells the _____ range of products. (wide)
4 Our staff are the _____ . (friendly)
5 Our internet provider has the _____ customer satisfaction rating. (high)
6 Power Energy have the _____ customer service. (bad)
7 Our team respond to customers the _____ . (fast)
8 They have the _____ customers. (happy)

Functional language

5 Complete the presentation with the words in the box.

| aim | first | morning | move | start | talk about | tell |

So, good ¹_____ , everyone. I'm Ray Wilson, the Finance Director.
The ²_____ of today's presentation is to ³_____ you about the company finances.
⁴_____ , I'll explain this year's finances and then I'll ⁵_____ next year.
Let's ⁶_____ with this year. As you can see, we had a very good year.
OK, let's ⁷_____ on to next year. We think our profits will grow …

93

8 REVIEW

Vocabulary

1 Choose the correct option.
1. Nur is very ____. She always completes tasks on time.
   a analytical   b motivated   c organised
2. Sandro has good ____ skills. He expresses his ideas well when speaking and writing.
   a analytical   b communication   c language
3. Lucas speaks fluent English and Portuguese and some German. His ____ skills are excellent.
   a communication   b IT   c language
4. Beatrice works well with other people. She's a good ____.
   a hard-working   b team worker   c communication
5. Kelly understands statistics. She is very ____.
   a analytical   b hard-working   c organised
6. Hugo wants to do well at work. He's very ____.
   a hard-working   b motivated   c organised
7. Sakura is a ____ student. She always does her homework.
   a hard-working   b motivated   c organised
8. Mohammad uses many software programs. He has good ____ skills.
   a communication   b IT   c language

2 Complete the sentences with the words in the box.

| advertisements candidates choose degree |
| essential qualifications useful vacancy |

1. We're interviewing three _____ tomorrow.
2. I'd like an assistant with experience, but it isn't _____.
3. He's studying at university for a _____ in marketing.
4. We can't decide which person to _____ for the job.
5. She reads the job _____ online every day.
6. Our customer service agents need good communication skills. It's _____ for the job.
7. We have a _____ in the IT department at the moment.
8. What _____ do you need to be an accountant?

Grammar

3 Write sentences using the Present Perfect Simple.
1. She / write / many emails and reports in English / .
   _____
2. I / never / manage / an international project / .
   _____
3. you / ever / give / presentations to clients / ?
   _____
4. He / not / have / much experience managing staff / .
   _____
5. she / ever / be / to Japan for business / ?
   _____
6. We / work / with many large manufacturers / .
   _____

4 Complete the sentences with the Present Perfect Simple form of the verbs in the box.

| be not go not buy make send take |

1. I _____ to head office once or twice.
2. She _____ language courses before.
3. We _____ many goods from this supplier. They are expensive.
4. They _____ our order late again!
5. This company _____ sofas and chairs for thousands of customers.
6. Paul _____ to the sales conference. He's in the office.

5 Complete the dialogues with the Past Simple or Present Perfect Simple form of the verbs in brackets.
1. A: Have _____ (you/go) to the company's head office in Berlin?
   B: Yes. In fact, I _____ (go) there a week ago.
2. A: Has _____ (she/ever/speak) to the new supplier in China?
   B: Yes, once or twice. In fact, she _____ (speak) to them yesterday.
3. A: Have _____ (we/have) many international interns at the company?
   B: Yes, lots. For example, we _____ (have) an intern from the Netherlands last month.
4. A: Have _____ (they/ever/sell) their products to other countries?
   B: Yes, I hear they _____ (sell) a lot of goods in China last week.

Functional language

6 Put the words in the correct order to make job interview questions and answers.
1. about / Can / work experience / tell me / your / you / ?
   _____
2. have / excellent / skills / I / communication / .
   _____
3. good at / my team / motivating / I'm / .
   _____
4. you / your / motivated / have / staff / How / ?
   _____
5. want to / you / Why / our company / do / for / work / ?
   _____
6. Where / years / see yourself / five / do / you / in / ?
   _____
7. staff training / I've / a lot of / done / .
   _____

Pronunciation bank

The sounds of English

These are the sounds of standard British English and American English pronunciation.

Consonants	
Symbol	Keyword
p	**p**en
b	**b**ack
t	**t**ea
d	**d**ay
k	**k**ey
g	**g**et
tʃ	**ch**urch
dʒ	**j**ob
f	**f**act
v	**v**ery
θ	**th**ing
ð	**th**is
s	**s**oon
z	**z**ero
ʃ	**sh**ip
ʒ	plea**s**ure
h	**h**ot
m	**m**ore
n	**n**ice
ŋ	thi**ng**
l	**l**ight
r	**r**ight
j	**y**ou
w	**w**ork

Vowels		
Symbol BrE	Symbol AmE	Keyword
ɪ	ɪ	k**i**t
e	e	dr**e**ss
æ	æ	b**a**d
ʌ	ʌ	b**u**t
ʊ	ʊ	f**oo**t
ɒ	ä	j**o**b
ə	ə	**a**bout
i	i	happ**y**
u	u	sit**u**ation
iː	i	f**ee**l
ɑː	ɑ	f**a**ther
ɔː	ɔ	n**or**th
uː	u	ch**oo**se
ɜː	ɚ	f**ir**st
eɪ	eɪ	d**ay**
aɪ	aɪ	pr**i**ce
ɔɪ	ɔɪ	b**oy**
əʊ	oʊ	n**o**
aʊ	aʊ	h**ow**
ɪə	ɪr	n**ear**
eə	er	h**air**
ʊə	ʊr	s**ure**

Pronunciation bank

Lesson 1.1
The -s ending

1 🔊 P1.01 **Listen and repeat.**

/s/ **s**ell, **s**even, in**s**truction
/z/ **Z**, **z**ero, vi**s**it

2 🔊 P1.02 **Listen and repeat.**

/s/ write**s**, report**s**, visit**s**, client**s**
/z/ call**s**, customer**s**, give**s**, instruction**s**

3 🔊 P1.03 **Listen and repeat.**

1 She never writes /s/ reports /s/.
2 He often visits /s/ clients /s/.
3 She always calls /z/ new customers /z/.
4 He often gives /z/ us instructions /z/.

4A 🔊 P1.04 **Listen to the sentences. The -s endings in the words in bold are different to the -s endings in Exercise 3. Why?**

1 She sometimes **processes** /ɪz/ data for our **bosses** /ɪz/.
2 He often **discusses** /ɪz/ this subject at **conferences** /ɪz/.
3 She usually **analyses** /ɪz/ economic **changes** /ɪz/.
4 He rarely **finishes** /ɪz/ his **sentences** /ɪz/!

B Work in pairs. Practise saying the sentences in Exercise 4A.

5A Work in pairs. Look at the words in the box. Do the words end with /s/, /z/ or /ɪz/?

> address**es**   answer**s**   assistant**s**   email**s**   make**s**
> miss**es**   phone**s**   start**s**   space**s**   task**s**   travel**s**
> watch**es**

/s/ _____ assistants _____
/z/ _____
/ɪz/ _____

B 🔊 P1.05 **Listen and check. Then practise saying the words.**

Lesson 1.3
Questions

1A 🔊 P1.06 **Listen and repeat the weak and strong pronunciation of *are*, *do* and *does*.**

are   are   are   are
do   do   do   do
does   does   does   does

B 🔊 P1.07 **Listen and repeat the questions and answers.**

1 A: Are they your colleagues?
  B: Yes, they are.
2 A: Do you travel for work?
  B: Yes, I do.
3 A: Does he live in Germany?
  B: Yes, he does.

2A 🔊 P1.08 **Listen to the questions. Do they go up (↑) or down (↓) at the end?**

1 Are you busy now? ↑
  What time are you available? ↓
2 Are they at the meeting?
  Where are they?
3 Do you get to work by bus?
  How do you get to work?
4 Do they eat in the canteen?
  Where do they eat?
5 Does your office have quiet areas?
  What facilities does it have?
6 Does she work here?
  Which department does she work in?

B Work in pairs. Practise saying the questions and answers in Exercise 2A.

Lesson 2.2
/iː/, /ɪ/ and /aɪ/

1 Listen and repeat.

🔊 P2.01 /iː/ f**ee**l   m**ee**t   s**ee**   w**ee**k   cl**ea**n   **ea**ch
               l**ea**ve   t**ea**m

🔊 P2.02 /ɪ/ g**i**ve   f**i**lm   f**i**t   l**i**ft   qu**i**ck   s**i**x   w**i**th   g**y**m

🔊 P2.03 /aɪ/ fl**y**   wh**y**   l**igh**t   n**igh**t   l**i**ke   pr**i**ce
               s**i**te   wh**i**te

2 🔊 P2.04 **Listen and repeat.**

/iː/	→	/ɪ/	→	/aɪ/
f**ee**l	→	f**i**ll	→	f**i**le
f**ee**t	→	f**i**t	→	f**igh**t
s**ea**t	→	s**i**t	→	s**i**te
t**ea**m	→	T**i**m	→	t**i**me

Pronunciation bank

3A 🔊 P2.05 Listen and tick (✓) one word in each sentence with the /iː/ sound. Compare your answers with a partner.

1 They deliver meals on motorbikes.
2 You can order meat, fish or vegetable rice.
3 They supply drinks in one-litre bottles.
4 Can you buy some milk, please?
5 What size is the big green box?

B Listen again and (circle) the /ɪ/ sounds in the sentences in Exercise 3A. Compare your answers with a partner.

C Listen again and underline the /aɪ/ sounds in the sentences in Exercise 3A. Compare your answers with a partner.

D Listen again and check. Practise saying the sentences in Exercise 3A.

Lesson 2.3
/tʃ/ and /dʒ/

1 Listen and repeat.

🔊 P2.06 /tʃ/ **ch**airs **ch**eck **ch**oose ki**tch**en pi**ct**ure
             atta**ch** tou**ch** whi**ch**

🔊 P2.07 /dʒ/ **j**ob **j**ourney **j**ust sub**j**ect ur**g**ent
             bri**dg**e messa**g**e pa**g**e

2A 🔊 P2.08 We don't always pronounce the letters 'ch' as /tʃ/. Listen and underline the words with the /tʃ/ sound.

charge **ch**emical ex**ch**ange pur**ch**ase ma**ch**ine
resear**ch** s**ch**edule s**ch**ool te**ch**nical

B Listen again and repeat.

3 Which two words in Exercise 2A have both the /tʃ/ and /dʒ/ sounds?

4A 🔊 P2.09 Listen and complete the sentences. Write one word in each gap.

1 I have cheese _____ for _____ .
2 This is the _____ for the March conference.
3 We have ten _____ centres in China.
4 _____ _____ meeting is difficult.
5 _____ _____ are never cheap.

B Listen again. Practise saying the sentences in Exercise 4A.

Lesson 3.1
The -ed ending

1A 🔊 P3.01 Listen and repeat.

book → book**ed** /t/
help → help**ed** /t/
play → play**ed** /d/
clean → clean**ed** /d/
start → start**ed** /ɪd/
found → found**ed** /ɪd/

B How are the green past forms different from the other past forms in Exercise 1A?

2A 🔊 P3.02 Listen and tick (✓) the sentences you hear.

1 We **produce** it.
  We **produced** it. ✓
2 I **like** it.
  I **liked** it.
3 They **supply** it.
  They **supplied** it.
4 I **use** it.
  I **used** it.
5 We **want** it.
  I **wanted** it.
6 They **need** it.
  They **needed** it.

B 🔊 P3.03 Listen and repeat the sentences in Exercise 2A.

3A 🔊 P3.04 Listen and repeat. What is the last sound in these words, /t/, /d/ or /ɪd/?

1 finished   worked
2 started   expanded
3 prepared   delivered
4 opened   moved
5 clicked   placed
6 calculated decided

B 🔊 P3.05 Listen to the sentences. Then practise saying them in pairs.

1 She finished university and then worked for a bank.
2 They started a company and then expanded its market.
3 He prepared the order and delivered it.
4 We opened another shop and moved office.
5 I clicked on the link and placed an order.
6 We calculated the costs and decided not to produce it.

97

Pronunciation bank

Lesson 3.3
/ɜː/ and /ɔː/

1 Listen and repeat.

🔊 P3.06 /ɜː/ first third service perfect reserve
              learn early burger purchase return

🔊 P3.07 /ɔː/ floor more before bought board
              award launch small talk water

2A 🔊 P3.08 We often pronounce the letters *or* as /ɜː/ or /ɔː/. Listen and underline the words with /ɜː/.

forward north order passport word work world
worse worst New York

B Listen again and (circle) the words with /ɔː/.

C Listen again and repeat.

3A 🔊 P3.09 Listen and complete the sentences with one word. Do you say the missing words with /ɜː/ or /ɔː/?

1 I have an urgent report to write for _____ .
2 Complete a short _____ about your last purchase.
3 I bought this purse from an online _____ .
4 She does research and calls clients every _____ .
5 Do you _____ to walk to work?
6 Furniture is one of their most important _____ .

B Listen again. Practise saying the sentences in Exercise 3A.

Lesson 4.1
/ŋ/, /ŋk/ and /n/. The *-ing* ending.

1 Listen and repeat.

🔊 P4.01 /ŋ/ during evening sing spring thing
🔊 P4.02 /ŋk/ drink ink link pink think
🔊 P4.03 /n/ begin bin pin skin win

2 🔊 P4.04 Listen and repeat.

1 drinking   thinking
2 winning   beginning
3 working   learning
4 reading   repeating
5 flying   driving
6 walking   talking

3 🔊 P4.05 Listen and repeat.

1 They're **drinking** tea and **thinking**.
2 She's **winning** at the **beginning**.
3 I'm **working** and **learning**.
4 He's **reading** and **repeating**.
5 We're **flying** or **driving**.
6 They're **walking** and **talking**.

4A 🔊 P4.06 Listen and complete the sentences with one word.

1 Things are going well and the business is _____ .
2 I don't think the _____ is winning new clients.
3 They're emptying the bins and _____ during the break.
4 There's no black ink in it so it's _____ in blue and pink.
5 We're _____ our spring holidays this evening.
6 The link isn't working because you're _____ in the wrong PIN.

B Work in pairs. Practise saying the sentences in Exercise 4A.

Lesson 4.4
/ɪə/ and /eə/

1 Listen and repeat.

🔊 P4.07 /ɪə/ ear here dear we're year cereal
🔊 P4.08 /eə/ air hair where they're airport rarely

2 🔊 P4.09 Listen and repeat.

   /ɪə/   /eə/
1 ear   air
2 here   hair
3 we're   where
4 really   rarely

3A 🔊 P4.10 Listen and (circle) the /ɪə/ sound in the sentences. Compare your answers with a partner.

1 The meeting room is near the stairs.
2 The engineer needs to repair the machine.
3 What's the rent per square metre here?
4 I hear they're ordering new computer chairs.
5 The instructions for the warehouse workers aren't clear.

B Listen again and underline the /eə/ sound in the sentences in Exercise 3A. Compare your answers with a partner.

C Practise saying the sentences in Exercise 3A.

Pronunciation bank

Lesson 5.1
/æ/, /e/ and /eɪ/

1 Listen and repeat.

🔊 P5.01 /æ/ b**a**ck b**a**dge ch**a**t h**a**ve c**a**ncel exp**a**nd h**a**ppy t**a**blet

🔊 P5.02 /e/ p**e**n s**e**t t**e**ll w**e**nt att**e**nd b**e**tter exp**e**ct m**e**ssage

🔊 P5.03 /eɪ/ br**ea**k gr**ea**t s**a**me tr**a**de aw**ay** del**ay** det**ai**l expl**ai**n

2 🔊 P5.04 Listen and repeat.

	/æ/	/e/
1	bad	bed
2	had	head
3	man	men
4	sat	set

	/e/	/eɪ/
5	get	gate
6	let	late
7	men	main
8	sell	sale

3A 🔊 P5.05 Listen and tick (✓) one word in each sentence with the /æ/ sound. Compare your answers with a partner.

1 The trade fair was an attractive event.
2 We offered fresh fruit and cake on the stand.
3 The hotel was a great place to relax.
4 They met their visitors on the station platform.
5 We launched an app and a special social media page.

B Listen again and circle the /e/ sounds in the sentences in Exercise 3A. Compare your answers with a partner.

C Listen again and underline the /eɪ/ sounds in the sentences in Exercise 3A. Compare your answers with a partner.

D Practise saying the sentences in Exercise 3A.

Lesson 5.3
/θ/ and /ð/ vs. /s/, /z/, /f/, /v/, /t/, /d/

1 Listen and repeat.

🔊 P5.06 /θ/ **th**ink **th**irty **th**rough bir**th**day some**th**ing mon**th**ly Eliza**be**th sou**th**

🔊 P5.07 /ð/ **th**en **th**ey **th**is **th**ese clo**th**es ano**th**er toge**th**er wi**th**

2A 🔊 P5.08 Listen and underline the words you hear.

1	thing	sing
2	three	free
3	mouth	mouse
4	three	tree
5	they	day
6	clothing	closing

B 🔊 5.09 Listen and repeat the words in Exercise 2A.

3A 🔊 P5.10 Listen and complete the sentences. Do you say the missing words with /θ/ or /ð/?

1 We would _____ like to thank you for the invitation.
2 I have other plans for _____ the tenth.
3 Are there any delivery charges _____ the EU?
4 Because of the _____ most flights are cancelled this morning.
5 We have more than three thousand customers in the _____ .
6 The Smith _____ opened that clothes shop in 1935.

B Listen again. Work in pairs. Practise saying the sentences in Exercise 3A.

Lesson 6.2
/ɑː/ and /ʌ/

1 Listen and repeat.

🔊 P6.01 /ɑː/ **a**re b**a**r d**a**rk f**a**r f**a**st h**a**rd p**a**rt **a**nswer m**a**rket reg**a**rds

🔊 P6.02 /ʌ/ b**u**t c**o**me c**u**p d**u**st f**u**n l**o**ve pl**u**s c**ou**ntry l**u**ggage S**u**nday

2A 🔊 P6.03 Tick (✓) the pairs of words with the same vowel sound. Listen and check.

1	March	much
2	track	truck
3	run	one
4	plan	plant
5	half	staff
6	pack	park
7	gas	glass
8	can't	last

B Listen again and repeat.

99

Pronunciation bank

3A 🔊 P6.04 Listen and circle the /ɑː/ sounds in these sentences. Compare your answers with a partner.

1 There aren't enough electric cars or buses in the city.
2 How can we encourage more customers to start using smart technologies?
3 I discussed with the production department how to hit the target.
4 To get a refund provide your passport and credit card numbers.

B Listen again and underline the /ʌ/ sounds in the sentences in Exercise 3A. Compare your answers with a partner.

C Work in pairs. Practise saying the sentences in Exercise 3A.

Lesson 6.3
/uː/ and /ʊ/

1 Listen and repeat.

🔊 P6.05 /uː/ blue choose do due June too improve reduce

🔊 P6.06 /ʊ/ cook could full look put would sugar woman

2A 🔊 P6.07 We often pronounce the letters oo as /uː/ or /ʊ/. Tick (✓) the pairs of words with the same vowel sound. Listen and check.

1 book   took
2 good   food
3 cool   school
4 noon   soon

B Listen again and repeat.

3A 🔊 P6.08 Listen and complete the sentences. Do you say the missing words with /uː/ or /ʊ/?

1 No chemicals are _____ produce fruit here.
2 Our _____ T-shirts always look cool on you.
3 This shampoo isn't sold _____ supermarkets.
4 The good _____ is that we'll move to a bigger room soon.
5 Ask the woman at the reception to make a _____ for two nights.
6 We might _____ sales in the future due to the distribution problems.

B Listen again. Work in pairs. Practise saying the sentences in Exercise 3A.

Lesson 7.2
/əʊ/ and /aʊ/

1 Listen and repeat.

🔊 P7.01 /əʊ/ ago both coach home over Poland soap

🔊 P7.02 /aʊ/ cloud found mouse pronounce pound round south thousand

2A 🔊 P7.03 We often pronounce the letters ow as /əʊ/ or /aʊ/. Tick (✓) the pairs of words that have the same vowel sound. Listen and check.

1 allow   now
2 brown   snow
3 down   town
4 grown   own
5 know   how
6 slow   show

B Listen again and repeat.

3A 🔊 P7.04 Listen and complete the sentences. Do you say the missing words with /əʊ/ or /aʊ/?

1 _____ files open slowly on this computer.
2 How long does the mobile site of the hotel take to _____ ?
3 They sold the house at a _____ of ten thousand pounds.
4 There's no progress _____ a good plan.
5 We chose new _____ and brochures for the show.
6 The _____ quality is so low that you can't understand announcements.

B Work in pairs. Practise saying the sentences in Exercise 3A.

Lesson 7.3
/p/, /b/, /f/ and /v/

1 Listen and repeat.

🔊 P7.05 /p/ parcel petrol applicant support lamp rep
🔊 P7.06 /b/ beans busy about distribution job
🔊 P7.07 /f/ fee feature difficult offer life safe
🔊 P7.08 /v/ value view advert level drive receive

2A 🔊 P7.09 Listen and underline the words you hear.

1 back   pack
2 bin   pin
3 few   view
4 safe   save
5 past   fast
6 copy   coffee
7 blog   vlog
8 best   vest

B 🔊 P7.10 Listen and repeat the words in Exercise 2A.

Pronunciation bank

3 🔊 P7.11 Listen and repeat.
1 **p**owerful **b**atteries
2 e**x**pensive **b**reakfast
3 **v**ery comforta**b**le
4 **p**repare a **b**rief
5 im**p**rove **p**erformance
6 com**p**etiti**v**e **b**usiness

Lesson 8.2 ▶

The vowel /ɒ/. The letter 'o' as /ɒ/, /əʊ/ and /ʌ/.

1 🔊 P8.01 Listen and repeat.

/ɒ/ cl**o**ck g**o**t s**o**ft t**o**p wh**a**t bec**au**se l**o**gical **o**perate p**o**sitive q**u**ality

2A 🔊 P8.02 Tick (✓) the pairs of words with the same vowel sound. Listen and check.

/ɒ/	/?/
1 c**o**st	m**o**st
2 c**o**llege	kn**o**wledge
3 g**o**ne	d**o**ne
4 H**o**lland	P**o**land
5 l**o**st	p**o**st
6 s**o**lve	s**o**ld
7 s**o**rry	w**o**rry
8 w**a**nt	w**o**n't

B Listen again. Practise saying the words in Exercise 2A.

3A 🔊 P8.03 Tick (✓) the letters o with the /ɒ/ sound. Listen and check.
1 The c**o**mpany has pr**o**blems finding m**o**tivated people.
2 She studied econ**o**mics and s**o**cial media marketing in L**o**ndon.
3 They paid a l**o**t of m**o**ney for the pr**o**gram.
4 The ph**o**t**o** was taken in my **o**ffice last m**o**nth.
5 I d**o**n't like the c**o**lours of their pr**o**ducts.
6 The **o**ther m**o**del weighs two kil**o**s.

B Circle the letters o with the /əʊ/ sound in Exercise 3A. Listen and check.

C Underline the letters o with the /ʌ/ sound in Exercise 3A. Listen and check.

D Work in pairs. Practise saying the sentences in Exercise 3A.

Lesson 8.3 ▶
Silent letters

1 🔊 P8.04 Listen and repeat the words. Why are some letters in green?

autum**n** de**b**t ex**h**ibition hang **k**now lis**t**en sci**e**nce wal**k** We**d**nesday **w**rite

2A 🔊 P8.05 Listen and circle the silent letters.
1 c u p b o a r d
2 h a l f
3 k n i f e
4 o f t e n
5 p s y c h o l o g y
6 s t r o n g
7 w o u l d
8 w r o t e

B Listen again. Practise saying the words in Exercise 2A.

3A 🔊 P8.06 Listen and complete the sentences with one word. Which letters are silent in the missing words?
1 She was very _____ at the interview.
2 He _____ a lot about our company.
3 Can we _____ about your experience?
4 I didn't get the right _____ .
5 You have the _____ information.
6 It took several _____ to interview everyone.

B Listen again. Work in pairs. Practise saying the sentences in Exercise 3A.

101

Grammar reference

1.1 Facts and routines

Present Simple

We use the Present Simple to talk about facts – things that are generally true, or true at the time.

I**'m** an Admin Assistant.
He **works** in London.
They **come** from Japan.

Present Simple + adverbs of frequency

We use the Present Simple with adverbs of frequency to say how often we do things. In a sentence, the adverb is after the subject (e.g. **I**) and before the verb (e.g. **arrive**):

I / You / We / They	always / usually / often / sometimes / rarely / never	arrive	at 9 o'clock.
He/She / She		arrives	

I never do something. = I don't do something.
I rarely do something. = I don´t do something very often.

Spelling

Most verbs: arrive – arrive**s**, start – start**s**, work – work**s**
Verbs ending with **-s**, **-sh**, **-ch**: miss – miss**es**, finish – finish**es**, watch – watch**es**
Verbs ending with **-y**: play – play**s**, stay – stay**s**, hurry – hurr**ies**

Present Simple *to be*

We can use the verb *to be* to describe facts and temporary states.
I**'m** from the UK. (fact)
How **are** you?
I**'m** fine. (temporary state)
The verb *to be* is an irregular verb.

Positive	Short form		Long form		
Singular	I**'m**	an IT Specialist.	I am		a Digital Designer.
	You**'re**		You	are	
	He**'s**/ She**'s**		He/ She	is	
	It**'s**	a good job.	It	is	a good job.
Plural	We**'re**	Engineers.	We	are	Sales Assistants.
	You**'re**		You		
	They**'re**		The		

Negative	Short form		Long form		
Singular	I**'m** not	an Engineer.	I am not		a Finance Officer.
	You**'re** not / You **aren't**		You are not		
	He/She**'s** not / He/She **isn't**		He She	is not	
	It**'s** not / It **isn't**	a good job.	It	is not	a good job.
Plural	We**'re** not / We **aren't**	Managers.	We You They	are not	Admin Assistants.
	You**'re** not / You **aren't**				
	They**'re** not / They **aren't**				

1 Look at the table. Write sentences.

	Mike – Admin Assistant	Lisa – Engineer	Joe – IT Specialist
Go to meetings	often	often	never
Work from home	sometimes	often	rarely
Start work at 8.00	usually	always	usually
Go to the factory	never	often	often

1 Mike and Lisa / meetings   _____
2 Joe / work from home   _____
3 Mike and Joe / start work at 8.00   _____
4 Lisa / work from home   _____
5 Lisa and Joe / go to the factory   _____
6 Lisa / start work at 8.00.   _____
7 Mike / go to the factory   _____
8 Joe / go to meetings   _____

1.3 Questions

Wh- questions with *be*		
Where	is	your desk?
	are	the computers?

Wh- questions with other verbs			
What	do	you they Engineers	do?
	does	he/she it	

Yes/No questions with *be*		
Am	I	late?
Is	he/she it	an Engineer?
Are	you	an Admin Assistant?
	we they	Admin Assistants?

Short answers		
Yes,	I	am.
	he/she it	is.
	you we they	are.

Short answers – short form		
No,	I	**'m** not.
	he/she it	is**n't**.
	you we they	**are**n't.

Short answers – long form		
No,	I	am not.
	he/she it	is not.
	you we they	are not.

Yes/No questions with other verbs			
Do	I you we they	**go** to meetings?	
Does	he/she		
Does	it the meeting	**start**	at 11 a.m.?

Yes,	I you we they	do.
Yes,	he/she it	does.

102

# Grammar reference

Short answers – short form		
No,	I / you / we / they	don't.
	he/she/it	doesn't.

Short answers – long form		
No,	I / you / we / they	do not.
	he/she/it	does not.

1 Write questions using the prompts.
1 You / an Engineer / ? _____
2 Paolo and Imran / go to meetings / ? _____
3 When / you start work / ? _____
4 Where / the kitchen / ? _____
5 Helena / an IT Specialist / ? _____
6 Your boss / work from home / ? _____
7 How / Ewan get to work / ? _____
8 What / their names / ? _____

1.4 Subject and object questions

Subject questions
We don't use **do** or **does** with subject questions.
Who manages the production department?
↓
Tomas manages the production department.
Who is the Project Manager?
↓
Elena is the Project Manager.

Object questions
We use **do** or **does** with object questions.
What does Tomas do?
Tomas manages the production department.
We can also use *is/are* in object questions.
What is Elena's job?
Elena is a Project Manager.

1 Choose the correct words.
1 Who *answers / does answer* the phone?
2 When *is / does* the meeting start?
3 When *are / do* your meetings?
4 Why *does David need / needs David* a projector?
5 Who *work / works* in the Madrid office?
6 How *get you / do you get* to work?
7 Where *is / does* your office?
8 Where *are / do* you have planning meetings?

2.1 Things you can and can't count

	Countable nouns	Uncountable nouns
Positive	We have **a** new customer. We have **some** new customer**s**. We have **a lot of**/**many** new customer**s**.	We have **some** time. We have **a lot of** time.
Negative	We don't have **any** customer**s**. We don't have **many** customer**s**. We don't have **a lot of** customer**s**.	We don't have **any** time. We don't have **much** time. We don't have a **lot of** time.
Questions	Do we have **a** new customer? Do we have **any** new customer**s**? Do we have **many** /**a lot of** new customer**s**? **How many** customer**s** do you have?	Do we have **any** time? Do we have **much** / **a lot of** time? **How much** time do you need?

Nouns can be countable or uncountable.

Countable nouns
Countable nouns have singular and plural forms:
Singular: *a customer,* **one** *customer*
Plural: **some** *customer***s***,* **two** *customer***s***,* **twenty** *customer***s**
We use the quantifiers (***a/an***, ***some***, ***any***, ***many***, ***a lot of***) with countable nouns.
some = an amount, large or small
many/a lot of = a large amount

Uncountable nouns
Uncountable nouns do not have plural forms: ***some*** *time,* ***some*** *money,* ***some*** *food*. This means we cannot count them.
We use the quantifiers (***some, any, much, a lot of***) with uncountable nouns.
much = a large amount
We can use exact measures and numbers or approximations (***about, over, a lot of, not much, not many***) to answer ***How much … ? / How many … ?*** questions.
Q: How many *new customers do you have?*
A: Over *fifty.*
A: *We have* **a lot of** *customers in the morning.*
Q: How much *time do you need?*
A: About *two hours.*
B: Not much.

1 Choose the correct option.
1 *How many / How much* pasta do you sell?
2 *How many / How much* people work here?
3 *How many / How much* does it cost?
4 *How many / How much* work do you have?
5 I have *a lot of / many* time for meetings today.
6 Do we have *much / many* orders today?
7 I don't have *much / any* new emails this morning.
8 We don't have *much / many* food in the warehouse.

103

Grammar reference

2.2 can/can't

We use **can/can't** to say when something is possible/not possible.
We use **Can … ?** in questions to ask if something is possible.

Positive	We **can** deliver the order on Monday. I **can** send you a price list.
Negative	They **can't** deliver today. We **can't** send the order today.
Questions	**Can** you deliver on Monday? **Can** I have your order number, please?
Answers	Yes, we **can**. / Sorry, we **can't**. Yes, certainly. It's PN967M. / I'm sorry, I don't know it.

1 Put the words in the correct order.

1 I / How / help / can / you / ?
   _____

2 see / I / can't / prices / the
   _____

3 send / you / a / new / catalogue / We / can
   _____

4 boxes / order / 300 / Can / small / we / ?
   _____

5 deliver / can / your / on / order / We / Friday
   _____

6 send / can't / boxes / any / We / white
   _____

2.3 Saying something exists

We use **there is/there are** to say that people or things exist.
We often use contractions **(there's, there isn't, there aren't)** when speaking and writing informal messages to people we know well. In formal business emails, websites, etc. we don't generally use contractions.

Positive	There is/are			
	There	is	an/one some/no	order. furniture.
	There	are	a lot of/five/many/some	chairs.
Negative	There isn't/aren't			
	There	isn't/ is not	a	discount.
	There	aren't/ are not	a lot of/much/any	information. charges.
Question	Is/Are there … ?			
	Is	there	a/one a lot of/much/any	problem? paper?
	Are		a lot of/many/any	boxes?
Short answers	Yes,	there	is. are.	
	No,		isn't / is not. aren't / are not.	

a/an

We use **there is** + **a/an** + single countable noun in positive sentences, negative sentences and questions.
There's an order.   There isn't a delivery charge.   Is there a discount?

some

We use **there are** + **some** + plural countable nouns in positive sentences.
There are some problems. (unspecified quantity)
There are two problems. (specified quantity)
We use **there is** + **some** + uncountable nouns in positive and negative sentences.
There is some equipment.   There isn't any furniture.

any

We use **there isn't** + **any** + uncountable nouns in negative sentences and **is there** + **any** + uncountable nouns in questions.
There isn't any A4 paper.   Is there any coffee in the machine?
We use **there aren't** + **any** + plural countable nouns in negative sentences and **are there** + **any** + countable nouns in questions.
There aren't any computer chairs.   Are there any printers?

There isn't a = There is no
There isn't a discount. = There is no discount.
There isn't any = There is no
There isn't any work now. = There is no work now.
There aren't any = There are no
There aren't any deliveries today. = There are no deliveries today.

1A Complete the sentences and questions with *there is, there are, is there* or *are there*.

1 _____ _____ some deliveries today.
2 _____ _____ a meeting this morning.
3 _____ _____ some new computer equipment.
4 _____ _____ some visitors in reception.
5 _____ _____ an email from them?
6 _____ _____ any messages for me?
7 _____ _____ any water in that bottle?
8 _____ _____ any pens on the desk?

B Write sentences 1–4 in Exercise 1A in the negative form.

1 _____
2 _____
3 _____
4 _____

3.1 Talking about the past (1)

The Past Simple

We use the Past Simple to talk about completed actions and events in the past. We often use specific time references (e.g. *in 2017, last year*) to say when the action happened.
*I started the business **in 2017**.*
*We launched the new product **last year**.*

Past Simple positive	
I/You/We/ They He/She	start**ed** the business in 2017. launch**ed** the new product last year. appl**ied** for the job last week.

104

Grammar reference

For negative forms of Past Simple regular verbs, see p.106, 3.3 Talking about the past (2).

Spelling of Past Simple regular verbs

To form the Past Simple of regular verbs, we add **-ed** to the end of the verb.

Spelling of Past Simple verbs ending in ...				
consonant	-e	vowel + -y or -w	consonant + -y	vowel + consonant
work – work**ed** start – start**ed**	produc**e** – produc**ed** hir**e** – hir**ed**	st**ay** – stay**ed** sh**ow** – show**ed**	app**ly** – app**lied** stu**dy** – stu**died**	st**op** – sto**pped** pl**an** – pla**nned**

1 Complete the sentences with the Past Simple positive form of the verbs.
1. He _____ (start) his job two years ago.
2. They _____ (work) at TechHub last year.
3. You _____ (finish) high school in 2018.
4. We _____ (develop) new products at the factory.
5. She _____ (study) in London.
6. They _____ (show) us the new offices yesterday.
7. I _____ (plan) the schedule. It's ready.
8. The company _____ (hired) a new manager.

Past Simple Yes/No questions

In Past Simple Yes/No questions, we use the auxiliary verb **did**. We don't change the main verb (e.g. *start, win*) to the Past Simple. We also reply with **did/didn't**.

Did you start the business in 2017? Yes, I did.
Did they hire a new Manager? No, they didn't.

Did	I/you/we/ they/he/she	**start** the business in 2017?	Yes, No,	I/you/we/ they/he/she	**did.** **didn't.**

Object questions

In Past Simple object questions, we use the Past Simple auxiliary verb **did**. We don't change the main verb (e.g. *start, win*) to the Past Simple.

When did you start?
What did you win?

See Unit 1.4 Subject and object questions, p.103, for a further explanation of object questions.

Object questions					Answers	
When	did	I/you/ we/they/ he/she	**start**?		I/You/ We/They/ He/She	**started** in 2018.
How	did	they	**expand** their market?		They	**created** products in different languages.
Where	did	he	**work** in 2010?		He	**worked** at Microsoft.
Who	did	you	**hire** for the job?		I	**hired** Clara Sanchez.
Why	did	they	**move** last year?		They	**moved** because they needed more space.
What	did	she	**study** at university?		She	**studied** business management.

Subject questions

In Past Simple subject questions, the main verb form for regular or irregular verbs is in the Past Simple. We do not use *did*.

*Who **started** the business?*
*Who **won** the contract?*

See Unit 1.4 Subject and object questions, p.103, for a further explanation of subject questions.

Subject questions		Answers
Who	**started** the business?	Three friends.
	designed the product?	Our Designer, David.
What	**happened** at work yesterday?	We had a meeting about the new design.
Which ... e.g. Which company	**launched** the iPhone?	Apple. Apple launched the iPhone.
Which employee	**started** last week?	David Lansbury. David Lansbury started last week.

2 Read the dialogues. Choose the correct option.

A: ¹*Who signed / Did you sign* the contract?
B: My manager.

A: Where ²*stayed / did you stay* at the conference?
B: We stayed at the Park Hall Hotel.

A: ³*Who designed the car? / What did you design?*
B: Karl Shultz was the designer.

A: ⁴*What designed John? / What did John design?*
B: John designed the tables and chairs.

3 Put the words in the correct order to make questions.
1. company / did / expand / the / range / its / ?
   _____
2. 2014 / did / in / start / university / you / ?
   _____
3. jobs / change / did / in / she / 2019 / ?
   _____
4. the company / who / started / ?
   _____
5. how / they / workplace / improve / did / their / ?
   _____
6. you / last year / work / where / did / ?
   _____
7. launched / last year / the HJ laptop / which company / ?
   _____
8. close / she / why / did / the shop / ?
   _____
9. who / a new computer / ordered / ?
   _____

Grammar reference

3.2 Giving instructions

We use the imperative to give instructions or orders to one person or a group of people.

Turn on your computer, then enter the password.
Go to reception and complete a form.

We can add *please* to be polite.

Please leave by 6.00 p.m.
Please don't move the boxes.

Positive

We use the infinitive verb form (e.g. *remove*, not *removes*) for the singular or plural imperative. We don't use subject pronouns (e.g. *you, they*).

Come to the office. ~~You come to the office.~~
Remove everything from your desk.
Come to the office at 10 o'clock, please.
Please leave by 6 o'clock.

Negative

We use the same negative form (e.g. *don't* not *doesn't*) for the singular or plural imperative.

Don't use this desk. ~~Doesn't use this desk.~~
Don't change desks.
Don't use this desk, please.
Please don't move these boxes.

1 Correct the mistakes in the sentences.

1 Please to help me.
   _____

2 Comes in and sits down, please.
   _____

3 Don't using your mobile phone here, please.
   _____

4 You are choose a new chair.
   _____

5 Doesn't take photos here, please.
   _____

6 Writes your name on your desk.
   _____

3.3 Talking about the past (2)

Irregular verbs in the Past Simple do not have an **-ed** ending.

Common irregular Past Simple verbs

be – was/were	have – had
build – built	hit – hit
buy – bought	make – made
go – went	spend – spent
grow – grew	win – won

For a list of irregular verbs, see page 114.

1 Choose the correct form (Present Simple or Past Simple form) to complete the sentences.

1 These days, I usually *spend / spent* about €100 per month travelling to work.
2 Last week, I *buy / bought* a new computer for €700.
3 Last month, we *have / had* problems at the factory.
4 We all *make / made* mistakes sometimes.
5 My grandfather *grow / grew* the business from one shop to 100.
6 The company *builds / built* over fifty offices every year.
7 Did you *win / won* the company tennis match?
8 They *has / had* two meetings yesterday.
9 We *go / went* to the new offices two days ago.
10 The first car we produced thirty years ago *is / was* very different to the others.

Past simple negative

In the Past Simple negative, we use **did not/didn't** + verb. We don't change the main verb to the Past Simple.

I worked at a car company in 2017.
I didn't work at a car company in 2017.

I/You/We/ They/ He/She	did not/didn't start	the business in 2017.
	did not/didn't win	the contract.
	did not/didn't arrive	at the hotel until 11.00 p.m.

2 Complete the sentences with the negative Past Simple form of the verbs in brackets.

1 He _____ (start) his job two years ago.
2 They _____ (work) at TechHub last year.
3 You _____ (finish) high school in 2018.
4 We _____ (grow) the business last year.
5 She _____ (go) to university in London.

4.1 Talking about arrangements

The Present Continuous

We use the Present Continuous to talk about definite arrangements in the future. These are usually fixed because someone arranged them or agreed to them, e.g. a meeting, a hotel booking, a flight.

I'm meeting the team later.
She's visiting the Paris office on Monday.
They're going to Munich next month.

We use time references with the Present Continuous to say when the arrangement is happening in the future.

I'm renting a car next week.
He's not visiting the office on Monday.
Are you flying to Munich tomorrow?

Positive/Negative			Yes/No questions		
I	'm / 'm not	renting a car next week.	Am	I	flying to Munich tomorrow?
He/ She/It	's / isn't		Is	he/she/ it	
You/ We/ They	're / aren't		Are	you/ we/ they	

106

Grammar reference

Wh- questions			
When	am	I	
How	is	he/she/it	travelling to Munich?
Why	are	you/we/they	

Short answers – Positive		
Yes,	I	am.
	he/she/it	is.
	you/we/they	are.

Short answers – negative		
No,	I	'm not. / am not
	he/she/it	isn't. / is not.
	you/we/they	aren't. / are not.

Spelling the Present Continuous	
add -ing	look → looking, go → going, meet → meeting
-e, add -ing	come → coming, have → having, make → making
consonant x2, add -ing	get → getting, stop → stopping, run → running

1 Complete the sentences using the Present Continuous and the words in brackets.

1 _____ (I / go) to Prague next week.
2 _____ (she / not stay) at a hotel.
3 _____ (we / visit) the office on Monday.
4 _____ (they / not rent) a car.
5 _____ (I / not meet) customers next week.
6 _____ (he / fly) to London tomorrow.
7 _____ (She / book) a flight to Porto.
8 _____ (they / start) the meeting at 9.00.

2 Complete the dialogues with the correct form of *be* and the verbs in the box in the Present Continuous. Use one verb twice.

> fly   go   rent   meet   stay

A: ¹_____ he ²_____ ?
B: No, he ³_____ . He's going by train.
A: ⁴_____ they ⁵_____ a car?
B: Yes, they ⁶_____ .
A: ⁷_____ I ⁸_____ in a hotel?
B: No, you ⁹_____ .
A: When ¹⁰_____ I ¹¹_____ ?
B: Next Monday.
A: Who ¹²_____ you ¹³_____ ?
B: I ¹⁴_____ customers.

4.2 will / won't

Promises and agreements
We also use *will / won't* to make promises and to agree to do (or not do) something.

*Thanks for the invitation. I **will (I'll) confirm** on Friday.*
*I **will not (won't) forget** to send the list.*

Decisions
We use *will / won't* to make decisions at the moment of speaking.

A: *What time is lunch?*
B: *I'll check the break times.*
*My flight is cancelled. I'**ll stay** in a hotel tonight. I **won't** go home.*

Offers
We also use *will* to make offers.

A: *I can't use this computer.*
B: *I'll try and fix it for you.*

A: *I'm really busy. I don't have time for lunch.*
B: *Don't worry, I'll get something from the canteen for us.*

We use an infinitive verb after *will / won't*.

	subject	will/won't	infinitive
Positive	I/You/We/They/He/She/It	will ('ll)	phone you tomorrow. check the details. send it immediately.
Negative	I/You/We/They/He/She/It	won't (= will not)	forget to call. charge for Wi-Fi access. miss the deadline.

1 Complete the responses with *will* and a verb.

> be   do   get   help   (not)be   open(x2)   phone   send

1 A: I don't have time to phone the client.
  B: I _____ her for you.
2 A: Can you talk to the catering manager?
  B: Certainly, I _____ it now.
3 A: It's hot in this office.
  B: Yes, it is. I _____ a window.
4 A: I can't operate this data projector.
  B: Don't worry. The assistant _____ you.
5 A: Can you send our order as soon as possible?
  B: Certainly. We _____ it tomorrow.
6 A: There's no paper in the photocopier.
  B: I _____ some from the computer shop.
7 A: I really need to eat, but there's another meeting at 12.30.
  B: Don't worry, there _____ lunch at the meeting.
8 A: Can I come to the bank after work?
  B: I'm sorry, it _____ possible after 5.30. The bank _____ again at 9am tomorrow.

107

Grammar reference

4.3 Things happening now

The present continuous

We use the Present Continuous to describe activities happening now.

What **are** you **doing**?
I**'m reading** a book.
I**'m writing** a report.
I**'m having** lunch.

We often use time references with the Present Continuous to say something is happening now.

I**'m working** at home **today**.
She**'s waiting** for the delivery **at the moment**.
Is she **giving** a presentation **right now**?

Positive/Negative		
I	'm 'm not	writing a report at the moment.
He/ She/It	's isn't is not	
You/ We/ They	're aren't are not	

Yes/No questions		
Am	I	giving a presentation right now?
Is	he/ she/it	
Are	you/ we/ they	

Wh- questions			
What	am	I	working on today?
	is	he/she/it	
	are	you/we/they	

Short answers – positive		
Yes,	I	am.
	he/she/it	is.
	you/we/they	are.

Short answers – negative		
No,	I	'm not. am not.
	he/she/it	isn't. is not.
	you/we/they	aren't. are not.

1 Choose the correct words.

1 I *'m / 's* working at my desk.
2 She *aren't / isn't* giving a presentation.
3 We *'re / 'm* looking after the new employees.
4 A: *Is / Are* you giving a presentation?
   B: Yes, I *am / 'm*.
5 A: *Is / Are* she meeting customers?
   B: No, she *isn't / is*.
6 What *they are / are they* working on?
7 They *aren't / isn't* finalising the sales figures.
8 She *'s / 're* meeting the sales team.

4.4 Making suggestions

We use **try + verb + -ing** to make suggestions for actions when there is a problem.

A: My phone doesn't work.
B: **Try charging** it.
A: I can't hear you, it's too loud. **Try phoning** me from another room.
B: OK.

Try	**turning** off your video. **unmuting** your microphone. **calling** me back.

1 Complete the dialogues with the correct form of the words in the box.

add   call   hang   turn (x2)   unmute

A: My screen is frozen.
B: Try ¹_____ up.

A: You're breaking up.
B: Try ²_____ off your audio.

A: I can't see you.
B: Try ³_____ on your video.

A: I can't see Dave.
B: Try ⁴_____ him to the call.

A: The connection isn't very good.
B: Try ⁵_____ me back.

A: I can't hear you.
B: Try ⁶_____ your microphone.

5.1 Talking about intentions

going to

We use **going to** to talk about future intentions. An intention is an aim; something you want to do or plan to do in the future, but the event is not definite at the time of speaking.

Positive/Negative

	Subject + be	going to	verb
Positive	I am He/She/It is You/We/They are	going to	**have** a bigger stand. **launch** a new product. **arrive** at 10 o'clock.
Negative	I'm not He/She/It isn't You/We/They aren't		

Yes/No questions

be + subject	going to	verb	Short answers
Am I **Is** he/she/it **Are** you/ we/they	going to	**have** a bigger stand? **launch** a new product? **arrive** at 10 o'clock?	Yes, I am. Yes, he/she/it is. Yes, you/we/they are. No, I'm not. No, he/she/it isn't. No, you/we/they aren't.

Wh- questions

Question word(s)	be + subject	going to	verb?
When Why	am I is he/she/it are you/we/they	going to	have a bigger stand? launch a new product?
How many	exhibitors are	going to	be at the trade fair?

1 Complete the sentences and questions with *going to* and the verb in brackets.

1. How many people _____ (attend) the presentation?
2. We _____ (not start) the meeting until 11 o'clock.
3. She _____ (set up) the stand in the morning.
4. _____ (they, launch) any new products this year?
5. The exhibition centre _____ (not, provide) free Wi-Fi.
6. When _____ (we, have) the next sales conference?
7. I _____ (send) you the details by email.
8. He _____ (not change) the brochures for this year's trade show.

5.3 Invitations with *would* and *want*

Do you want to … ? is an informal way of making offers and inviting people to do something, e.g. by social media or with people we know well.

Do you want to join me for lunch?

Would you like to … ? is a polite way of making offers and inviting people to do something, e.g. by formal email, or when speaking to people we don't know well. We do not use *love to* in questions for offers or invitations.

Would you like to join us for dinner?

Yes/No questions

Would/Do	subject	like/want	to	verb / verb phrase
Would	you	like	to	join us for lunch?
Do		want		see the factory?

Short answers

Thank you (very much). I would love to.
Yes, that would be* good/great.
Thanks! I'd love to.
Yes! Sounds good.

I would love to or *that would be good/great* are formal and polite ways of saying 'yes' to an invitation.

Thanks! I'd love to and *Yes! Sounds good* are examples of informal short responses to an informal invitation.

*be is not used with *to* after *would*.

We do not use *I wouldn't like to* to say 'no' to invitations. Instead we can say:

Thank you very much for the invitation, but I am not available today. (formal)
I am (very) sorry, but I cannot come because I have a meeting. (formal)
Thanks for the invitation, but I'm not free today. (informal)
Sorry, but I have other plans. (informal)

Wh- questions

Question word(s)	would	subject	like	to	verb / verb phrase
When					see the factory?
Where	would	you	like	to	go for lunch?
What time					start the meeting?

Would like to in a positive statement is also a formal and polite way of making offers and inviting people. You can also respond to the the invitation with a positive statement.

Positive

Subject	would	verb	to	verb / verb phrase
We/ Management	would	like	to	invite you to join us for lunch. show you the factory.
I	'd	like/ love	to	join you for dinner on the 29th.

1 Complete the invitations with the words in the box.

> but join like love sorry
> what would (x2) want you

1. **A:** Would you ¹_____ to join us for coffee?
   B: I'm very ²_____ , but I have a video conference in a few minutes.
2. **A:** ³_____ they like to visit the other departments?
   B: Yes, that ⁴_____ be good.
3. **A:** Do you ⁵_____ to see the new brochures?
   B: Thanks! I'd ⁶_____ to.
4. **A:** Would ⁷_____ like to walk to the restaurant?
   B: Thank you for the invitation, ⁸_____ I'll take a taxi.
5. **A:** ⁹_____ would you like to do this evening?
   B: I'd love to visit the old town.
6. **A:** What time would you like to have lunch?
   B: About 1 o'clock. Would you like to ¹⁰_____ me?

Grammar reference

6.1 ▸ Speculating about the future

will/won't/might/might not

We use **will/won't/might/might not** to speculate about the future.

There will be more electric cars soon.
Robots might help with everyday tasks.
We won't need more cash.

We use *will* when we are certain about something happening in future; *won't* when we think something is impossible in future; and *might/might not* when we think something is possible in future, but we don't know for certain.

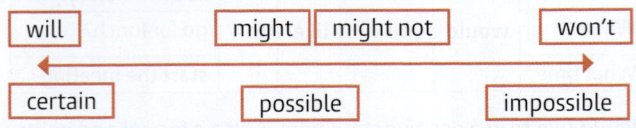

will		might	might not		won't
certain			possible		impossible

We can use **I think** and **I don't think** at the start of a sentence to speculate about the future. It is more natural to say *I don't think we will/we'll …* than *I think we won't …* .

I think there will be more electric cars soon.
I don't think we will need cash.

will/won't

	subject	will/won't	infinitive
Positive	I/You/He/She/It/We/They	will	use more robots.
	There		be more electric cars.
Negative	I/You/He/She/It/We/They	won't / will not	want these jobs.
	There		be many shops.

might / might not

	subject	might/might not	verb
Positive	I/You/He/She/It/We/They	might	use more robots.
	There		be more electric cars.
Negative	I/You/He/She/It/We/They	might not	do these jobs.
	There		be many shops.

1 Put the words in the correct order to make sentences.

1 might / in / Robots / offices / work
   _____.

2 think / might / many / disappear / I / shops
   _____.

3 exist / in / the future / jobs / won't / Many
   _____.

4 people / from / think / most / will / home / I / work
   _____.

5 might / be / many / There / drivers / not
   _____.

6 think / petrol / I / there / any / be / will / don't
   _____.

7 I / be / there / more / think / electric vehicles / will
   _____.

6.3 ▸ Describing production

The Present Simple Passive

We often use the Present Simple Passive to describe products, processes and procedures, e.g. a manufacturing or production process.

The cotton is grown in India. Then, it is sent to the factory.

The Present Simple Passive is formed with the verb **be** and a past participle. For a list of past participles, see p.114.

Positive: Singular			
Object	is	past participle	
The cotton	is	grown	in India.
Our coffee		sold	direct to you.
The T-shirt		made	in Morocco.

Positive: Plural			
Object	are	past participle	
Our clothes	are	made	with 100 percent organic cotton.
Farmers		paid	a fair price.
The beans		shipped	to our warehouse.

We use the Present Simple Passive when it is not necessary to know who does an action, or when we don't know who does the action.

The subject/agent/doer is not important in the Present Simple Passive so the emphasis changes to the object.

Passive: *The **cotton** is grown in India.* (no subject) [object]
Active: ***Farmers** grow the **cotton** in India.* [subject, object]

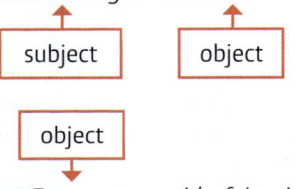

Passive: ***Farmers** are paid a fair price.* (no subject) [object]
Active: ***We** pay **farmers** a fair price.* [subject, object]

We can use *by* when we want to indicate who does an action. However, the emphasis is still on the object.

Active: ***Our creative team** design **the shoes**.* [subject, object]
Passive: ***The shoes** are designed by **our creative team**.* [object, subject]

The main focus of the passive sentence is the object of the verb and it comes first in the sentence, in this example 'the shoes'. In the active sentence the subject (our creative team) is the main focus and it comes first in the sentence.

Grammar reference

1 Choose the correct option to complete the sentences.
1. These oranges *grow / are grown* by farmers in Spain.
2. No animal products *use / are used* in our restaurant.
3. The company *makes / is made* the jeans from organic cotton.
4. We *sell / are sold* our eggs direct to the customer.
5. Our factory workers *pay / are paid* higher wages than in other factories.
6. No sugar *add / is added* to produce our fresh fruit juices.
7. The packaging *produced / is produced* from recycled materials.
8. We *buy / are bought* all our products from ethical suppliers.

7.1 Comparing (1): Comparatives

Comparative adjectives

We use comparative adjectives to say how two things are different.

*My laptop is **cheaper** than yours.*
*My new laptop is **better** than my old one.*
*The security is **more advanced** than other systems.*

We often use the verb **to be** with a comparative adjective and **than**.

Object	to be	comparative adjective	than	object
My laptop		cheaper		your laptop.
This car	is	nicer	than	that one.
The security		more advanced		other systems.

We don't need to use **than + object** when we know what the other object is.

A: Do you like your new car? Or do you prefer the old car?
B: The new car is nicer. (The new car is nicer than the old car)

We can also use other verbs (e.g. **takes**, **has**, **looks**) with comparatives.

*My new phone **takes longer** to charge. The design **looks worse**.*
*This laptop **has** a **bigger** database than my old one.*

Spelling comparative adjectives

One syllable: add *-er*	cheap → cheap**er** strong → strong**er**
Two syllables ending in *-y*: add *-ier*	easy → eas**ier** noisy → nois**ier** busy → bus**ier**
Two or more syllables: use *more*	expensive → **more** expensive powerful → **more** powerful
Irregular	bad → worse good → better
Adjectives ending in consonant + vowel + consonant: double the final consonant and add *-er*	big → big**ger** thin → thin**ner**

1 Complete the sentences with the correct form of the words in the box.

big   bright   cheap   easy   fast   long   small   expensive

1. Our new office is _____ than our old one. We save $500 a month.
2. The screen's _____ than other laptops. It's only 25 cm.
3. The battery lasts _____ than other phones – more than fifteen hours.
4. This phone is £300 more _____ than the other one.
5. We have a _____ database than our competitors.
6. My new car's _____ than my old one. It can go at 150 km per hour.
7. The screen on this TV is _____ than my old one.
8. This car is _____ to drive than other models.

7.3 Comparing (2): Superlatives

Superlative adjectives

We use superlative adjectives to say that one thing has more or less of a quality that any other thing in the same group.

*Our new AX laptop is lighter than the BX and the CX models. The AX is **the lightest** laptop.*
*5G mobile data is bigger than 4G data and 3G data. 5G data is **the biggest**.*
*The new Six Plus sports car is more powerful than the 4 Plus and 3 Wheeler. It is **the most powerful**.*

We use **the** with the superlative adjective to describe the object.

*My car is **the best**.*
*This laptop is **the most expensive** in the shop.*

You can also use other verbs (e.g. **have**, **offer**, etc.) with **the** and superlative adjectives.

*We **offer the best** value for money.*
*Our cars **have the most powerful** engines.*

Spelling superlative adjectives

One syllable: add *-est*	hard → the hard**est** cheap → the cheap**est**
Two syllables ending in *-y*: change *y* to *i* and add *-est*	easy → the eas**iest** happy → the happ**iest** noisy → the nois**iest**
Two or more syllables: use *most*	expensive → the **most** expensive powerful → the **most** powerful
Irregular	good → the best bad → the worst fun → the most fun
Adjectives ending in consonant + vowel + consonant: double the final consonant and add *-est*	big → the big**gest** thin → the thin**nest**

111

Grammar reference

1 Complete the sentences with the superlative form of the words in brackets.

1 We were _____ (reliable) company last year.
2 Our staff are _____ (friendly) in the industry.
3 This is _____ (secure) system in the world.
4 We have _____ (big) database in recruitment.
5 This is the _____ (light) phone on the market.
6 We have _____ (good) customer service.
7 Their products are _____ (bad). Don't buy them.
8 This is _____ (advanced) software in the world.

8.1 Talking about experiences

The Present Perfect

We use the Present Perfect Simple to talk about experiences in our lives. We do not say when they happened.

I've worked for a bank.
I've been to Paris.

We often use **ever** in questions with the Present Perfect Simple. It means 'at any time in your life'.

*Have you **ever** worked in this industry?*

We often use **never** with the Present Perfect Simple. It means 'at no time in my life'.

*I've **never** worked abroad.*

Positive

Subject	have/has	past participle	
I/You/We/They	have / 've	worked	on international projects.
He/She/It	has / 's		in this industry.

Negative

Subject	have/has not	past participle	
I/You/We/They	have not / haven't	worked	on international projects.
He/She/It	has not / hasn't		in this industry.

Yes/No questions

Have	Subject	past participle	
Have	I/You/We/They	worked	on international projects?
Has	He/She/It		in this industry?

Short answers

Yes, I/you/we/they **have**.	Yes, he/she/it **has**.
No, I/you/we/they **haven't**.	No, he/she/it **hasn't**.

Wh- questions

Question word(s)	have	subject	past participle
Where	have	I/you/we/they	worked?
	has	he/she/it	

Past participles

- To form past participles of most regular verbs, add -d or -ed.
  *deliver**ed**, export**ed**, help**ed**, liv**ed**, start**ed**, work**ed***
- When a regular verb ends in -y, form past participles in two ways.
  - When a verb ends in a vowel and -y, add -ed:
    *employ – employ**ed**, play – play**ed**, stay – stay**ed***
  - Change -y to -i and add -ed when the verb ends in a consonant and -y:
    *carry – carr**ied**, copy – cop**ied**, study – stud**ied**, try – tr**ied***
- One group of irregular past particles are the same as the irregular past simple forms.
  bought, had, made, put, sent, sold
- Another group of irregular past particles is different from the irregular Past Simple forms. For irregular past forms, see p.114.

Common irregular verbs

Infinitive	Past Simple	Past Participle
be	was/were	been
give	gave	given
go	went	gone*
grow	grew	grown
speak	spoke	spoken
take	took	taken
write	wrote	written

Contractions

've = have   haven't = have not
's = has   hasn't = has not

We often use contractions in spoken English and informal writing. The full forms (**have/has/have not/has not**) should be used in formal writing.

*been or gone?

The past participle of *go* is *gone*. *Gone* means the trip is not completed. However, to say the trip was completed, we use *been*.

A: *Where's the manager this week?*
B: *She's **gone** to Paris for work.*
(She is in Paris now.)

A: *Has she ever travelled for business?*
B: *Yes, She's **been** to Paris for work.*
(She was there at some time in the past, but is not there now.)

1 Complete the sentences and questions using the Present Perfect. Use contractions where possible.

1 I _____ (have) several jobs in sales.
2 He _____ (change) companies three times in his life.
3 I _____ (never/go) to China on business.
4 He isn't in the office today. He _____ (go) to visit some clients.
5 We _____ (not study) at university.
6 They _____ (not write) many blogs in English.
7 She _____ (not design) lots of websites.

8 I _____ (not have) much experience managing staff.
9 _____ she _____ (give) presentations at conferences?
10 _____ he _____ (buy) products from this supplier in the past?
11 _____ they (ever/deliver) _____ the orders on time?
12 _____ we _____ (sell) materials to these markets before?

8.3 ▶ Talking about experiences and completed past events

The Present Perfect Simple and the Past Simple

We often use the Present Perfect Simple and the Past Simple together to talk about experiences.

We often start with a question in the Present Perfect Simple to ask someone if something happened at a point in their life, e.g. *Have you ever travelled for work?* If the answer is *yes*, we use the Past Simple to ask for extra information about this experience, e.g. when/why/where it happened.

A: *Have you ever travelled for work?* (Present Perfect Simple)
B: *Yes, I have, once or twice.*
A: *When was the last time you travelled for work?* (Past Simple)
B: *It was last year. I went to Manchester.* (Past Simple)

Common time expressions used with the two tenses to talk about life experiences include:

Past Simple	two days ago, an hour ago, from 2019 to 2020, in 2009, in January, last year, last night
Present Perfect Simple	in the past, ever, many times, never, once, twice

1 Put the time expressions in the box in the correct column. Some can be used with either tense.

> a few days ago   before   ever   five minutes ago
> from 2016 to 2018   in 2017   in November   last month
> last week   many times   never   three times   yesterday

Past Simple	Present Perfect Simple

2 Complete the dialogues with the Past Simple or Present Perfect Simple form of the verb in brackets.

1 **A:** Have you ¹_____ (ever / write) an email in English?
   B: Yes, I've ²_____ (write) lots of emails in English.
   A: Who ³_____ (you write) the last email to?
   B: I ⁴_____ (write) to a customer in the Netherlands yesterday.
   A: Why ⁵_____ (you write) to the customer?
   B: Because they ⁶_____ (want) a price list.

2 **A:** Have you ⁷_____ (ever / travel) for work?
   B: Yes, I ⁸_____ (travel) many times for work.
   A: When ⁹_____ (be) your last trip? Where ¹⁰_____ (you / go)?
   B: It ¹¹_____ (be) last January. I ¹²_____ (go) to Zurich.
   A: Where ¹³_____ (you / stay)?
   B: In a small hotel in the city centre.
   A: What ¹⁴_____ (you / do) there?
   B: I ¹⁵_____ (visit) clients, ¹⁶_____ (give) a sales presentation and ¹⁷_____ (have) dinner with them in the evening.
   A: ¹⁸_____ (you / have) a good time?
   B: Yes, I did. Zurich is beautiful, but it was very cold.

Irregular verbs list

	INFINITIVE	PAST SIMPLE	PAST PARTICIPLE
P9.01	be [biː]	was/were [wɒz/wɜː]	been [biːn]
P9.02	become [bɪˈkʌm]	became [bɪˈkeɪm]	become [bɪˈkʌm]
P9.03	begin [bɪˈgɪn]	began [bɪˈgæn]	begun [bɪˈgʌn]
P9.04	break [breɪk]	broke [brəʊk]	broken [ˈbrəʊkən]
P9.05	bring [brɪŋ]	brought [brɔːt]	brought [brɔːt]
P9.06	build [bɪld]	built [bɪlt]	built [bɪlt]
P9.07	buy [baɪ]	bought [bɔːt]	bought [bɔːt]
P9.08	can [kæn]	could [kʊd]	been able to [biːn ˈeɪbl tə]
P9.9	catch [kætʃ]	caught [kɔːt]	caught [kɔːt]
P9.10	choose [tʃuːz]	chose [tʃəʊz]	chosen [tʃəʊzn]
P9.11	come [kʌm]	came [keɪm]	come [kʌm]
P9.12	cost [kɒst]	cost [kɒst]	cost [kɒst]
P9.13	cut [kʌt]	cut [kʌt]	cut [kʌt]
P9.14	do [duː]	did [dɪd]	done [dʌn]
P9.15	drink [drɪnk]	drank [dræŋk]	drunk [drʌŋk]
P9.16	drive [draɪv]	drove [drəʊv]	driven [drɪvn]
P9.17	eat [iːt]	ate [et/eɪt]	eaten [iːtn]
P9.18	feel [fiːl]	felt [felt]	felt [felt]
P9.19	find [faɪnd]	found [faʊnd]	found [faʊnd]
P9.20	fly [flaɪ]	flew [fluː]	flown [fləʊn]
P9.21	forget [fəˈget]	forgot [fəˈgɒt]	forgotten [fəˈgɒtn]
P9.22	get [get]	got [gɒt]	got [gɒt]
P9.23	give [gɪv]	gave [geɪv]	given [gɪvn]
P9.24	go [gəʊ]	went [went]	gone [gɒn]
P9.25	grow [grəʊ]	grew [gruː]	grown [grəʊn]
P9.26	have [hæv]	had [hæd]	had [hæd]
P9.27	hear [hɪə]	heard [hɜːd]	heard [hɜːd]
P9.28	hit [hɪt]	hit [hɪt]	hit [hɪt]
P9.29	keep [kiːp]	kept [kept]	kept [kept]
P9.30	know [nəʊ]	knew [njuː]	known [nəʊn]
P9.31	learn [lɜːn]	learned [lɜːnd]/ learnt [lɜːnt]	learned [lɜːnd]/ learnt [lɜːnt]
P9.32	leave [liːv]	left [left]	left [left]
P9.33	let [let]	let [let]	let [let]
P9.34	lose [luːz]	lost [lɒst]	lost [lɒst]
P9.35	make [meɪk]	made [meɪd]	made [meɪd]
P9.36	meet [miːt]	met [met]	met [met]
P9.37	pay [peɪ]	paid [peɪd]	paid [peɪd]
P9.38	put [pʊt]	put [pʊt]	put [pʊt]
P9.39	run [rʌn]	ran [ræn]	run [rʌn]
P9.40	say [seɪ]	said [sed]	said [sed]
P9.41	see [siː]	saw [sɔː]	seen [siːn]
P9.42	sell [sel]	sold [səʊld]	sold [səʊld]
P9.43	send [send]	sent [sent]	sent [sent]
P9.44	set [set]	set [set]	set [set]
P9.45	show [ʃəʊ]	showed [ʃəʊd]	shown [ʃəʊn]
P9.46	sit [sɪt]	sat [sæt]	sat [sæt]
P9.47	speak [spiːk]	spoke [spəʊk]	spoken [ˈspəʊkən]
P9.48	spend [spend]	spent [spent]	spent [spent]
P9.49	take [teɪk]	took [tʊk]	taken [ˈteɪkən]
P9.50	teach [tiːtʃ]	taught [tɔːt]	taught [tɔːt]
P9.51	tell [tel]	told [təʊld]	told [təʊld]
P9.52	think [θɪŋk]	thought [θɔːt]	thought [θɔːt]
P9.53	understand [ˌʌndəˈstænd]	understood [ˌʌndəˈstʊd]	understood [ˌʌndəˈstʊd]
P9.54	win [wɪn]	won [wʌn]	won [wʌn]
P9.55	write [raɪt]	wrote [rəʊt]	written [rɪtn]

Additional material

Lesson 1.2 > 7

Student A

1 You need to schedule a planning meeting by Friday 29 March with Student B. Write an email.
- Say that you need to have the meeting for one hour.
- Say when you are available.
- Ask when Student B is available.

Monday 25 March
At factory all day (every week)
Tuesday 26 March
Wednesday 27 March
Sales meeting (all day)
Thursday 28 March
Management meeting (all day)
Friday 29 March

2 Read Student B's email and write a reply. Try to agree a time and place to meet.

3 Continue exchanging emails until you agree a time for the two meetings.

Lesson 3.1 > 6

Student A

Part 1

Read the information. Answer Student B's questions.

Liu Qing – Didi Chuxing

2000: Bachelor's degree, Computer Science, Peking University

2002: Master's Degree, Harvard University, computer science

2002: Starts work – first job at Goldman Sachs, Asia

2014: New job – Chief Operating Officer of Didi Chuxing, a ride-sharing app

2018: Is in Forbes' list of China's Top 100 Businesswomen

Part 2

Ask Student B questions to complete the timeline.

Arash Ferdowsi – Dropbox

¹ _____ : Finishes high school, begins study at MIT

June 2007: Launches ² _____ – a file-hosting service

September 2007: ³ _____ with no degree

2007–2016 – Works as ⁴ _____ of Dropbox

⁵ _____ : New job: Member of management team and board of directors

BUSINESS WORKSHOP 1 > 2B

Student A

You are Maria Alvarez and you work for *U-Trav-L*. You want to interview Angela Lawrie. Make an arrangement by email.

1 Wait for Angela's email response. Send a short reply.
- In your reply, explain you are not available in the last week in March. Suggest Wednesday 2 April.

2 Wait for Angela's second response and reply again.
- You are available on:
  Tuesday 1 April
  Wednesday 2 April
  Thursday 3 April
  Friday 4 April.

Is she available on any of these dates? If yes, write a short email and confirm you can meet on that date.

BUSINESS WORKSHOP 1 > 5A

Student A

You are Maria Alvarez. You want to interview another business professional. Ask Student B the questions and make notes. Then swap roles.

Questions	Answers
1 What is your name?	
2 Which department do you work in?	
3 What do you do?	
4 Where do you work?	
5 How do you get to work?	
6 How long is your journey to work?	
7 How often do you travel abroad?	
8 Where do you travel to?	
9 Why do you travel for work?	
10 Do you work when you're on the train or plane?	
11 What's your favourite travel destination?	

Lesson 2.2 ▶ 5

Student B

Roleplay 1: You work for Eco Boxes.
- Look at the catalogue.
- Answer the phone and take the customer's order.
- You need to know:
  - the customer's name and company name.
  - details of the order (quantities and colours).
- Use the phrases in Exercise 3 to help you.
- You need to tell the customer:
  - You only have yellow boxes in stock.
  - Delivery cost: €5 all orders under €50, free of charge over €50
  - Delivery time: three working days

ECOBOXES: Salad and sushi boxes

PRODUCT	REFERENCE NUMBER	SIZE	COLOUR	QUANTITY	PRICE	PRICE PER 100
Small salad and sushi box	SUB01	57 x 115 x 75 mm	Two colours – white and yellow	25 units	€5	€20
Big salad and sushi box	SUB02	70 x 225 x 95 mm	Two colours – white and yellow	20 units	€7	€30

Roleplay 2: You are the customer.
- Look at the catalogue.
- Phone your partner and order some boxes. You would like to order 500 white sandwich boxes and 1,000 white burger boxes.
- You want to know:
  - the prices, colours and delivery cost.
  - the total cost of the order.
  - if you can have the delivery in two days.

Use the phrases in Exercise 3 to help you.

ECOBOXES: Sandwich and burger boxes

PRODUCT	REFERENCE NUMBER	SIZE	COLOUR	QUANTITY	PRICE	PRICE PER 100
Sandwich box	SAB01	57 x 115 x 75 mm	Two colours _____, _____	20 units		€17.50
Burger box	BBB03	70 x 225 x 95 mm	Two colours _____, _____	20 units		€22.50

Lesson 3.4 ▶ 4B

Answer these questions about the project in Exercise 4A before you write your dialogue.

1 How did it go in general? Well? Badly?
2 What went well? Which stages? Why? Who did a good job?
3 What didn't go well? Which stages? Why? What were the problems?

BUSINESS WORKSHOP 1 ▶ 4B

Questions	Answers
1 What is your name?	Angela Lawrie
2 Which department do you work in?	Marketing
3 What do you do?	Marketing Manager for technology start-up company
4 Where do you work?	London
5 How do you get to work?	Train
6 How long is your journey to work?	50 minutes
7 How often do you travel abroad?	Every two weeks
8 Where do you travel to?	At the moment: Germany, Poland, India, China, Japan, Canada and Mexico
9 Why do you travel for work?	To try and get new business in these markets; to talk to customers; to promote our products
10 Do you work on the train or plane?	Yes, I try to use the time to do work.
11 What's your favourite travel destination?	Mexico – there are some beautiful beaches and everyone is so friendly.

BUSINESS WORKSHOP 1 ▶ 3

Student B

Arrange a time to meet at the office.

You are Angela Lawrie. You agreed to meet Maria Alvarez on Friday 4 April, but now she is not available.

Look at your calendar for next week. When are you available? Take a phone call from Maria and arrange a new date.

APRIL	Mon 7	Tue 8	Wed 9	Thu 10	Fri 11
11.00				Budget meeting	
12.00		Factory all day			
1.00					
2.00				Planning meeting	Progress meeting
3.00					

Lesson 2.4 > 5

Student A

You represent Robert's Cleaning Services. Use the table to ask and answer questions.

Questions for customer	Information to tell customer
How / rooms are / to clean? What / you want the cleaner to do? How / days / you need a cleaner? What time / you want the cleaner to come?	Your company: – can clean a small office in two hours a day. – does not clean windows (not in the contract). – charges €20 an hour on weekdays / €25 an hour at the weekend. – charges €3 a week for cleaning products.

Lesson 1.2 > 7

Student B

1 You need to schedule a budget meeting by Friday 29 March with Student A. Write an email.
- Say that you need to have the meeting for one hour.
- Say when you are available.
- Ask when Student A is available.

Monday 25 March	
Tuesday 26 March	
At the factory (every week)	
Wednesday 27 March	
Client meetings – all day	
Thursday 28 March	
Friday 29 March	
Morning: Working at home	

2 Read Student A's email and write a reply. Try to agree a time and place to meet.
3 Continue exchanging emails until you agree a time for the two meetings.

Lesson 2.4 > 6

Student A

You need a catering service for your office party. Use the table to ask and answer questions.

Questions for the catering company	Information to tell the catering company
How many catering staff / there? / they clean the office after the party? / you supply plates and glasses? How / do you charge?	– You want a cold buffet for twenty-five people. – The party is at 1 p.m. next Friday. – You have a kitchen where the catering staff can work. – You want the catering staff to clean the room after the party.

BUSINESS WORKSHOP 1 > 2B

Student B

You are Angela Lawrie and you work as a Marketing Manager in a technology start-up company. You want to be in *U-Trav-L* magazine.

1 Write a short reply to Maria Alvarez's email on page 16.
- In your reply, explain that you usually work on finance results in March, but you are available for one day during the last week of the month. Suggest Friday 28 March.

2 Wait for Maria's email response. Reply again with a short email.
- In your reply, explain you usually work from home on Wednesdays so you can't meet on 2 April.
- Tell her you can meet on Friday 4 April. Suggest 2.00 p.m.

3 Read Maria's final response. When can she meet?

BUSINESS WORKSHOP 1 > 5A

Student B

You own a business and Maria Alvarez wants to interview you. Complete the questionnaire about you and your business travel and answer Maria's questions. You can invent your answers. Then swap roles.

Questions	Answers
1 What is your name?	
2 Which department do you work in?	
3 What do you do?	
4 Where do you work?	
5 How do you get to work?	
6 How long is your journey to work?	
7 How often do you travel abroad?	
8 Where do you travel to?	
9 Why do you travel for work?	
10 Do you work when you're on the train or plane?	
11 What's your favourite travel destination?	

> Additional material

BUSINESS WORKSHOP 1 ▶ 3
Student A

Phone and arrange a time to meet at the office.
You are Maria Alvarez. You agreed to meet Angela Lawrie on Friday 4 April, but now you can't.

Look at your calendar for next week. When are you available? Phone Angela to arrange a new date.

APRIL	Mon 7	Tue 8	Wed 9	Thu 10	Fri 11
11.00					Presentation
12.00	Working from home all day		Management meeting all day		
1.00					
2.00					
3.00				Training	

BUSINESS WORKSHOP 3 ▶ 4
Student A

1 Choose the correct words to complete the questions.
   1 How did the project *go / went* , generally?
   2 What *go / went* well, in particular?
   3 What did you *do / did*?
   4 What *are / do* you need to change?
   5 What *did / was* the problem?
   6 What *didn't go / wasn't* well?

2 You are a writer for a business blog. Interview João Silva. Use the questions in Exercise 1 and complete the notes.

> How the project went:
> What went well:
> What didn't go well:
> What the problem was:
> What João did:
> What the João wants to do next:

Lesson 5.3 ▶ 7

A very important client is going to visit your company on Thursday next week. You are organising the visit. Write an email invitation to the client.

- Invite the client to have a tour of the company. (*Include information on the departments or buildings you'd like to show him/her, and what time.*)
- Also invite the client to join you for lunch or dinner on Thursday. (*Include information on where, when and who with.*)

Use more formal phrases in your email.

Lesson 5.2 ▶ 5
Student B

Take turns to take and leave phone messages. Use some expressions from Exercise 3A.

Phone call 1	Phone call 2
You represent the conference centre. You are the Receptionist at Wallace Hotel Conference Centre. Angela Mulligan, the Assistant Manager of the centre, is on holiday today. Answer the phone and take a message for her. You want to know the caller's name, company and the date of the conference.	**You are the client.** Your name is _____ . (invent a name) You work for_____ . (choose a company) You are going to attend a meeting at Stanford Conference Centre, London on _____ . (choose a date) Phone the Stanford Conference Centre. Leave a phone message for Henri Dupont, the Centre Manager.

BUSINESS WORKSHOP 3 ▶ 1B
Student A

Write questions. Ask Student B.

1 Who / start Software de Jogo?
   _____
2 Who / João and Manuela hire / January?
   _____
3 When / create Software de Jogo?
   _____
4 Where / rent an office?
   _____
5 When / launch *Vai-Vai* in Portuguese?
   _____

Lesson 2.2 ▶ 1
Student B

Look at the order form. Ask Student A questions to complete the information.

> What's the customer name?
> How many do you need?
> What's the customer reference number?

ORDER NUMBER	S342091BE
CUSTOMER NAME	2
COMPANY ADDRESS	187 High Street, Burham
CUSTOMER REFERENCE NUMBER	4
PRODUCT	Green 1-litre bottles
PRODUCT CODE NUMBER	GB100463Y
QUANTITY	6

118

BUSINESS WORKSHOP 2 > 4A

Student B

1. You work for Carter-Villiers caterers. Anita Patterson at Benham Engineering phones to make an order.
   - Look at your order form.
   - Prepare the questions to ask the customer.
   - Ask and answer questions and take the customer's order.

   What's the (company name)?
   How many people are there for canapés?
   How many (sandwich platters) do you want?

   Carter-Villiers CATERERS

   Company name [1] Benham Engineering
   Delivery date [2] _____
   Order details
   Number of people for canapés [3] _____
   Number of sandwich platters: [4] _____
   Type of platters: [5] _____ meat
   [6] _____ fish [7] _____ vegetarian
   Number of cake platters [8] _____
   Number of cut fruit platters [9] _____
   Delivery time [10] _____
   Total cost: £1,007 (before discount), £956.65 with five percent discount
   No delivery charge.

   ---

2. Compare your information. Are all the details of the order correct?

Lesson 5.3 > 6

Student A

A Write an informal invitation message on social media. Use the information below.

You met your sales targets last month. Invite your colleagues to dinner tonight to celebrate.
- Include some useful phrases from this lesson.

B Respond to other invitation messages only in social media messages.

Lesson 3.1 > 6

Student B
Part 1
Ask Student A questions to complete the timeline.

Liu Qing – Didi Chuxing

2000: Bachelor's degree, Computer Science, [1] _____ University
2002: Master's Degree, Harvard University, subject – [2] _____
[3] _____ : Starts work – first job at [4] _____ , Asia.
[5] _____ : New job – Chief Operating Officer of Didi Chuxing, a ride-sharing app
2018: Is on Forbes' list of China's [6] _____

Part 2
Read the information. Answer Student A's questions.

Arash Ferdowsi – Dropbox

2004: Finishes high school, begins study at MIT
June 2007: Launches Dropbox – a file-hosting service
September 2007: Finishes university at MIT with no degree
2007–2016: Works as Chief Technology Officer of Dropbox
2016: New job: Member of management team and board of directors

BUSINESS WORKSHOP 2 > 5

Student B

1. You work for Benham Engineering. You want to arrange an extra cleaning service with Best Cleaning Services.
   - Read your information.
   - Have a meeting with Student A from Best Cleaning Services.
   - Write the cost of the service in your notes.
   - Make a business agreement.

   You want the cleaner to:
   - work two extra hours on 14 March.
   - start after 5.30 p.m.
   - clean the conference room and staff kitchen after the party.
   - clean the tables, empty bins and vacuum the carpet in the conference room, wash the plates and glasses and clean the kitchen floor.

   What is the cost of this extra service? _____

2. Compare your information. Are all the details of the agreement correct?

Additional material

Lesson 2.4 ▶ 6

Student B

You represent a catering service. A new client wants catering for an office party. Use the table to ask and answer questions.

Questions for the client	Information to tell the client
you want a hot or cold buffet? How / people / there for the party? What day / the party? What time / the party? / there a kitchen at the client's office?	Your company: – can provide hot and cold buffets. – provides two catering staff for cold buffets and three for hot buffets for groups of 20–30. – does not clean rooms after a party. – provides all plates and glasses. – charges €20 per person for cold buffets and €27 for hot buffets.

BUSINESS WORKSHOP 3 ▶ 1B

Student B

Write questions. Ask Student A.

1 Where / *Vai-Vai* / instant success?
   _____
2 Who / hire in August?
   _____
3 When / move to Brazil's Silicon Valley?
   _____
4 Why / hire a product manager and two more engineers?
   _____
5 How many games / produce from December?
   _____

BUSINESS WORKSHOP 5 ▶ 4B

Student B

> What do you think of … ?

> Do you like … ?

Topic	You think
Conference	It's a bit boring. The meeting rooms are very comfortable.
Hotel	You're not a guest in the hotel. It's a beautiful old building.
The city	You live in Nottingham. The old city centre and castle are very interesting. Invite your colleagues to visit the city.
The dinner	The food is delicious but it's sometimes cold.

BUSINESS WORKSHOP 8 ▶ 5

Student A

Look at your candidate profile information. Complete the sentences with the Present Perfect Simple.

Full name: _____
Job: Operations Manager

Skills summary
Organised and hard-working
I have experience in the transport industry.
I ^{1}_____ (work) in busy transport offices.
I ^{2}_____ (organise) deliveries in the UK and Europe and I ^{3}_____ (manage) administration staff and drivers.

Experience
Operations Manager
L&H Transport Services
Manchester
September 2019 to present day

I am responsible for transport operations between the UK and Europe in this small family transport company. I manage two administration assistants and twelve drivers. I deal with clients on the phone and email every day.

Intern/Work experience
January to March 2019
L&H Transport Services
Manchester

As an intern, I provided administration support to the General Manager of the company and her team.

Education
BSc (Hons) Business Administration

BUSINESS WORKSHOP 6 ▶ 2

Student B

You are the Sales Manager at Natural. Student A wants to buy your products. Read the information and prepare for the roleplay. Then discuss the order.

- Ask what products your customer wants to order.
- Ask what quantity he/she wants.
- Agree the price, delivery date and payment terms.

	You would like	You can accept
Price	$350 to $400 per 100 units.	$300 to $350 per 100 units.
Delivery date	Up to a week from now.	Five days from now.
Payment	Payment by bank transfer when the order is made.	Fifty percent when the contract is signed and fifty percent by bank transfer when the order is delivered.

Lesson 4.1 ▶ 6

Student A

Look at your travel arrangements. Have a conversation with Student B and arrange a time to meet.

Trip to Frankfurt and Athens

Tuesday	
Morning:	Train to Frankfurt
Afternoon:	Meet suppliers
Evening:	
Wednesday	
Morning:	Meet Angela at the apartment
Afternoon:	
Evening:	Dinner with Mr Brandt
Thursday	
Morning:	
Afternoon:	Have lunch with Frankfurt colleagues, until 2 p.m. Available after 2pm.
Evening:	Fly to Athens

Lesson 6.2 ▶ 5

Student B

Phone call 1: You are the Customer Services Agent

- Answer phone call.
  Customer Services, …
- Ask about the problem.
  How can I … ?
- Ask for the order number.
  Can I have … ?
- Say what you will do.
  We'll …
  I'll …
- Be polite.
  I'm (very) sorry about …
- Ask if they need anything more / End the call.
  Can I help you with …

Delivery normally takes three to four days. You can ask your manager to use express delivery in special cases.

Phone call 2: You are the client

The office digital printer isn't working. You need a technician today. It's urgent.

- Phone customer services.
  Good morning, …
- Explain the problem.
  There's a problem with …
- Ask when they can send a technician.
  When will … ?
- Explain that it is urgent. You need it to work as soon as possible.
  We need …

BUSINESS WORKSHOP 4 ▶ 4C

Student B: Karl

Continue your call with Alex. Look at your calendar. Find a time that you can both meet.

- Your presentation is on Thursday evening at 6.00 p.m. so you need to practise it together before then.

Day	Monday	Tuesday	Wednesday	Thursday	Friday
MORNING		Flight EX499, arrives midday		Meet customers	Flight EX376, departs 8.30 a.m.
AFTERNOON				Attend a talk	Attend a talk
EVENING	Flight EX499, arrives 9.00 p.m. CANCELLED	Attend a networking event		Give company presentation with Alex 6.00 p.m.	
HOTEL (FOUR NIGHTS)					

Continue the conversation.

Alex: *That's much better! I can hear you now. We need to arrange a meeting about our presentation.*

Karl: *Yes, we need to practise. I'm arriving on …*

Lesson 6.4 ▶ 5

Student A

You are the Buyer for a children's clothing company. Student B is the Sales Manager for a clothes manufacturer. Read the information and prepare for the roleplay. Then discuss the order.

It is 28 April and you want children's jumpers for the autumn season.

	You would like	You can accept
Price	£4.50 per jumper. You want 100 jumpers in total.	£4.50 to £5 an item.
Delivery date	8 July	Up to 16 July.
Payment	Payment by bank transfer when the order is delivered.	Twenty-five percent when the contract is signed and seventy-five percent by bank transfer when the order is delivered.

Additional material

Lesson 5.2 ▶ 6

Student B
Take turns to make phone calls.

Phone call 1	Phone call 2
You represent the conference centre. You are Angela Mulligan at Wallace Hotel Conference Centre. Phone the client who left a message in Exercise 5. You want to know: • how many people are going to attend the conference. • how many participants are going to stay at the hotel. • when the client is going to confirm the names and numbers. • what catering the client is going to need. • what equipment the client is going to need in the room.	**You are the meeting organiser.** Use the same name and company as for Exercise 5. • About 15–17 people are going to attend your meeting. • Promise to confirm the number of participants and their names next Monday morning. • You are going to have a coffee break at 11.00 a.m. and lunch at 1.30 p.m. • You need a projector, screen and Wi-Fi connection in the room. • You need a list of hotels near the conference centre. Henri Dupont, the Manager at Stanford Conference Centre phones you.

Lesson 2.4 ▶ 5

Student B
You need a cleaner for your office. Use the table to ask and answer questions.

Questions for cleaning company	Information to tell the cleaning company
How / time does the cleaner need? How much / you charge? you supply cleaning products? How / is that?	– It's a small office, 70 square metres: two offices, a small kitchen and toilet. – Cleaning tasks: clean the floor, clean the kitchen and toilet, clean the desks and clean the windows. – You want a cleaner three days a week (Tuesday, Thursday and Saturday) after 6 p.m.

Lesson 5.3 ▶ 6

Student C

A Write an informal invitation message on social media. Use the information below.

You got a promotion at work. Invite your colleagues to go for lunch at a restaurant.
• Include some useful phrases from this lesson.

B Respond to other invitation messages only in social media messages.

BUSINESS WORKSHOP 5 ▶ 2

Student B
You work at the Trent Hotel and Conference Centre. Look at the notes below.

• Your client at Hopkins Financial Services phones you.
• Answer the phone and introduce yourself.
• Discuss the conference details.

Good [morning/afternoon/evening], Trent Conference Centre. [Your name] speaking. How can I help you?

Event	Hopkins Financial Services annual sales conference
Dates	27 and 28 May Start time? *What time is the sales conference going to start?* Finish time?
Participants	How many people / going to / attend / the conference?
Hotel guests	How many people/ going to / stay at the hotel on nights of 26 and 27 May?
Catering	What time / going to / have / morning coffee break / lunch /afternoon coffee break?
Meeting rooms	How many rooms / you going to / need?
Equipment	• all meeting rooms have data projectors, screens, sound systems and Wi-FI connections • assistant at conference centre / going to / help with equipment?

Lesson 4.1 ▶ 6

Student B
Look at your travel arrangements. Start a conversation with Student A and arrange a time to meet.

Schedule for Frankfurt

Tuesday	
Morning:	
Afternoon:	Meet sales team from 1–5 p.m.
Evening:	Dinner with Sales Team Manager
Wednesday	
Morning:	
Afternoon:	Meeting with clients all afternoon
Evening:	
Thursday	
Morning:	Project update meeting
Afternoon:	
Evening:	Busy

Additional material

BUSINESS WORKSHOP 4 ▶ 4C

Student A: Alex

Continue your online meeting with Karl. Look at your calendar. Find a time that you can both meet.

- Your presentation is on Thursday evening at 6.00 p.m. so you need to practise it together before then.

	Monday	Tuesday	Wednesday	Thursday	Friday
MORNING	Flight AF212, arrives 11.00 a.m.	~~Meeting with Karl~~ CANCELLED	Meet customers		Flight AF799, departs 9.30 a.m.
AFTERNOON		Meet customers		Lunch with customers	
EVENING	Dinner			Give company presentation with Karl 6.00 p.m.	
HOTEL (FOUR NIGHTS)	Hotel City Park				

Continue the conversation.

Alex: *That's much better! I can hear you now. We need to arrange a meeting about our presentation.*

Karl: *Yes, we need to practise. I'm arriving on …*

Lesson 6.4 ▶ 5

Student B

You are the Sales Manager for a clothes manufacturer. Student B is the Buyer for a children's clothing company. Read the information and prepare for the roleplay. Then discuss the order.

It is 28 April and your client wants children's jumpers for the autumn season. Production takes eight to ten weeks. An order received by 2 May can be ready by 1 July and delivered on 23 July.

	You would like	You can accept
Price	£5.50 per jumper for orders under 200.	£5 to £5.50 an item for orders of 100+. There is no discount for orders under 100.
Delivery date	23 July	You might deliver earlier (20 or 21 July). You can offer a discount of five percent for delivering after 16 July.
Payment	Fifty percent when the contract is signed and fifty percent when the order is delivered.	Thirty percent when the contract is signed and seventy percent by bank transfer when the order is delivered.

BUSINESS WORKSHOP 7 ▶ 2

Group A

You work for Seven Seas Ships. You are presenting your new ship, *The River Queen*, at the International Cruise Show.

1 Number the parts of the presentation in the correct order.

a OK. So let's start with the size. *The River Queen* is 160 metres long and 25 metres wide. Each ship has three decks and 95 rooms. ____

b Now, let's talk about delivery times. We can deliver a ship to you six months after you order it. That's the fastest delivery time in the industry. Costs will depend on what you want, but it's about $4.5 million. ____

c First I'll talk about the size of the ship. Then I'll talk about the special features and finally, I'll talk about delivery times . ____

d Good morning everyone and thanks for coming. Today, we'd like to present our new cruise ship, *The River Queen*. ____

e Now, let's move onto the special features. Each ship has three bars and two restaurants. We also have a swimming pool on the top deck, which is great for a ship of this size. ____

2 Practise reading the presentation in your groups.

BUSINESS WORKSHOP 8 ▶ 5

Student D

Look at your candidate profile information. Complete the sentences with the Present Perfect Simple.

Full name: _____
Job: Transport and Logistics Assistant

Skills summary

Motivated team player with excellent IT and problem-solving skills.
I ¹_____ (organised) transport and logistics for a major construction company since university.
I ²_____ (work) to deadlines on many projects in this role.

Experience

Transport and Logistics Assistant
KLP Construction
April 2018 to present date

I coordinate the transportation of machinery for the company. I communicate with drivers, project managers in other departments and machinery hire companies. I assist the Senior Logistics Manager.

Education

BA (Hons) Sociology

Additional material

Lesson 8.4 ▶ 5
Student A

Roleplay 1
INTERVIEWER
You are the interviewer. You need a new Sales Manager for a mobile phone company.
Make questions and interview the candidate.
1. Can / tell me / work experience?
2. What / main strengths?
3. / you had any experience managing staff?
4. How / you motivated your staff?
5. Why / you want / to work for this company?
6. Why / you want / leave your current job?
7. Where / you see yourself / five years?
8. / you have / questions / me?

Roleplay 2
JOB CANDIDATE
You are a candidate for the job of Production Manager at a car factory.
Use the ideas (1–8) to answer the questions. You can change or add any ideas you want.
1. Assistant Production Manager in car parts factory / degree in engineering
2. Organised, analytical, problem-solving skills
3. Managed fifty staff in the production department
4. Help staff when they have problems, training sessions
5. Want more responsibility, company has a good reputation
6. More career opportunities
7. Want to work in project management
8. Skills and experience of your ideal candidate?

BUSINESS WORKSHOP 5 ▶ 4B
Student C

What do you think of … ?
Do you like … ?

Topic	You think
Conference	It's very good. You liked all the presentations. Good equipment in the rooms.
Hotel	You're a guest in the hotel. Your room is a bit small. You drove here. It's near the motorway, but not near the city centre. It's a bit boring.
The city	You want to visit the old city centre and castle. You heard it's interesting.
The dinner	You don't like it. The food is very bad.

Lesson 7.1 ▶ 11
Student B

1 Complete the questions with the correct form of the words in brackets. Then ask the questions to Student A.
1. Which phone is _____ (heavy)?
2. Which phone has a _____ (bad) battery?
3. Which phone is _____ (thin)?
4. What are the special features of each model?
5. Which phone is _____ (cheap)?

2 Use the information in the table to answer Student A's questions.

Product name	Super K family car	Super S sports car
Weight	1,590 kilogrammes	1,985 kilogrammes
Engine	1.4 litres	1.6 litres
Top speed	200 kilometres per hour	260 kilometres per hour
Features	Large space for luggage, advanced safety features.	Advanced safety features, very comfortable for tall drivers.
Price	£38,500	£42,000

Lesson 8.1 ▶ 5

| What employers want | Tick (✓) your rating | | Your examples |
	I'm good at this.	I need to work on this.	
analytical			
communication skills			
hard-working			
IT skills			
language skills			
motivated			
organised	✓		On Monday morning I always make a plan for the week.
team worker			

Lesson 5.3 ▶ 6
Student B

A Write an informal invitation message on social media. Use the information below.

Your department/company is going to move to another town. Invite your colleagues to visit the new location next week.
• Include some useful phrases from this lesson.

B Respond to other invitation messages only in social media messages.

Additional material

BUSINESS WORKSHOP 7 ▶ 2
Group B

You work for Saffron Ship Company. You are presenting your new ship, *The Star Sailor*, at the International Cruise Show.

1 Number the parts of the presentation in the correct order.

a First I'll talk about the size of *The Star Sailor*. Then I'll talk about the special features and finally, I'll talk about delivery times. ____

b OK. Now, let's talk about delivery times. We can deliver a ship to you one year after you order it. That's fast for ships of this size. The estimated cost is $5 million. ____

c Good morning everyone and thanks for coming. Today, we'd like to present our new cruise ship, *The Star Sailor*. ____

d Now, let's move onto the special features. The ship has five bars and three restaurants. We have three swimming pools on the top deck and a dance floor on the second deck . ____

e OK. So let's start with the size. *The Star Sailor* range is 230 metres long and 40 metres wide. Each ship has five decks and 150 rooms. ____

2 Practise reading the presentation in your groups.

Lesson 5.2 ▶ 6
Student A
Take turns to make phone calls.

Phone call 1	Phone call 2
You are the conference organiser. Use the same name and company as for Exercise 5. • About 60–65 people are going to attend the conference. • You don't know how many participants are going to stay at the hotel. • Promise to confirm this and send the names by Tuesday afternoon. • People are going to arrive at 9.30 a.m. You want tea and coffee when they arrive and you're going to have lunch at 1 o'clock. • You want a projector, screen and audio equipment in the room. Angela Mulligan at Wallace Hotel Conference Centre phones you.	**You represent the conference centre.** You are Henri Dupont, the Manager at Stanford Conference Centre. Phone the client who left a message in Exercise 5. You want to know: • how many people are going to be at the meeting. • when the client is going to confirm the names and numbers of participants. • what catering the client is going to need. • what equipment the client needs. Offer to send the client a list of hotels near the conference centre.

BUSINESS WORKSHOP 3 ▶ 4
Student B

1 Complete the sentences.

| didn't hit | fixed | had | grew | want to | went |

a We _____ our target of 100,000 sales.
b It _____ well.
c We _____ problems with the English translation.
d We _____ the problems.
e We _____ our range of games from one to five.
f We _____ create more games.

2 Answer the interviewer's questions. Use the sentences in Exercise 1 and the notes below.

A: How did it go, generally?
B: It went well.
A: What went well, in particular?
B: We grew our range of games from one to five.

> Project went well
> Grew one to five games
> Didn't hit target (100,000)
> Problems with English translation
> Fixed problems
> Next: More games!

BUSINESS WORKSHOP 8 ▶ 5
Student B

Look at your candidate profile information. Complete the sentences with the Present Perfect Simple.

> Full name: _____
> Job: Transport Manager
>
> **Skills summary**
> Enthusiastic and motivated team worker
> I ¹_____ (had) experience in the transport department of a large supermarket chain. I ²_____ (recruit), ³_____ (train) and ⁴_____ (manage) drivers.
>
> **Experience**
> Transport Section Manager
> Helford Supermarkets
> July 2018 to present day
> My team is responsible for delivery of food and drink to hundreds of our supermarkets across the country.
>
> **Education**
> BA (Hons) Economics and Politics

125

Additional material

BUSINESS WORKSHOP 6 ▶ 3B

Student B

You are the Customer Services Agent at Natural. Student A is the customer. Read your information. Answer the phone and talk to Student A about the problem.

- Answer the phone call.
  Customer Services, …
- Ask about the problem.
  How can I … ?
- Ask for the order number.
  Can I have … ?
- Say what you will do.
  We'll …
  I'll …
- Be polite.
  I'm (very) sorry about …
- Ask if they need anything else. / End the call.
  Can I help you with … ?

Delivery usually takes three to four days. You can ask your manager to use express delivery in special cases.

Lesson 7.1 ▶ 11

Student A

1 Use the information in the table to answer Student's B questions.

Product name	GIT 200 phone	GIT 250 phone
Weight	185 grams	200 gram
Battery life	338 hours	400 hours
Size	156 x 74.3 x 9 mm	158 x 75 x 8mm
Features	Better camera than any other model, advanced security software.	Longer battery life than any other model, larger memory than any other model.
Price	£399	£420

2 Complete the questions with the correct form of the words in brackets. Then ask the questions to Student B.
1 Which car is _____ (light)?
2 Which car has a _____ (powerful) engine?
3 Which car is _____ (fast)?
4 What are the special features of each model?
5 Which car is _____ (expensive)?

Lesson 8.4 ▶ 5

Student B

Roleplay 1

JOB CANDIDATE

You are a candidate for the job of Sales Manager at a mobile phone company.

Use the ideas in (1–8) to answer the questions. You can change or add any ideas you want.

1 Assistant Sales Manager for IT company, degree in business
2 Excellent communication skills, IT skills, presentation skills
3 Manage ten sales staff
4 Good at motivating the team, organise team sports events, prizes for top sales staff and group meals
5 Big multinational company, good reputation
6 Opportunity for promotion and career progress
7 Working in an office abroad for company – perhaps Japan or somewhere in Asia
8 Possible to transfer to other countries?

Roleplay 2

INTERVIEWER

You are the interviewer. You need a new Production Manager for your car factory.

Make questions and interview the candidate.

1 Can / tell me / work experience?
2 What / main strengths?
3 / you had any experience managing staff?
4 How / you motivated your staff?
5 Why / you want / to work for this company?
6 Why / you want / leave your current job?
7 Where / you see yourself / five years?
8 / you have / questions / me?

Lesson 2.1 ▶ 8B

1 Complete the following statements about your company or a famous company that provides a service.
This company sells/~~provides~~ many _____*phones*_____ .
They have/use a lot of _____ .
They also offer some _____ .
They don't sell/provide any _____ .
They don't sell/provide much _____ .
They don't sell/provide/offer many _____ .

2 Work in pairs. Read your statements. Can your partner guess the company? Can you guess your partner's company?

BUSINESS WORKSHOP 2 > 5

Student A

You work for Best Cleaning Services. Benham Engineering wants an extra cleaning service.

- Look at your notes.
- Complete the questions for the customer.
  1. date / you want the extra cleaning service?
  2. how many / extra hours?
  3. time / you want the cleaner to come?
  4. which rooms / you want the cleaner to clean?
  5. what / you want the cleaner to do?
- Talk to the customer and complete your notes.
- Have a meeting with Student B. Make your business agreement.

> **BEST CLEANING SERVICES**
> Company name ¹Benham Engineering
> Date of extra service: ²_____
> Number of extra hours: ³_____
> Time: ⁴_____
> Places to clean: ⁵_____
> Jobs to do: ⁶_____
> The charge is £24 an hour for extra cleaning services.

Compare your information. Are all the details of the agreement correct?

Lesson 8.3 > 6

You are Jay Peters. You are a Chemical Engineer. You live in Antwerp, Belgium.
You have a Master's in Project Management from Drumford University. You studied there from 2015 to 2017. You also have a BSc (Hons) Degree in Chemical Engineering. You studied this degree at the same university from 2012 to 2015.
You work for Danotex Chemicals in Birmingham, UK, as a Senior Project Manager. You have been there since March 2019. You are responsible for special projects across the UK and Europe. You organise and lead project teams, motivate team members, write reports for senior managers and give presentations.
From May 2017 to February 2019 you were a Project Manager for CUG Engineering Group. You were responsible for engineering projects in the UK and managed a team of engineers.
You are a motivated, organised and analytical Chemical Engineer. You have worked on international project teams in the chemical industry. You are a team worker and have excellent IT, problem-solving and communication skills.

BUSINESS WORKSHOP 8 > 5

Student C

Look at your candidate profile information. Complete the sentences with the Present Perfect Simple.

> Full name: _____
> Job: Warehouse and Logistics Manager
> **Skills summary**
> Organised, excellent communication skills
> I ¹_____ (plan) and ²_____ (manage) logistics, warehouse and transportation in different industries. I ³_____ (have) experience in managing and motivating teams.
> **Experience**
> Warehouse and Logistics Manager
> Mayland Pharmaceuticals
> Sheffield
> February 2019 to present day
> I manage the warehouse and logistics for the company's largest factory. I am responsible for deliveries and orders. I recruit and train warehouse staff and drivers. I manage a large warehouse team.
> Assistant Operations Manager
> Parsons Foods
> Sheffield
> March 2015 to January 2019
> I organised the transportation to clients from the company's warehouse.
> **Education**
> BSc (Hons) Business and Management

Lesson 5.3 > 6

Student D

A Write an informal invitation message on social media. Use the information below.

It's your birthday. Invite your colleagues to join you for coffee and cake this morning.

- Include some useful phrases from this lesson.

B Respond to other invitation messages only in social media messages.

Lesson 5.1 > 8

1 Your manager asks you to attend an industry trade show next month with a colleague. Choose six things you intend to do there.

- check my work email ☐
- do some exercise in the hotel gym ☐
- go to a networking event ☐
- get/provide some freebies ☐
- have dinner with colleagues ☐
- launch an app ☐
- meet an important client for lunch ☐
- set up your company's stand ☐
- visit other stands ☐
- watch presentations ☐
- visit the town ☐
- work on the stand ☐

2 Complete your diary with six things you are going to do at the trade show.

Session	Tuesday	Wednesday	Thursday
Morning	set up the company stand		
Afternoon			
Evening			final evening party

3 Work in pairs. Tell your partner about your intentions at the trade fair and answer their questions. Then swap roles.

A: On Tuesday, I'm going to…
B: Are you going to visit other stands?

Videoscripts

1.1.1 N = Narrator LW = Liz Warnock
EJ = Ellen James MC = Muj Choudhury
N: What do you do at work? This is the working day of three people. They work for three different companies: an event management school, a pharmaceutical research company and a tech company.
LW: My name is Liz Warnock and I'm the Student Services Manager at the Event Academy. I usually start work at 8.30 and finish at five, but I sometimes finish work later. When I'm in the office, I check emails and answer the phone, and I have a meeting with my manager on Mondays. I sometimes go to meetings in London. I never teach students and I rarely travel abroad for work. I take a break around eleven and I have lunch around one.
EJ: My name is Ellen James. I work at Small Pharma, a pharmaceutical research company and I'm a Senior Research Manager. I don't drive to work. I always cycle to and from work. I usually start work at 9.30 and I finish at 5.30. On Mondays I don't come into the office – I always work at home on Mondays. On Tuesdays I finish work at 3.30 and I collect my daughter from school. At work, I analyse data. I email other researchers and I make phone calls. I sometimes go to conferences, but I never work in a lab. My manager and I work in the same office and we often have meetings. My manager arrives at work at ten and he leaves at six. I usually have lunch at one and I either eat at my desk or in the kitchen.
MC: My Name is Muj Choudhury and I'm the Chief Executive Officer of a tech company, Voice IQ. I usually start work at 7.30 in the morning and I finish at around eight in the evening. We have offices around the country and on Monday mornings I always speak to my team. I usually go to our Manchester office on Thursdays and Fridays. I often write reports and I never do company accounts. I sometimes travel for work. We have an office in Sri Lanka, so I sometimes go there and I occasionally go to California to meet with my investors. Sam is our Chief Marketing Officer. Sam starts work at 8.30 and he finishes at 8 o'clock. Sam sometimes visits Voice IQ customers.

1.4.1 MH = Max Hartmann IN = Izabela Nowak
MS = Maria Stavrou
MH: Maria, this is Izabela. She's our Office Manager here in London. Izabela, this is Maria, from the Madrid office. Can you show her around, please?
IN: Of course, no problem. Nice to meet you, Maria.
MS: Nice to meet you, too, Izabela.
MH: See you later.
IN: Which department do you work in?
MS: The sales department.
IN: So, who's your manager?
MS: Monica Lopez. She's the Regional Sales Director for Southern Europe. And I'm a Sales Manager for Spain.
IN: Oh, yes, I know Monica. She often visits this office.
MS: Right.
IN: Do you travel for work a lot?
MS: Yes, I do. I visit clients and I work with the local sales teams.
IN: What are your plans for this visit to our office?
MS: We usually have a planning meeting with the other sales teams when we visit. I give a presentation about my work, and they give an update on their activities.
IN: Well, I hope the meetings go well. Shall we?

1.4.2 IN = Izabela Nowak JM = Josie Marr
MS = Maria Stavrou
IN: Hi, Josie.
JM: Hi.
IN: Maria, Do you know Josie?
MS: No, I don´t.
IN: Josie, this is Maria.
MS: Nice to meet you, Josie.
JM: Good to meet you, Maria.
MS: What do you do, Josie?

JM: I'm an Admin Assistant.
MS: And which department do you work in?
JM: I work in office facilities, but I work with all the departments.
MS: Oh, OK. And who manages that team?
JM: Pietro Russo. Do you know Pietro?
MS: No, I don't.
JM: What about you, Maria? What do you do?
MS: I am a Sales Manager with the Madrid team. I do research, analyse sales data, write reports, visit clients …
JM: That's interesting. I also help the sales team here in London. I help the team process orders – and I make calls and write a lot of emails to the team!
MS: You're obviously very busy then! Nice to meet you.

2.1.1 N = Narrator JL = Jodie Lundie
MM = Maxwell McKenzie
N: Every day The Good Eating Company serves breakfast and lunch to lots of customers at this café in London. How much food do they use and who supplies it? The Good Eating Company talks about orders, deliveries and popular food at one of their cafés.
JL: My name is Jodie Lundie and I'm Operations Manager for The Good Eating Company. The Good Eating Company runs cafés and restaurants throughout London and Ireland. We run around twenty-eight cafés and restaurants.
MM: I'm Maxwell Mckenzie and I'm one of the development chefs here at Good Eating Company. Six people work at this café. We serve tea and coffee throughout the day. We also serve freshly prepared breakfast and lunch, as well as snacks.
N: How much coffee do you sell at this café each week?
MM: We sell five different types of coffee. We serve over 500 cups of coffee a week. And we use over eight kilos of coffee beans. We sell a lot of flat whites, but we don't sell many espressos.
N: Who supplies your food and drink?
JL: We order from many different suppliers that we contact directly. Some of our suppliers are from abroad and some are from the UK. Where possible, we like to use local suppliers. 'Please can I place an order for tomorrow?' We like to place our orders by telephone in order to build a relationship with our suppliers.
N: How many deliveries do you have for this café each week?
JL: We have about twenty-five deliveries every week. We have a lot of deliveries in the morning but we do not have many in the afternoon. The deliveries of our fresh produce normally arrive any time between 5 a.m. and 9 a.m.
N: How much produce do you use at this café each week?
MM: We use over twenty kilos of potatoes; we use over thirty kilos of carrots and ten kilos of lettuce. We use over 300 eggs per week. We use them to make omelettes or scrambled eggs.
N: What do customers buy for lunch?
MM: Some customers buy just a sandwich; some customers buy a salad and some fruit, and lots of customers buy just a hot dish.
N: What do you buy for lunch?

2.4.1 IN = Izabela Nowak RH = Robert Harris
IN: Please, take a seat. Would you like a tea or coffee?
RH: No, thank you. OK, let me just check … So, there's the reception area, one big office, two meeting rooms and the staff kitchen area on this floor. And then, upstairs there's another big office and four individual offices.
IN: Yes, that's right. And there are two staff toilets, one on each floor, and the stairs.
RH: Two staff toilets and the stairs. And… what do you want the cleaner to do, exactly?
IN: OK. Well, erm, clean the desks, empty the bins and clean the floors.
RH: And… clean the two staff toilets and the kitchen area?

IN: Yes, yes. Can the cleaner wash the coffee cups?
RH: Yes, of course. And the office windows? Do you want us to clean the windows?
IN: No. We have a specialist company to clean the windows.
RH: And… how many days do you need a cleaning service?
IN: Five days, Monday to Friday. How many cleaners are there?
RH: It's usually one cleaner for an office of this size. What time do you want the cleaner to come?
IN: We usually start at 8.30 in the morning. And people usually go home at 5.30 p.m. How about coming before we start work? Can the cleaner do that?
RH: Yes, that's fine. The cleaner can do that. Before … 8.30 in the morning.
IN: How much time does the cleaner need?
RH: About three hours a day. So, fifteen hours a week.
IN: And… how much is that for fifteen hours a week?
RH: £300.
IN: Can you provide the cleaning products?
RH: Yes, we can.
IN: Does the price include cleaning products?
RH: No, it doesn't. There's a small charge for those.
IN: How much is that?
RH: It's £10 a week. So, the total per week is £310. We send an invoice each month.
IN: OK, we can agree to that.
RH: Is there a place for the cleaning products?
IN: Yes, there is a cupboard in the kitchen. There is cleaning equipment in there. When can the cleaner start?
RH: How about… next Monday?
IN: That's fine.

3.1.1 N = Narrator LJS = Leona Janson-Smith
MD = Morgan Dudley JD = Julie Deane
MK = Max Karie
N: Postmark is a company based in London. It sells quality cards and gifts. The Cambridge Satchel Company makes and sells bags. These are their stories.
LJS: My name is Leona Janson-Smith and I am a director at Postmark.
N: Who started the business?
LJS: My husband, Mark, started the business in 2004. He wanted to sell really good quality cards at a great price. After two years, in 2006, the annual turnover was approximately £120,000. Last year it was approximately £1.3 million.
N: How many stores and how many employees do you have?
LJS: We now have four stores and employ twenty-four people.
N: Postmark hired Morgan Dudley as Head of Operations in 2015. Morgan has a lot of experience in sales. Leona thinks this was an important decision for the business. Morgan helped them to expand the business.
MD: My name's Morgan Dudley. I studied fashion design in South Africa from 2003 to 2006.
N: When did you arrive in the UK and what did you do?
MD: I arrived in the UK in 2008 and I started as a Sales Assistant.
N: When did you join Postmark?
MD: I joined Postmark in 2013. I started as a Sales Associate and then I managed a store; and then I moved on to Head of Operations. I love the small business environment. Leona and Mark really look after their team and you're allowed a lot of flexibility.
JD: My name is Julie Deane. I created The Cambridge Satchel Company. I started the company in 2008 with £600. Four years later the company was valued at £40 million. When I started Cambridge Satchel there were brown bags, dark brown bags and black bags. But we then moved into a range of different colours. I decided to start a factory in 2011. We have 155 employees. Now we have shops in Cambridge, London, Oxford, Brighton and Edinburgh.

129

Videoscripts

MK: My name is Max Karie and I am Head of Special Projects with Cambridge Satchel Company. Before I joined The Cambridge Satchel Company, I had my own shop. I joined The Cambridge Satchel Company in 2012 to manage the sales of bags and accessories to other shops.
N: Max's job changed when The Cambridge Satchel Company opened their first shop in London.
MK: I started to work on store design, which is the look and feel of the shop. My new job was to design our first shop. What I most enjoy about The Cambridge Satchel Company is that I have the freedom to work on creative projects and that is a real joy.

3.4.1 WJ = William James HS = Haru Sakai
EM = Ellen Morgan
WJ: Congratulations, Ellen and Haru. I saw the winter collection in the shops! I talked to customers and they really like it. They made a lot of very positive comments.
HS: Thanks, William. Ellen's designs are great.
WJ: Yes, well done, Ellen.
EM: Thanks, I'm very happy!
WJ: As you know, I set this meeting up because I wanted to talk to you about the production process of the winter collection.
EM: Yes, of course.
WJ: So, let's begin with your views. How did it go, generally?
EM: I think it went well.
WJ: Haru?
HS: Yes. I think so, too.
WJ: OK, let's start with the positives. What went well, in particular? Ellen?
EM: Well, the teamwork was really good. It was difficult at first, but then I started to ask questions. Everyone helped me … and answered my questions! I learnt a lot.
HS: Yes, we have a great team.
WJ: Great. That's important.
EM: And I'm very happy with the design of the jackets. And you said the shops like it, too. So, we created a good design, I think.
WJ: Yes, I can see that. I have to ask … what didn't go well? Anything? Haru, what was your experience?
HS: Well. Yes, there were one or two problems with the jackets. We had some problems with the supplier. First, there was a problem with the quality of the material.
WJ: So, what did you do?
HS: We changed to a different supplier. We got the right quality material from them.
WJ: OK, I see.
HS: But then, we had a problem with the manufacturer.
WJ: What was the problem?
HS: They didn't meet the deadline, so we delivered the jackets to the shops a few days late.
WJ: Why did this happen?
HS: Well, we didn't communicate the new dates for delivery of material to the manufacturer.
WJ: So, what do we need to change?
HS: Communicate the dates to everyone. We need to have regular update meetings with both manufacturers and suppliers.
WJ: I see.
HS: It was OK in the end. And the jackets are in the shops.
WJ: Yes, great work. Everyone's really happy with them!

4.1.1 N = Narrator CD = Claire Derrick
MD = Michaela Drake
N: In some jobs, employees travel for work. There are lots of different reasons for visiting other countries on business – for example, to visit clients or customers, to see colleagues in a different location, or to go to a conference. Claire works at the Event Academy, an event management school, and she often travels for work.
CD: My name is Claire Derrick and I am the Principal for the Event Academy. I travel quite often around Europe for work and I often travel in the UK. My next trip is to Oxford. I'm travelling with my colleague.
N: How are you getting there?
CD: We're renting a car because it's quicker than going by train. It takes about two hours. We're travelling there and back in one day.
N: Where are you meeting your client?
CD: We're meeting our client at his office in central Oxford. After Oxford I'm going to Manchester for two days for a conference. I'm going by train to Manchester and I'm staying in a hotel for one night.
N: What are you planning to do in the evening?
CD: In the evening, I'm planning to meet some friends and go to a restaurant.
N: Michaela works at Shed Collective, a digital design company.
MD: My name's Michaela Drake and I am an Operations and Client Director for Shed Collective. I travel quite regularly, sometimes within the UK, often near London, but sometimes also travel internationally. I'm travelling to Hong Kong for two weeks in September. On this trip I'm travelling alone, but previously I went to Hong Kong with two colleagues.
N: How are you getting there?
MD: I'm travelling to Hong Kong by aeroplane from London Heathrow airport to Hong Kong airport. I booked my flight one month ago and I booked it online.
N: Where are you staying?
MD: I'm staying in a hotel in central Hong Kong.
N: Why are you going to Hong Kong?
MD: I'm working with my client at their offices in central Hong Kong. It's in a tall building and it's on the 35th floor. Our client is opening a sports stadium and we're building the website for the sports stadium.
N: What are you planning to do in the evening?
MD: Some evenings I'm planning to do some sightseeing in Hong Kong and some evenings the client is taking me to restaurants. And I'm planning to do a cable car trip up a mountain where you get a really good view across Hong Kong.

4.4.1
Conversation 1
HS = Haru Sakai   WJ = William James
HS: Hello?
WJ: Hi, Haru. How's it going!
HS: William! Hello? Can you hear me?
WJ: Yes, I can. But you can't hear me, can you?
HS: I can't hear you, William. Are you on mute? Try unmuting your microphone.
WJ: Oh! Yes, sorry, I am. How about now? Can you hear me?
HS: Yes, no problem! It's OK now.
WJ: OK, great. So, how's it going with the new jeans collection?
HS: I finally had a call from the material supplier. He's sending me some information later today.
WJ: That's good.
HS: I'll have a look, then I'll send it to you.
WJ: Fantastic. Now, what about …

Conversation 2
WJ = HS = Haru Sakai   William James
HS: William, Hello?
WJ: Hi, Haru.
HS: Are you there? The screen is frozen.
WJ: Are you there? The connection isn't very good.
HS: The connection isn't very good. You're breaking up.
WJ: Sorry, my internet connection is slow.
HS: Try turning off your video.
WJ: Sorry, can you repeat that, please?
HS: I said, try turning off your video. Let's have an audio call.
WJ: Hello? Can you hear me?
HS: Yes, I'm here.
WJ: Ah, yes, that's much better.
HS: OK, good.
WJ: We need to talk about the new designs. The client wants to change some details.
HS: OK, Ellen has a few ideas. She's working on two more designs. I have some drawings to show you.
WJ: Oh, great! Tell me more about that …

Conversation 3
WJ = William James   MS = Maria Stavrou
MH = Max Hartmann
WJ: Hi, Maria.
MS: Hi, William.
WJ: Where's Max?
MS: Just a second. I'm adding him now.
WJ: Sorry, what did you say?
MS: I'm adding Max to the call.
WJ: Oh, OK.
MS: Hello, Max.
MH: Hi, Maria. Hi, William.
WJ: Maria, I can't see Max.
MS: Max, we can't see you.
MH: Sorry. My camera isn't working.
MS: Oh, OK. No problem. You can stay on audio.
MH: OK.
MS: I'm sharing my screen now. Can you see it?
MH: Yes.
WJ: Not yet. My internet connection is slow.
Oh, OK, there it is. I can see it now.
MS: So, let's discuss these sales figures.
WJ: You have all the data now?
MS: Yes, I do.
WJ: Great.
MS: You can see the sales so far this year …

4.4.2 WJ = William James
MH = Max Hartmann
WJ: Hello Max.
MH: Hello, William.
WJ: I can't hear you. Try unmuting your microphone.
MH: Sorry.
WJ: That's better.
MH: The connection isn't very good. Now the screen is frozen. Try turning your video off.
WJ: Can you hear me?
MH: Can you repeat that, please?
WJ: You're breaking up!
MH: Hang up! I'll call you back!
WJ: OK. Max?
MH: Hi, William.
WJ: Ah, that's much better!

5.1.1 N = Narrator   MR = Martyn Roberts
N: Graduate Fashion Week is a fashion exhibition. It takes place every year in London and shows the best work by fashion students from all over the world. It needs a lot of planning.
MR: I'm Martyn Roberts. I'm the Managing Director of Graduate Fashion Week. Graduate Fashion Week is the world's largest and leading event for fashion graduates. Our show is going to open next week and it's going to be our 28th year. Our event is going to run for four days and it runs from 2 June to 5 June.
N: How many visitors are going to attend?
MR: We're going to have 30,000 visitors during those four days. It's a big event and there are more and more visitors each year. So many visitors are going to be coming. We print thousands and thousands of badges, brochures and lanyards.
N: What services are you going to provide?
MR: For our visitors, we're going to have bars and cafes as well as lots of fun things to do on our exhibition stands.
N: Who is going to have stands at the exhibition?
MR: There are going to be thirty-eight stands from our UK universities as well as forty international universities.
N: Popular brands like Givenchy, Ralph Lauren and LVMH are going to have stands at the exhibition. The exhibition is going to be huge. The building is 10,000 square metres and the catwalk hall is going to have seats for over 400 people. There are going to be three floors with exhibitions, sponsor stands, as well as the catwalk. The international section is going to show work from some of the graduates – fashion, accessories and shoes.
N: What else is going to happen at the exhibition?

MR: There are going to be talks from all different people from the industry as well as twenty-four catwalk shows. And on our final evening we're going to have our gala awards show.
N: Good luck! We hope the event is going to be a great success!

5.4.1 JA = Julia Anderson   MH = Max Hartmann
JA: Max?
MH: Julia! How lovely to see you. I heard you were here. How are you?
JA: Very well thanks, and you?
MH: Good, good. Shall we get a coffee?
JA: That would be great.
MH: When did you arrive?
JA: Well, I went to Paris yesterday. I had some business meetings there and I flew here this morning.
MH: That sounds like a busy schedule.
JA: It is, but now I'm here I can relax and enjoy the conference.
MH: Yes, the conference will be great. By the way, what are you doing for lunch? Would you like to join me and my colleagues? I'll introduce you to Maria Stavrou, our new Sales Manager for your region.
JA: Thanks, I'd love to join you.
MH: Great! We're going to meet here at 12.30 and go to the restaurant.
JA: Sounds good. I'll see you back here.
MH: Absolutely.

5.4.2 MH = Max Hartmann   MS = Maria Stavrou   JA = Julia Anderson
MH: Oh, by the way, Julia Anderson is going to join us for lunch. She works for Urban Fashion.
MS: That's an important client for us.
MH: That's right. It's a good opportunity for you to meet her.
MH: Ah. Hello, Julia. Thanks for joining us.
JA: Thank you for inviting me.
MH: Let me introduce you to Maria, our new Sales Manager for your region.
JA: Hello, Maria. Nice to meet you.
MS: It's a pleasure to meet you, too.
MH: That was William. He's going to be five minutes late. Sorry about that.
JA: That's OK.
MH: So, what do you think of the trade fair?
JA: I think there are some good presentations. And I like some of the exhibitors' stands.
MS: Yes, I agree. I saw a presentation about the impact of technology on our industry this morning. It was very good.
MH: Yes, that sounds interesting.
JA: Yes, it does. So, where are you staying?
MH: At the Mason Park Hotel.
JA: That's where I am. Do you like the hotel?
MH: Well, it's comfortable and it's near a park.
JA: Yes, but it isn't near the city centre.
MS: Yes, it's a bit boring there. I wanted to visit the old town. I hear it's beautiful.
MH: Well, how about getting a taxi and having dinner in the city centre tonight? We can walk through the old town first.
MS: I'd love to.
MH: Would you like to join us?
JA: I'm sorry, but I can't. I have plans for this evening.
MH: Of course. No problem. So …

6.1.1 N = Narrator   LJS = Leona Janson-Smith   SM = Steve Morris   KM = Kate Morton   LFA = Lisa Francesca Anand
N: Technology has a big impact on our lives. But how will it change products and services in the future?
LJS: My name is Leona Janson-Smith and I'm a Director at Postmark. I think shops will still exist in ten years. I think there will be more online shopping, but people will still want to look at the things they're buying and touch and feel them. I think that in the future there will be robot shop assistants. Cash will become less and less popular and we will pay for things with our phones, our watches and with contactless credit cards. Packaging will change in the future. There will be less packaging on all products bought in store to reduce waste.
SM: My name is Steve Morris and I'm the CEO of the Morgan Motor Company. In the next five to ten years, electric cars and motorbikes will become very popular. Many people will buy them because they are good for the environment and they reduce pollution in our cities. Many people will choose to share cars. I think there might be driverless cars on the streets within the next five to ten years. Over the next ten years, Morgan will think about developing electric and hybrid cars. We won't plan to develop driverless cars, but we will continue to make exciting sports cars.
KM: I'm Kate Morton. I'm Trading Director for Fashion and Retail Personnel. I think technology will have an impact on clothes and soon we might go into a store and find clothes that change colour. We'll shop online and we'll try on clothes via an app on our mobile phones. In the next five to ten years, manufacturers will use recycled materials to make clothes and this will be better for the environment. People won't buy as many clothes, but if we need a new shirt or dress, then we might rent instead.
LFA: I'm Lisa Francesca Anand and I'm a travel journalist. I think hotels will be different in many ways in the future. There won't be a reception desk because guests will check in online. And when they arrive at the hotel, they will go straight to their room and open their door using an app on their smartphone. Guests will order food and drink via an app, and robots might deliver this to their rooms. Smart technology will also help hotels to save energy and reduce waste.

6.4.1 ED = Eduardo Dias   MS = Maria Stavrou
ED: The T-shirt designs are really nice, and we're definitely interested. Could we talk about price now?
MS: Yes, of course. So, how many T-shirts do you want to order?
ED: For this first order, we'd like 1,000, please.
MS: Well, for 1,000 T-shirts, the price is two euros fifty per T-shirt.
ED: That's quite expensive for a new brand in our stores. Can you give us a lower price? How about two euros per T-shirt?
MS: I'm afraid I can't agree to that. Because we're an ethical company, we pay a fair price to our cotton suppliers. And our T-shirts are 100 percent organic cotton. So, the price is two euros fifty on all orders below 2,000.
ED: OK, so 1,000 T-shirts, that's … 2,500 euros in total.
MS: Yes, that's right.
ED: OK, but could we pay 25 percent on signature and 75 percent on delivery?
MS: I'm sorry, I'm afraid for new clients it's 50 percent on signature and 50 percent on delivery.
ED: I see, 50 percent on signature and 50 percent on delivery. OK. When can you deliver the order?
MS: It might be… at the end of March.
ED: The end of March? We'd really like the order sooner. Can you deliver them by the 17th of March?
MS: Sorry, that's not possible. How about the 25th of March?
ED: The 25th of March?
MS: Yes.
ED: Does delivery usually take four weeks?
MS: No, it usually takes two weeks. The problem is, we had so many orders for that T-shirt last week, we have to request more from manufacturing.
ED: Hmm. I really wanted them sooner. OK. Is there a discount?
MS: How about 5 percent? That's 125 euros.
ED: How about 10 percent? 250 euros? What do you think?
MS: Well, I'm … OK, I think that's OK. What sizes do you want?
ED: We'd like 250 small T-shirts, 500 medium and another 250 large, all in black.
MS: OK. That's 250 small, 500 medium and 250 large.
ED: Yes, that's right.
MS: All black?
ED: Yes, only black.
MS: Only black. That's fine. I think we can do that.
ED: Great! We'll pay by bank transfer. Thank you.

7.1.1 N = Narrator   TB = Toby Blythe   GC = Graham Chapman
N: The Morgan Motor Company is a British car manufacturer that produces sports cars.
TB: I'm Toby Blythe and I'm Marketing Manager for Morgan Motor Company.
GC: My name is Graham Chapman. My job title is Technology Director.
TB: We make five different models of sports car. The Morgan Plus 4 was launched in 1950 and it's our most popular sports car. The Morgan Plus Six is a newer model. We launched it in 2019.
GC: The Plus Six is a brilliant car. The Plus Six has a much larger and more powerful engine than our Plus 4 model. The Plus Six goes faster than the Plus 4. The top speed of the Plus Six is 270 km per hour. The top speed of the Plus 4 is 170 km per hour.
TB: The Plus Six is more spacious than the Plus 4, making it more comfortable for taller drivers. The space behind the seats is bigger in the Plus Six, so there's more room for luggage. The Plus Six is wider and longer than the Plus 4.
GC: The Plus Six is heavier than the Plus 4. The Plus Six is 1,050 kilos where the Plus 4 is 900 kilos. The wheels – there's a very big difference. The Plus Six has bigger wheels than the Plus 4. The Plus Six uses nineteen-inch wheels, the Plus 4 uses fifteen-inch wheels.
TB: The Morgan Plus 4 is cheaper than the Plus Six. The Plus 4 costs £45,000 and the Plus Six costs £78,000. Morgan also make a three-wheeled sports car. The first model was produced in 1909. And the new model was launched in 2011. The 3 Wheeler is smaller and lighter than the Plus 4, but the top speed is around the same. It costs £39,000. The 3 Wheeler is hugely exciting to drive. There is nothing else on the road quite like it!

7.4.1 JP = Jonathan Potts   MH = Max Hartmann
JP: So, good morning. I'm Jonathan Potts. I'm Sales Director at Web Trade Builder. Thank you for attending this presentation. The aim of today's presentation is to introduce our company and services. First, I'll tell you a bit more about the company's history. Then, I'll explain our products and services and how we can help you. Finally, we'll have a question and answer session at the end.
So, let's start with more information about the company. Web Trade Builder started in 2001, and we are the biggest provider of e-commerce services in Europe. We're based in Birmingham, in the UK, and have offices in Madrid and Frankfurt. We provide a range of products and services for e-commerce, including websites, payment systems and secure payment wallets. We currently have over 20,000 clients and can offer the fastest, most secure payment packages on the web.
So, let's move on to our products and services. First, let's look at our website solutions. If you have a website, you can add our online shop to it. If you don't have a website, we can build a complete website, including an online shop.
Now let's talk about our credit card system. We created a secure credit card payment system that can manage payments from every country in the world. We can design a system that allows your customers to pay faster, wherever they are in the world. We can also store their details on our payment database, which is the most secure system in the world.
First, I told you about our company, then I told you about our products, and finally, I talked about the services that we offer. OK. So that's the end of my presentation. Does anyone have any questions?
MH: Yes. I'd like to ask…

131

Videoscripts

8.1.1
**N = Narrator   JW = James Warwick
PB = Polly Barnes   DC = Dan Cullen-Shute**

N: People need different skills and experience in their jobs.
JW: My name is James Warwick. I'm a Senior Content Developer for an education company.
PB: My name is Polly Barnes and I am the Client Services Director at Creature, which is an advertising agency. I manage a team of people who speak to our clients every day.
N: What skills and personal qualities are important in your job?
JW: For my job I need communication skills to talk to customers. I also need analytical skills to assess information, analyse data and solve problems.
PB: You need to be able to understand people and communicate very well and you have to be able to express ideas very clearly. When you're working with an international team, you need to be good at communicating, reliable, but also have a positive attitude and to be funny and friendly.
N: How many companies have you worked for?
JW: I've worked for five different companies in the past, as a teacher and an editor, and I've also managed my own company.
PB: I've worked for three different advertising agencies.
N: Have you ever lived and worked abroad?
JW: I've lived and worked in three different countries. I was an English teacher in Malta from 2012 to 2014. I ran my own business in Valencia in Spain for two years from 2014 to 2016. And then I moved to Singapore. I worked as an editor for nine months in 2017. I've never worked in the USA or in South America, but I'd really like to.
PB: I've worked in Amsterdam and Eindhoven and Germany, and in Paris. In Paris I spent three months working on a television project where we made television and radio ads in French.

N: To own or run a business also requires particular skills. Dan Cullen-Shute is Chief Executive Officer at Creature.
DC: My name's Dan Cullen-Shute and I'm the Chief Executive Officer here at Creature. We're an advertising agency that I set up eight years ago with some friends. I've worked for three large businesses before I started Creature, so Creature is my fourth job. I manage the business. I have to be organised and decisive 'cause I have to make the final decision on what we do and what we don't do. To talk fluently or write well about ideas, and understand those ideas, is important. The team at Creature are a group of very hard-working people. We all work very closely together, and I think that ability to work well with people as part of a team is hugely important.

8.4.1
MR = Matt Reece   AD = Angela Davis

MR: So, Angela, can you tell me about your work experience?
AD: Yes. Well, I work as a team leader in customer services for a retail company. I started my working life as a Shop Assistant and then I moved into customer services. I have a lot of experience dealing with customers.
MR: And what are your main strengths?
AD: I have excellent communication skills, both speaking and writing, but I think the most important skill is listening, really listening to your staff and customers.
MR: Yes, that´s an important skill for customer services.
AD: I think I also have good problem-solving skills, as that's part of my job every day. It's essential to listen to customers and my team and help to solve their problems.
MR: What other skills do you have?
AD: I have good IT skills, because we deal with customers via many digital channels these days. And I have good people skills; I'm good at motivating my team to do their job well. That's essential when you manage Customer Service Advisors.
MR: How have you helped to motivate staff?
AD: Well, there are lots of ways to do that. I've always set goals with staff and when they meet those goals, we celebrate, for example. It's important to have a good team spirit. The job can sometimes be stressful, when customers get angry.
MR: Yes, you're right. And, have you ever organised training sessions?
AD: Yes, I've done a lot of staff training and given presentations.
MR: What about staff? Have you ever had any problems with difficult people in your teams?
AD: Yes, there have sometimes been problems between team members. I usually ...
MR: Yes, that's true. Why do you want to work for our company, Angela?
AD: I want to progress in my career and your company has an excellent reputation for customer service.
MR: Why do you want to leave your current job?
AD: I enjoy my work and I've learnt a lot, but your organisation has more opportunities.
MR: Where do you see yourself in five years?
AD: I'd like to develop my skills and do more staff training.
MR: Do you have any questions for me?
AD: Yes, I do. What training opportunities are there with this job?
MR: Well, we have an excellent management training programme. We'll train you in all our products and processes. We'll also provide on-the-job training.
AD: Sounds great! Another question I want to ask is about ...

Audioscripts

1.01 S = Susan D = David
S: Hi, David.
D: Oh hi, Susan. How are things?
S: I'm fine, thanks, but we need to change the date of the new project planning meeting, sorry. Are you available on Friday the 29th, in the morning?
D: Sorry, no, I'm not. I have a presentation on Friday morning until eleven. Let me check my calendar after eleven. Er … then I have a phone call with the Berlin office at noon, for an hour. I'm available in the afternoon. How about Friday afternoon?
S: Sorry, I'm afraid I'm busy then. I meet clients on Friday afternoon from two o'clock. Er … wait. How about lunchtime on Friday?
D: Friday lunchtime is good. I'm available. Er … what time, exactly?
S: I usually have lunch at one o'clock. How about then?
D: Sounds good. Shall we meet in your office?
S: Yes, that's fine. Then we can go to lunch for about an hour.
D: OK, so new project planning meeting at one o'clock on Friday the 29th. See you then.
S: Thanks. See you then.

1.02
1 We need to change the date of the new project planning meeting.
2 Are you available on Friday 29th, in the morning?
3 How about Friday afternoon?
4 Sorry, I'm afraid I'm busy then.
5 Friday lunchtime is good. Shall we meet in your office?
6 I usually have lunch at 1 o'clock. How about then?
7 Yes, that's fine. Then we can go to lunch for about an hour.
8 See you then.

2.01 L = Laura I = Igor
L: Eco Boxes. Laura speaking. How can I help you?
I: Hello, my name is Igor Mazur. I'm calling from Polka Café.
L: Sorry, can you spell your surname for me, please?
I: Yes, it's M-A-Z-U-R. It's pronounced 'Mazur'.
L: And the name of the café?
I: It's Polka. That's P-O-L-K-A.
L: Thank you, Mr Mazur. Can I have your CRN?
I: Erm, what is my CRN?
L: It's your customer reference number.
I: Ah, yes, it's 19-00-01-36-78.
L: Thank you. How can I help you?
I: I'd like to order some of your new takeaway boxes but I can't see the prices in the online catalogue.
L: I see. Do you have the product reference numbers?
I: Yes, I have them here – TGB01, TGB02 and TGB03. How much are the three boxes?
L: The TGB01 costs £2.50 for twenty-five boxes. The TGB02 costs £3 for twenty boxes and the TGB03 costs £2 for ten.
I: So that's £2.50 for the small ones, £3 for medium and £2 for the large size.
L: Yes, that's right.
I: What are the two colours?
L: Natural and white.
I: And how much does delivery cost?
L: It's free delivery for orders over £100. How many boxes do you need?
I: 400 of the white TGB01 boxes and 500 of the natural TGB02 boxes. Can you deliver by Monday 26th?
L: I'm very sorry, we can't. We don't have any white boxes in stock. But we can send the natural ones by Monday.
I: OK, I'd like to order those now, please.
L: Certainly, I'll put your order on the system.
I: How much is that in total?
L: The total cost is £115 including tax. Delivery is free of charge for this order. Can I help you with anything else?
I: No, that's fine. Thank you for your help. Goodbye.
L: You're welcome. Goodbye.

2.02
1 Eco Boxes. Laura speaking. How can I help you?
2 Can you spell your surname for me, please?
3 I'd like to order some of your new takeaway boxes.
4 Do you have the product reference numbers?
5 How much are the three boxes?
6 How much does delivery cost?
7 How many boxes do you need?
8 Can you deliver by Monday 26th?
9 I'm very sorry, we can't. We don't have any in stock.
10 Certainly, I'll put your order on the system.

2.03
1
A: Is there any photocopy paper in the office?
B: Yes, there's some pink A4 paper. Here you are.
A: No, I need white paper. Is there any white paper?
B: Sorry! No, there isn't. I'll order some now.
2
C: Three new employees start work today. Are there any desks and computer chairs for them?
D: Yes, there's some new furniture in the warehouse.
C: Is there any office equipment for them?
D: No, there isn't. What exactly do they need?
C: Three phones, three computers and a printer.

3.01 A = Andrew C = Claudia
A: OK, Claudia. So, the first item on today's meeting agenda is the office move. Do you have the plans for the office move next Thursday?
C: Yes, I do. Finally!
A: Oh, that's great! The ten new employees we hired, well, they all start on Monday. And this office is really small. We definitely need new, bigger offices …
C: We do! And I think the new location is great for us. There are lots of good restaurants nearby, and the new office has much better facilities.
A: Oh, that's good to know as well! Anyway, I need to write to all staff before I leave work later. So, what's the plan?
C: OK. Well on Thursday, I need everyone in the office by 9.00 a.m.
A: OK, no problem.
C: They need to put all their desk items in boxes. And these boxes need to stay in the office on Thursday.
A: Right …
C: At 12.30, you can send staff home. We don't want any staff in the office after 12.30.
A: So, there's no work on Thursday afternoon?
C: No. There's no space. And no work on Friday morning either.
A: Really? OK. That's great for them!
C: Yes, it is! OK, so on Friday, please ask them to arrive at 1.00 p.m. When they arrive, they need to find a desk with their name on it and their personal desk items.
A: OK …
C: And these desks are permanent. Please tell staff that they can't change desks.
A: Of course, no problem.
C: So, the only thing after that is the office party to celebrate!
A: OK. So, what are the plans for that?
C: Well, I arranged for food and drinks to arrive at the new office for 6.00 p.m. The party can start then!
A: That sounds great! I'm looking forward to it.

4.01 B = Bea D = Dom
B: Dom, I booked a flight for your trip to Japan, on Japan Airlines.
D: Thanks, Bea. What about my hotel?
B: I need to book a hotel room for you tomorrow.
D: Am I going by plane from Osaka to Tokyo?
B: No, you aren't flying. You're going by train. It's only two-and-half hours by train – the trains are very fast in Japan.
D: Where am I staying? For a two-week visit, I usually rent an apartment.
B: Yes, that's what we're doing. It isn't big, but it's very comfortable. And it's near the office.
D: OK. Where am I meeting customers?
B: In the office. There's a meeting room there.

4.02 P = Pietro B = Barbara
P: When are you flying to Munich?
B: I'm flying on Monday.
P: Is Claudia meeting you at the airport on Monday?
B: No, she isn't. She's meeting me at the hotel on Tuesday morning. We're visiting the factory in the afternoon.
P: Are the area managers visiting the factory with you?
B: Yes, they are.
P: And when are you travelling to Augsburg?
B: On Wednesday morning. I'm going by train.

4.03
1
This is an announcement for passengers on flight AI663 to Rome. The flight is delayed due to technical problems. We currently expect a delay of about one hour. Passengers, please wait for more announcements.
2
This is a customer announcement for passengers on platform ten. We are sorry to announce that the 10.15 service to Paris is cancelled. This is due to bad weather. We apologise to all customers travelling on the 10.15 service to Paris.
3
We're sorry to announce that the 12.25 service to Leeds on platform seven is delayed by approximately thirty minutes due to a problem with the train. Please listen for more announcements. We are sorry for the delay to your journey.
4
We are sorry to announce that flight EY825 to New York JFK is cancelled tonight. All passengers please go to the customer service desk for more information. We apologise for the cancellation of flight EY825 to New York JFK.
5
This is a gate change announcement for passengers. Flight CA2424 to Abu Dhabi is now departing at gate ten. All passengers currently at gate seven for flight CA2424 to Abu Dhabi, please go to gate ten.
6
This is a platform change announcement. The 12.16 service to Brussels is now departing from platform nine. That's platform nine for the 12.16 service to Brussels.
7
Attention departing passengers. The airport is very busy today. Please allow forty-five minutes to go through security. Thank you.
8
All arriving passengers, please follow the signs for passport control. Passengers with connecting flights, please follow the signs for flight connections. For more information, visit the airline information desks.

4.04
1
Attention departing passengers. The airport is very busy today. Please allow forty-five minutes to go through security. Thank you.
2
This is a customer announcement for passengers on platform ten. We are sorry to announce that the 10.15 service to Paris is cancelled. This is due to bad weather. We apologise to all customers travelling on the 10.15 service to Paris.
3
We are sorry to announce that flight EY825 to New York JFK is cancelled tonight. All passengers please go to the customer service desk for more information. We apologise for the cancellation of flight EY825 to New York JFK.

Audioscripts

4
We're sorry to announce that the 12.25 service to Leeds on platform seven is delayed by approximately thirty minutes due to a problem with the train. Please listen for more announcements. We are sorry for the delay to your journey.

4.05
1
This is an announcement for passengers on flight AI663 to Rome. The flight is delayed due to technical problems. We currently expect a delay of about one hour. Passengers please wait for more announcements.
2
This is a gate change announcement for passengers. Flight CA2424 to Abu Dhabi is now departing at gate ten. All passengers currently at gate seven for flight CA2424 to Abu Dhabi, please go to gate ten.

4.06
We are sorry to announce that flight EX499 to Tokyo is cancelled tonight due to bad weather. All passengers please go to the customer service desk for more information. We apologise for the cancellation of flight EX499 to Tokyo.

4.07
We're very sorry about the cancellation. We're putting you on the next flight to Tokyo. You're arriving in Tokyo at 12 o'clock midday tomorrow – that's Tuesday. And we're booking a hotel room for you tonight.

4.08 A = Alex   K = Karl
1
A: Hello? Karl? I can't hear you. Karl, are you there? I can't hear you. The connection isn´t very good. OK, I'll try …
K: I don't think the connection is very good. But I can hear you.
A: I still can't hear you. Try …
2
K: Hello? Er … can you hear me?
A: Hi, Karl. Yes, I can. That's better. Can you hear me?
K: Yes, I can. But the screen's frozen. Now I can't see you!
A: Oh, no!
K: My internet connection is slow. Sorry.
A: OK, try …

5.01 F = Finley   H = Hinata
F: Good morning, Wallace Hotel. This is Finlay speaking. How can I help you?
H: Hello, can I speak to Mary Duffy, the Conference Centre Manager?
F: I'm sorry, she's not available right now. She's in a meeting at the moment. Can I take a message?
H: Yes, can you tell her Hinata Nakamura phoned about our conference next month, on the 25th and 26th January?
F: Yes, certainly. Can you spell your name for me, please?
H: Sure, it's Hinata, that's H-I-N-A-T-A. And my surname is N-A-K-A-M-U-R-A.
F: Thank you, Ms Nakamura. And it's about the conference next month?
H: Yes, that's right.
F: And what's the company name?
H: It's Dallas Corporation Europe.
F: Sorry, could you say that again, please?
H: Dallas Corporation. That's D-A-L-L-A-S.
F: OK, thank you. And can I have your phone number?
H: Yes, my number is 0044 3584 751 059.
F: So, that's 0044 3584 751 059. I'll give her your message, Ms Nakamura.
H: Thank you very much.
F: Have a nice day!
H: You too. Goodbye.

5.02
1 How can I help you?
2 I'm sorry, she's not available right now.
3 Can I take a message?
4 Yes, can you tell her Hinata Nakamura phoned?
5 Can you spell your name for me, please?
6 And it's about the conference next month?
7 Sorry, could you say that again, please?
8 OK, thank you. And can I have your phone number?
9 So, that's 0044 3584 751 059.
10 I'll give her your message.

5.03 M = Mary   H = Hinata
M: Hello, Ms Nakamura?
H: Yes.
M: This is Mary Duffy, the Conference Centre Manager at Wallace Hotel. I'm sorry, I was in a meeting when you called earlier today.
H: Hello, Mrs Duffy. Thank you for calling me back. I just wanted to talk about next month.
M: Yes, of course. The conference on the 25th and 26th January. Now, how many participants are there going to be?
H: About 120 to 130.
M: And how many guests are going to stay at the hotel on the nights of the 25th and 26th?
H: Between forty-eight and fifty-five. I don't have the exact number, but I will confirm on Friday.
M: Thank you. Can you send me the list of participants and the names of the hotel guests on Friday?
H: Certainly. I'll send all the details by email on Friday morning. Does the conference room have a data projector, screen and sound system?
M: Yes, all the equipment you need is in the room.
H: Are we going to have some help with the equipment?
M: Yes, there´ll be an assistant from our team in the room with you. Don't worry, I'm sure she'll help you.
H: Oh good. You see, it's the first time I'm organising this event and I want everything to be perfect.
M: I understand. We will do our very best for you. What time do you want to have the breaks and lunch?
H: Well, we're going to start at nine. So, let's see … I think we'll have a break at 11 for tea and coffee. Then the buffet lunch at 1 p.m. and then another break at about 3.30.
M: OK, now there´s going to be another big event at the conference centre that day. I'll just check that the break times are different … . Yes, that's fine.
H: Thank you! And I won't forget to send the list of names and final numbers on Friday morning.
M: Bye for now, Ms Nakamura. I look forward to hearing from you.

5.04
1 Would you like to join us for dinner?
2 Do you want to see the factory?
3 Thank you very much. That would be nice.
4 Thanks! I'd love to.
5 I would like to join you, but I have a meeting.
6 Thanks for the invitation, but I'm not free today.
7 I'm very sorry, but I'm not available today.
8 Do you want to join us for coffee?

6.01
1 Gas and electricity are two common types of energy.
2 The air in this city is full of pollution.
3 Many people are buying electric cars today.
4 The land, water and air that people, animals and plants live in is the environment.
5 All machines need to use power, usually electricity.
6 Digital technology is changing how we live and work.
7 We recycle paper in our office. It's good for the environment.
8 There is a lot of plastic in the sea and it's bad for marine life.

6.02 M = Marek   C = Customer
M: Customer Service, Marek speaking. How can I help you?
C: Good morning. I'm calling from Patterson's Limited. There's a problem with the laptops you delivered yesterday. You sent the wrong model.
M: I'm sorry to hear that. Can I have your order number, please?
C: Yes, it's FT90087.
M: That's FT90087. I see you ordered fourteen of the CR673 laptops.
C: Yes, that's right, but we received the wrong model. These are the CR653 model.
M: I'm very sorry about the mistake. We'll change those for you. OK, can I just check your delivery address?
C: Yes, it's our office near Manchester airport. That's Patterson's Limited, 13 Northport Road, Manchester M19 5LH. When will you deliver them?
M: It might take three to four days.
C: Oh no! We need them as soon as possible. We have a lot of work here.
M: I understand this is important for you.
C: Is there anything you can do about it?
M: I don't know. I'll talk to my manager. One moment, please. OK. I can send them express delivery. They'll arrive within two days. You can return the other computers to the delivery driver.
C: Thank you!
M: Can I help you with anything else?
C: No, thank you for your help.
M: You're very welcome. Goodbye.

7.01 M = Misako   K = Karim
M: What do you think of your new laptop, Karim?
K: I don't know. It's not as fast as I expected. It's got a larger memory than my old one, but it feels slower. It's got a really good battery, though, and it's really light. I can carry it anywhere.
M: I know. It's so light! But for me, the main thing is the battery – it lasts for a really long time. I know what you mean about the memory. It takes a long time to open some video files. I don't think it's that large.
K: You're right, Misako. And I don't know about the security software. Waiwex says it has more advanced security software and should be more secure than older models, but I got a virus in the first week of using it.
M: Really? I think it's much more secure than my old one. It was probably your fault, Karim.
K: Well, only two years until the company gives us new ones again!

7.02 E = Ellie   T = Tom
E: Hi, Tom. Thanks for your email on the recruitment companies.
T: No problem. So which agency do we want to use? We're recruiting for two jobs at the Manchester office and one in London.
E: I'm not sure. All Recruit has a London office, and Jones doesn't. Is that a problem?
T: I don't think so, Jones is bigger. And they have offices near London.
E: Yes, that's true. But I can see that All Recruit offers a six-month guarantee on candidates.
T: Yes, that means, if the candidate leaves the company in the first six months, All Recruit will not charge us any fees. Jones only offers a three-month guarantee.
E: Right, and it says here All Recruit do background checks on candidates as well – does that mean a check on job history and their use of social media, that kind of thing?
T: That's correct, although Jones can also do that.
E: Ah, Yes, I can see that. But All Recruit also searches for candidates on professional networking sites …
T: … Yes, that would be useful.
E: … and then do candidate interviews with their expert consultants. So they will do everything for us and probably find the right people.
T: Yes, they will. The problem might be the cost.
E: Hmm. Good point. So, All Recruit charges a fee of 10–15 percent of the candidates first-year salary.

So, that's around 3,000 on a 30,000 salary. That could be expensive, you're right.
T: Well, the alternative is Jones. They charge a fixed fee of £399 for their standard service. It includes advertising and selection of CVs, but obviously no interview for that fee. They can do background checks for an additional fee.
E: OK. Maybe we just need the agency to advertise the job, check the candidate's background and then give us a list of ten candidates. We can do the interviews. I'd like to meet the candidates anyway.
T: Yes, exactly. But first, we need to know Jones' fee for background checks. I'll phone them now.
E: Great. If Jones are cheaper then All Recruit overall, let's use them.
T: OK, that sounds good. I'll let you know what they say.

8.01 E = Elsa D = Dan
D: Hello, Elsa. I'm just phoning about your email. How did the video interviews go?
E: Very well. A few technical problems at first with the video and sound quality as usual.
D: Yes, it's always the same.
E: The good news is, I have three excellent candidates for you to meet.
D: Sounds great! Tell me about them.
E: Well, first there's Vicki Grant. My impression of Vicki is she's very friendly and has good communication skills. She has all the essential skills, with three years' experience in sales and she manages a team of twelve staff.
D: Does she work in the chemical industry?
E: No, but she works in a related industry – pharmaceuticals. And she has a chemistry degree.
D: A chemistry degree! That's a useful qualification for the job.
E: Yes, I know. She doesn't speak German, but she's studied French and speaks it well and says she's happy to study German.
D: That's good to know.
E: Next there's Sam Gowan. My impression of Sam is he knows a lot about our company and products and he has good language skills. He also has three years' experience in sales and manages a team of eight staff.
D: Where does he work?
E: For a smaller company in our industry called, Centrin. Have you ever heard of them?
D: No, I haven't.
E: He has a business degree. He's worked in Germany and he says his German is excellent.
D: Ah, that's interesting. We work a lot with Germany.

E: And finally, the third candidate. His name's Isaac Lange. My impression is he's a good team worker and he has a friendly personality. He plays in a football team at weekends, so you have something in common.
D: Yes, we do!
E: He has more experience than Vicki and Sam – five years in sales – and he manages a bigger team of staff – twenty people. He works for a paint manufacturer, so it's a related industry. He's travelled a lot in Europe for work but says his German is basic. No university qualification.
D: That's no problem, it isn't essential for the job. The right experience and personality is more important to me.
E: Yes, I agree.
D: Well done, Elsa! It'll be difficult to choose the candidate. Can you contact them and arrange the interviews for next week? Tuesday morning is the best time for me.
E: Yes, OK. I'll do that, and I'll send you their full curriculums.
D: Thanks, I'd like to read them. And can you do the interviews with me? Two heads are better than one.
E: Certainly! I'll email you the details. Bye for now.
D: Cheers. Bye!

P1.05
/s/
assistants makes starts tasks
/z/
answers emails phones travels
/ɪz/
addresses misses spaces watches

P2.09
1 I have cheese sandwiches for lunch.
2 This is the agenda for the March conference.
3 We have ten regional centres in China.
4 Each budget meeting is difficult.
5 Digital projects are never cheap.

P3.09
1 I have an urgent report to write for Thursday.
2 Complete a short survey about your last purchase.
3 I bought this purse from an online store.
4 She does research and calls clients every morning.
5 Do you prefer to walk to work?
6 Furniture is one of their most important exports.

P4.06
1 Things are going well and the business is growing.
2 I don't think the advertising is winning new clients.
3 They're emptying the bins and cleaning during the break.
4 There's no black ink in it so it's printing in blue and pink.
5 We're booking our spring holidays this evening.
6 The link isn't working because you're putting in the wrong PIN.

P5.10
1 We would both like to thank you for the invitation.
2 I have other plans for Thursday, the tenth.
3 Are there any delivery charges within the EU?
4 Because of the weather most flights are cancelled this morning.
5 We have more than three thousand customers in the north.
6 The Smith brothers opened that clothes shop in 1935.

P6.08
1 No chemicals are used to produce fruit here.
2 Our popular T-shirts always look cool on you.
3 This shampoo isn't sold through supermarkets.
4 The good news is that we'll move to a bigger room soon.
5 Ask the woman at the reception to make a booking for two nights.
6 We might lose sales in the future due to the distribution problems.

P7.04
1 Video files open slowly on this computer.
2 How long does the mobile site of the hotel take to load?
3 They sold the house at a discount of ten thousand pounds.
4 There's no progress without a good plan.
5 We chose new posters and brochures for the show.
6 The sound quality is so low that you can't understand announcements.

P8.06
1 She was very calm at the interview.
2 He knew a lot about our company.
3 Can we talk about your experience?
4 I didn't get the right answer.
5 You have the wrong information.
6 It took several hours to interview everyone.

Pearson Education Limited
KAO Two, KAO Park, Hockham Way, Harlow
Essex, CM17 9SR, England
and Associated Companies throughout the world

www.english.com/businesspartner

© Pearson Education Limited 2020

All rights reserved; no part of this publication may be reproduced, stored in a retrieval system, or transmitted in any form or by any means, electronic, mechanical, photocopying, recording, or otherwise without the prior written permission of the Publishers.

First published 2020
Tenth impression 2024
Coursebook and eBook with Online Practice and Digital Resources
ISBN: 978-1-292-39294-3
Set in Burlingame Pro
Printed in Slovakia by Neografia

Acknowledgements

The publishers are very grateful to the following advisers and teachers who contributed to the initial research and commented on earlier versions of this material:
Senay Akar-BenBey, Eric Altman, Sean Banville, Fiona Benson, Katrin Beringer, Selena Caamano, Veronika Caspers, Alina Blitek-Dąbrowska, Darryl Boon, Janet Bowker, Julie Bradshaw, Nicole Brunnhuber, Norman Cain, Veronika Caspers, Adrian Crawley, Kevin Davis, Monja de Silva, Louise Dixon, Aaron Dods, Magdalena Dolińska, Analía Duarte, John Duplice, Dagmar Elmendorf, Jens Andreas Faulstick, Marina Fella, Anna Firek, Amanda Franklin, Sally Fryer, Danuta Galecka-Krajewska, Małgorzata Gepta, Rafał Głowacz, Monika Grodkiewicz, Angelika Gruszka, Krystyna Hat, Petra Harder, Timothy Hill, Kate Hoerbe-Montgomery, Imelda Hogan, Carol Hogg, Agnieszka Humiecka, Jackie Jays, Greg Januszko, Magdalena Jonczyk, Ilona Kaliszuk-Rogala, Agnieszka Kędzierawska, Tina Kern, Cornelia Kirsten, Wiebke Kloss, Mirosława Knapik-Jach, Mindy Krull, Jolanta Lacka-Badura, Kelly Leach, Brian Lewis, Jim Maloney, David Meier, Maria Mercado, Sarah Milanes, Wendy Miles, Yamataka Miwa, Rinako Miyata, Jadwiga Nabielska, Tina Nguyen, Seamus O'Shea, Daniel O'Donnell, Renata Pikiewicz, Maria Pophristova, Brian Power, Ilona Rogala, Agata Romańska, Fabienne Ronssin, Christine Schrempp, Ulrich Schuhknecht, Anna Maria Scordino, Tomasz Siuta, Ana Sliwa, Beata Świerczewska, Dennis Tachiki, Satoko Tachiki, Yasuo Tanaka, David Thorne, Christine Tracey, Karyn Weston, Carter Williams, Mark Wills, Philip Wilson, Martina Woff, Ewa Wójcik, Miwa Yamataka, Lidia Zielińska.

We are grateful to the following for permission to reproduce copyright material:

Photo acknowledgements

The publisher would like to thank the following for their kind permission to reproduce their photographs:

123RF.com: Goodluz 52, Kittipong Jirasukhanont 27; **Alamy Stock Photo:** Gunter Marx 76, Heritage Image Partnership Ltd 67, Ian Dagnall 42, Interfoto 27, Justin Kase Zsixz 76, MIKA Images 58, Steven Gill 48; **Getty Images:** 10'000 Hours 14, 2Mmedia 38, Agencia Press South 49, AndreyPopov 24, Ansonmiao 42, Assalve 48, Bim 38, Bogdankosanovic 58, Boonchai Wedmakawand 7, Busakorn Pongparnit 10, Caiaimage/Trevor Adeline 7, Caziopeia 26, Cegli 58, Danchooalex 53, Daniel Allan 22, Den-Belitsky 38, Ezra Bailey 14, Geber86 82, Goodboy Picture Company 52, Grafissimo 38, Hemul75 12, Hero Images 54, Hraun 72, Imaginima 50, Indeed 65, Ismagilov 12, Jaimie Ho 17, Jotily 41, Juanmonino 58, Justin Geoffrey 24, KatarzynaBialasiewicz 24, Kentaroo Tryman 31, Krisanapong Detraphiphat 77, Kupicoo 12, Leon Neal / Staff 59, Littlehenrabi 62, LOOK Photography 13, Lucinda Merano / EyeEm 58, Luis Alvarez 33, M-imagephotography 52, Makoto Fujio 24, Martin Barraud 14, Maskot 70, MBI 23, 51, 75, Michael Blann 30, Miriam-doerr 58, Nd3000 7, NoSystem images 18, Pau Barrena 48, Paul Bradbury 86, Pekic 7, PhotoAlto/Ale Ventura 7, Pixelfit 10, Portishead1 82, Rawpixel 36, RicardoImagen 24, Roger Tully 7, Ruizluquepaz 26, SerrNovik 42, Shapecharge 81, Sofiaworld 66, Sofie Delauw 16, Stockcam 42, Svetikd 7, Szepy 42, Tassii 52, Teap 60, Tempura 81, 82, 82, Tramino 48, Westend61 58, 58, 86, Wittayayut 61, Yagi Studio 52; **Pearson Education Ltd:** Gareth Boden 28; **Shutterstock.com:** A G Baxter 12, Andrey_Popov 7, Aofchin 48, Baranq 32, Big Foot Productions 26, Denis Shpacov 63, Design56 20, DigitalMammoth 48, Drserg 48, Ekaterina Pokrovsky 10, Elle Aon 8, ESB Professional 60, Fun Fun Photo 37, Gajus 50, Giancarlo Liguori 47, Gorodenkoff 8, 8, ID1974 12, Just2shutter 7, Kamil Macniak 38, Kent Weakley 62, Kittima05 68, Look Studio 63, Mangostar 85, Marvent 18, MBI 8, Miguel G. Saavedra 57, Mnlva 50, Nordling 28, Paradoo 58, PixOfPOP 52, Romix Image 26, S-F 38, Samir_Niftaliyev 21, Svetlana Orusova 58, Winai Tepsuttinun 58.

Illustrations

Ben Hasler (nb Illustration) 34, 35, 40, 43, 62; Designers Collective 63 and all charts and graphs.

Lesson 1 videos:

Produced by ITN Productions

Cover Images: Shutterstock.com: Andrii Kondiuk

All other images © Pearson Education

Every effort has been made to trace the copyright holders and we apologise in advance for any unintentional omissions. We would be pleased to insert the appropriate acknowledgement in any subsequent edition of this publication.